Sinti and Roma:
Gypsies in German-Speaking Society
and Literature

Culture and Society in Germany
General Editors: Eva Kolinsky and David Horrocks, Department of
Modern Languages, Keele University

SINTI AND ROMA

*Gypsies in German-Speaking Society
and Literature*

Edited by Susan Tebbutt

Berghahn Books
NEW YORK • OXFORD

First published in 1998 by

Berghahn Books

©1998 Susan Tebbutt

Library of Congress Cataloging-in-Publication Data
Sinti and Roma: Gypsies in German-speaking society and lierature /
edited by Susan Tebbutt.
    p.   cm. -- (Culture and society in Germany : v. 2)
  Includes bibliographical references and index.
  ISBN (invalid) 1-57181-912-5 (alk. paper). -- ISBN 1-57181-922-3
(pbk. : alk. paper)
    1. Gypsies--Germany. 2. Germany--Ethnic relations.
  3. Gypsies--Germany--Social conditions. 4. German literature--History
and criticism. 5. Racism--Germany. 6. Gypsies in literature.
  I. Tebbutt, Susan.   II. Series.
DX229.S53 1998
305.891'497017531--dc21   98-10815
                          CIP

British Library Cataloguing in Publication Data

A catalogue record for this book is available from the British Library.

Contents

Tables

Preface and Acknowledgements

Until the late 1980s it was extremely uncommon to find any mention of the Sinti and Roma in studies of the culture and history of the German-speaking world. Since then a number of works have appeared in German. The aim of this volume is to introduce a wider English-speaking audience to the persecution and prejudice which the Sinti and Roma in German-speaking countries have faced over the centuries, and to highlight the contribution of the Sinti and Roma to German-speaking society and literature.

Special thanks are due to Daniel Strauß for his invitations to participate in symposia on 'Antiziganismus' at the Frankfurt Book Fair in 1994 and in Braunschweig in November 1997, to Professor Thomas Acton, Reader in Romani Studies at the University of Greenwich, and to Karl Stojka for his inspiring talk at the Spiro Institute in London. Thanks go to colleagues in the Department of Modern Languages at the University of Bradford for all their constructive comments. I am particularly grateful to Eva Kolinsky and David Horrocks, who have provided support throughout, and read and commented on the volume, to Sybil Milton for all her constructive comments and help, particularly with respect to historical terminology, and to Sarah Miles and Marion Berghahn for their editorial guidance. Finally, I would like to thank my daughter Clare for her support throughout the preparation of the volume.

Susan Tebbutt

Introduction

Sinti and Roma: From Scapegoats and Stereotypes to Self-Assertion

Susan Tebbutt

Scapegoats and Stereotypes

People in both the west and the east of Germany were asked in 1990 to rate the extent of their affinity to members of various ethnic groups on a scale of +5 to –5. As can be seen from the results below, there are certain differences as to which nations are liked the most, but citizens in both west and east place Jews, Poles, Turks and the Sinti and Roma at the bottom of the list. It is striking how much stronger the antipathy to the Sinti and Roma is than that towards any other ethnic group. The average scores are shown in Table 1.

Both the title of the article about the survey, 'Fremde als Sündenböcke' (Aliens/strangers/foreigners as scapegoats), and the subtitle, 'Attitudes to *Ausländer*' (foreigners), are misleading. Whereas it is easy to define, say, the Danish, Frisian or Sorb minority in Germany in terms of place of origin, the Sinti and Roma are far less homogeneous a group, since many have lived in Germany for generations, if not centuries, and have German nationality, and some have even fought for Germany in the First and/or Second World Wars. Like most minority groups, the Sinti and Roma are seen as a social category,[1] but within this broad classification there are vast differences not only in terms of ethnicity, but also with reference to income, employment, life-style, housing, education, language and religion.

Table 1: Aliens as Scapegoats: Attitudes to Foreigners

Affinity towards	West German results	East German results
French	+ 2.0	+ 2.6
Austrians	+ 1.7	+ 2.7
Citizens of the USA	+ 1.9	+ 1.2
Russians	+ 1.2	+ 0.8
Jews	+ 0.4	+ 1.3
Poles	- 0.2	- 0.4
Turks	- 0.2	- 0.8
Sinti and Roma	- 1.5	- 1.5

Source: Wilfried Schubarth, 'Fremde als Sündenböcke', *Spiegel Spezial* 1 / 1991, p.47.

Schubarth, the author of the article, highlights how the results reveal the Sinti and Roma to be the least popular ethnic group in both the old and the new federal states and correctly refers to them by their preferred nomenclature, 'Sinti and Roma' but then uses as a caption for the statistics the phrase 'In der Aversion gegen Zigeuner einig' (United in aversion to Gypsies[2]), and in so doing himself further perpetuates images of the stereotypical 'Zigeuner' (Gypsy).

Is the use or misuse of the term *Zigeuner* so important? It is difficult to find an appropriate English language equivalent, since in English the term 'Gypsy'[3] is either used pejoratively or conjures up romantic images which are also rooted in stereotypes. Although the term 'Traveller' is widely accepted in Great Britain by the Roma community, it refers more to a life-style than to ethnic origins and would be rejected by German Sinti and Roma.

Language not only reflects social reality, but may help to form it. Members of minority groups are particularly likely to be the butt of derogatory comments and discrimination. In common parlance the word *Zigeuner* has many negative connotations. Standard dictionaries, reference books and restaurant menus still contain offensive references to *Zigeunerschnitzel* (Gypsy chop), *Zigeunersteak* (Gypsy steak), and *Zigeunerblut* (lit.: Gypsy blood, a type of cheap red wine), whereas no-one would dream of calling a meat dish, say, 'Jew steak' or 'Jew chop'. In his collection of essays about Sinti and Roma in Germany, *Oh Django, sing deinen Zorn!* (Oh Django, sing about your anger!, 1993), Reimar Gilsenbach includes a critical vignette which he entitles 'Gypsy Steak'.

> GYPSY STEAK
> Markkleeberg. I am eating lunch in the Raschwitz Forest House Hotel. Six men sit down at the next table. [...] The waiter flicks open his notebook. The six agree on one and the same dish: 'Gypsy steak'.
> 'So it's six Gypsies, then?' the waiter asks.
> I look at the menu. What I find is: 'Steak done Gypsy-style'.
> The guests nod. One of them confirms it: 'Six Gypsies'.
> Let's assume the order had run: 'Six nigger steaks'.
> 'So it's six niggers?'

Gilsenbach then runs through the possibility that they might have asked for other dishes in this way, and wonders whether they would have not called in a solicitor to deal with a case of discrimination if they had seen a steak described as *Niggersteak* (steak nigger-style) or *Polackensteak* (steak Pole-style[4]) but he reiterated the fact that no-one raised an eyebrow when the conversation ran: 'Gypsy steak.' / 'So it's six Gypsies, then?'. Gilsenbach concludes that this must be considered acceptable: 'It's the waiter they turn to and not the solicitor. The six enjoy their food'.[5]

When Germans say someone leads a *Zigeunerleben* (Gypsy life) they are referring to someone with a nomadic, disorderly life-style, despite the fact that the great majority of the ethnic group are not nomadic at all and are extremely meticulous about cleanliness. The only travelling which over 90 percent of Sinti and Roma do today is during a short summer holiday, in the same way that the *Mehrheitsbevölkerung* (members of the majority ethnic group of the population)[6] also travel, but no-one would describe the Germans as nomadic. The verb *zigeunern* (there is no exact English equivalent, lit.: to Gypsy) is defined in the dictionary as 'to wander from place to place in a restless way'[7] and is often also used to mean 'to deceive'. (Another similar example would be the verb *türken* [lit.: to Turk] which is used in the sense of 'to feign'.) There are nouns associated with certain minority groups, and the ethnic term is often used as a term of abuse, thus *Pollack* (Pole) is used for an uneducated person, *Ostfriese* (East Frisian) for a simpleton and *Zigeuner* is used to refer to a vagabond or tramp. It is significant that there are jokes described as '*Türkenwitze, Judenwitze, Negerwitze* and *Zigeunerwitze*' (Turkish, Jewish, Negro and Gypsy jokes). In most cases the ethnic group is immaterial, and each is interchangeable.[8]

The German-language media rely heavily on preconceived ideas of who is a 'Gypsy', taking more note of the Roma who lead a nomadic life and of the latest arrivals from Eastern Europe who match their stereotypical image, than those less 'visible' Sinti and Roma who lead a life outwardly indistinguishable from that of the majority population. Visual images reinforce the linguistic clichés. The front cover of the weekly news magazine *Der Spiegel* (36/1990) shows an intimidating mass of dark-skinned people, including toddlers, staring sullenly at the camera. The caption 'Asyl in Deutschland: Die Zigeuner' (Political Asylum in Germany: The Gypsies) raises the question as to whether the Gypsies should be allowed to stay. The headline of the article, 'Alle hassen die Zigeuner' ('Everyone Hates the Gypsies'), has echoes of the Nazi past, and illustrates how animosity can be fanned by insensitive reporting.

In the 1990s the Press Association in Germany officially declared its commitment to the eradication of discrimination in the media, and in particular to the elimination of the practice of highlighting ethnic affiliation. Reporting of criminal events has long been one of the most important tools in reinforcing xenophobic and racist prejudices in readers' minds. Jürgen Bischoff, chairman of the German Journalists' Union in Hamburg, argues that a ban on discrimination does not impinge on the freedom of press:

> For years now it's precisely in this genre [crime reports] that the newspaper columns have been full of reports about Russian mafia-men, Kurdish drug-dealers and tribes of Roma on break-in sprees. [...] What reader today would take a blind bit of notice of an article about pickpocketing — unless the article mentioned the fact that the criminals were 'thought to be asylum seekers from Romania'.[9]

Bischoff goes on to say that the constant repetition of ethnic or religious characteristics, which have no, or only peripheral, relevance, contributes to the public discrimination against particular groups. He quotes the results of an opinion poll conducted in Germany in 1994 by the Emnid Institute, which found that 68 percent of the population did not wish to have Sinti and Roma as neighbours. In 1995 IG Medien (The Journalists' Trade Union) were campaigning for the revision of the existing Press Law in Hamburg to ensure that reporting did not have the effect of inciting discrimination on grounds of ethnicity, religion or gender.

In the case of public perceptions of the Sinti and Roma, the stereotypes are deep rooted. As the writer Luise Rinser points out in her provocative study of the treatment of Gypsies in Germany, *Wer wirft den Stein?* (Who's going to throw the stone?),[10] the Germans tend to associate the Gypsies with criminality, laziness, dishonesty and fraudulent practices.[11] She argues that it is easy to deconstruct these prejudices and demonstrate that the percentage of criminal or antisocial elements among the Gypsies is no higher than in other sections of the population, and that murders and violent attacks are almost unheard of among the Gypsy community. Although Gypsies are often accused of being prone to stealing, Rinser puts awkward questions to the Germans about who exactly it was who stole the jewellery, gold and musical instruments from the Gypsies in the concentration camps. Above all, she emphasises that Sinti and Roma are not objects to be examined through a magnifying glass and classified, but a stigmatised minority who still do not enjoy full human rights and whose heritage must be highlighted.

Who exactly are the Sinti and Roma?

Who exactly are the Sinti and Roma, and why are they are so very unpopular? There are many misconceptions and misunder-standings surrounding the identity and character of the Sinti and Roma, who originally came from the Punjab region of north India and belong to the Indo-European speaking peoples. 'Sinti and Roma' is the ethnic group's own preferred nomenclature, although there are other smaller groups of Romani people living in Germany belonging to other tribes such as the Kalderash or Lalleri. The term 'Rom' (plural 'Roma') is taken from the Romani language (which evolved from early modern Indo-Aryan) and means 'person'.

It is hard to gain accurate figures for the size of the Roma/ Gypsy populations in Europe, but 1994 statistics give some idea. Table 2 gives 'stable numbers' and is thus more indicative of the long-term picture than of recent population movements.

Over the centuries policies towards Roma/Gypsies in the whole of Europe have involved a negation of the ethnic group, their culture and their language. Policies of containment have given way in the second half of the twentieth century to efforts on the part of governments to bring about integration into the 'mainstream' or majority society. Despite the regulations which are intended to facilitate this assimilation, many laws, such as those

Table 2: Roma/Gypsy Populations Throughout Europe, 1994[12]

State	Minimum	Maximum
Austria	20,000	25,000
France	280,000	340,000
Germany	110,000	130,000
Hungary	550,000	600,000
Romania	1,800,000	2,500,000
Spain	650,000	800,000
Switzerland	30,000	35,000
United Kingdom	90,000	120,000
Total Europe (approx.)	7,000,000	8,500,000

pertaining to camping on land owned by a town, are applied selectively and enforced more strictly where Roma/Gypsies are concerned. As Jean-Pierre Liégeois, one of the leading European researchers into Roma/Gypsy issues and director of the Gypsy Research Centre in Paris writes: 'In other words, the sole fact of being a Roma/Gypsy, and being perceived as such, provokes discriminatory treatment which is backed up by law'.[13] Given the tendency towards homogenisation of national policies, the consequences for Roma/Gypsies are that the group is marginalised, frequently seen as scapegoats and rarely recognised as a minority with specific rights in the state. The relationship between the majority and the minority population is characterised by wariness and suspicion. As Ian Hancock says in the introduction to *The Gypsies of Eastern Europe*:

> While the Romani struggle to retain their identity has been one of keeping the barrier between Rom and Gadzo [non-Gypsy] firm, the increasingly complex structure of society makes such tactics less and less possible, or indeed desirable. Some Roma are beginning to recognize the fact that integration need not mean assimilation, and that acquiring mainstream skills and putting them to use within the Romani community need in no way jeopardize their integrity, but instead would allow them to deal with the mainstream more equably and to profit by doing so.[14]

In 1991 the European Commission held a hearing in which Roma/Gypsy delegates from fourteen states made statements about their situation. The great majority of Roma/Gypsies are citizens of the state in which they live, but are often marginalised, and prejudice and stereotypical images continue to justify attitudes and behaviour towards them. They are defined 'through an arbitrary process which fixes upon a term and strips it of any ethnic or cultural connotations with which it may be associated'.[15] This means that they are not seen as having any ethnic, linguistic or cultural roots, and what are in fact cultural questions are reclassified as 'social problems', with the focus often on the consequences of a situation, such as poor health, sub-standard housing, poverty or illiteracy rather than the causes of the problems, such as discrimination, the judicial system or inadequate provision.

It is, however, encouraging that more and more states in Europe are ratifying international conventions which facilitate the campaign against discrimination against Roma/Gypsies on ethnic and racial grounds. Despite the difficulties resulting from the upheavals in central and eastern Europe, and the alarming increase in violence against members of the Roma community in a number of European states, there are still grounds for optimism. There is clearly a need for partnerships with European institutions such as the Council of Europe and the European Union, with the aim of improving cooperation and exchange of information and fostering a recognition of the diversity and plurality of the Roma/Gypsy communities. The culture of most Roma/Gypsy groups is thriving, and political, social, cultural and educational organisations are supporting further developments and progress.[16]

Sinti and Roma in Germany today fall into three main groups. Firstly there are some 60,000 Sinti and Roma who are of German nationality. Romanies subdivide into many groups, including the Sinti (masculine singular 'Sinto', feminine singular 'Sintezza'), who settled in Germany some six hundred years ago, the first records dating back to 1407 (in Hildesheim). Roma is, however, not only the collective term for all Romanies, but also the term used to refer to those from Eastern Europe, many of whom came to Germany between 80 and 150 years ago, mainly from Hungary, and settled in the Ruhr area and Westphalia. Secondly there are a large number of eastern European Roma in Germany today who came to the Federal Republic of Germany (henceforth abbreviated as FRG) at the start of the 1970s seeking employment. The great majority of this group have a work permit and a permanent place of work in Germany. The third group consists of Roma from eastern Europe, who fled from persecution. Many arrived in Germany in the late 1980s. After the collapse of Communism,

Gypsies were blamed for many of the social and economic problems in the previously totalitarian states, and there was a massive influx into Germany of tens of thousands of refugees, particularly from Romania, with Gypsies from Yugoslavia swelling the numbers once Yugoslavia disintegrated into civil war. Given the circumstances in which they fled, many arrived in Germany with little more than the clothes they were wearing and the belongings they could carry with them.

Sinti and Roma are not confined to Germany, but have also lived in Switzerland since the fifteenth century. The continuity of discrimination can be traced over a period of five hundred years, from the bans and expulsions of Gypsies from Lucerne and Geneva in the 1470s to the cessation in 1973 of one form of injustice towards the minority.

> In 1926 the eminently respectable Pro Juventute foundation decided, in keeping with the theories of eugenics and progress then fashionable, that the children of *Jenische* ('Travellers') should wherever possible be resettled, in order to divert them into the mainstream of society; thus began a system of taking children away from parents without their consent, changing their names, and placing them in foster homes. These institutionalized abductions continued until 1973, by which time over 600 children had been forcibly removed.[17]

Since the sixteenth century Sinti and Roma have been living in the territory which today is Austria, the largest sub-group being the Roma, who have traditionally lived in Burgenland, the region closest to the border with Hungary. There are also some Lovara and Polish Roma and Sinti who have emigrated from Germany. In the period between the two World Wars the largest concentration of Roma was in Oberwart in the south of Burgenland, where they constituted some 8 percent of the population prior to their deportation.[18]

English-Language Research into the Gypsies/Roma in German Society and Literature

Angus Fraser's wide-ranging study entitled *The Gypsies*[19] provides a historical and social overview of the life and history of Gypsies in general, including many individual references to Gypsies in German-speaking countries over the centuries, but by far the most detailed English-language account of any aspect of the Sinti and Roma in German-speaking countries is that provided by Donald Kenrick and Grattan Puxon in their eminently readable, meticulously researched *Gypsies under the Swastika* (1995), a revised and extended edition of *The Destiny of Europe's Gypsies* (1972). Although the work includes a chapter on the historical roots of prejudice, it does not deal with events after the end of the Second World War. In *The Racial State: Germany 1933–1945* (1991) Michael Burleigh and Wolfgang Wippermann devote a whole chapter to 'The Persecution of Sinti and Roma, and Other Ethnic Minorities' in the Nazi period, and mention briefly the continued discrimination against Sinti and Roma in the postwar period, but they are more intent on demonstrating the comprehensive character of racism under the Nazis than focusing in detail on the Sinti and Roma. Henry Friedländer creates the linkage of fate between three victim groups, the Jews, the Gypsies and the disabled, in the chapter on the 'Gypsies' and the 'Note on Language' in *The Origins of Nazi Genocide: From Euthanasia to the Final Solution* (1995).

Sybil Milton's chapter entitled 'Holocaust: The Gypsies' in *Genocide in the Twentieth Century: Critical Essays and Eyewitness Accounts* edited by William S. Parsons, Israel W. Charny and Samuel Totten (1995) covers the Weimar period and the postwar Federal Republic and includes ten translated eyewitness accounts by German and Austrian Sinti and Roma survivors. One of the few other English-language works to contain some information about the conditions of German Gypsies in postwar Europe is Isabel Fonseca's *Bury Me Standing: The Gypsies and their Journey* (1995). Her racy travelogue about her impressions of living and travelling with Gypsies in Eastern Europe, interspersed with observations on the socio-political history of the ethnic group, contains a number of observations on Gypsies in Germany in the chapter entitled 'Zigeuner chips' (Gypsy crisps). Despite her extensive efforts to expose the roots of prejudice, Fonseca herself perpetuates stereotypes. Her journalistic, often flippant and patronising style reinforces negative views of the 'Gypsies' with sweeping statements such as: 'they appear to be the German *Volk*'s opposite: dirty, dark, devious, idle and aggressively antisocial. But then, more subtly, these people really do represent a *Volk*. They keep to themselves and they maintain their customs, their language, and their close-knit community, itself always prized above the individual', and her comment that the 'Gypsy is the quintessential stranger — and strangers are never benevolent'.[20]

For any English-language reader looking for a social anthropological account of the Romani way of life, Judith Okely's *The*

Traveller-Gypsies (1983), which relates primarily to Britain and Ireland, is more reliable and differentiated. Thomas Acton and Gary Mundy's *Romani Culture and Gypsy Identity* (1997) analyses Gypsy culture, art and music and issues to do with health and education with reference to both Britain and other countries. Thomas Acton's companion volume *Gypsy Politics and Traveller Identity* (1997) looks at the relationship between Gypsies and the state in countries as far apart as Bulgaria and Japan. Professor Ian Hancock of the University of Texas at Austin, who is the UN representative of the International Romani Union, has published over one hundred articles on Romani issues, but as is the case with *Romani Culture and Gypsy Identity and Gypsy Politics and Traveller Identity*, there is very little specific information on Roma in the German-speaking world. Although Sybil Milton's exhibition catalogue, *The Story of Karl Stojka: A Childhood in Birkenau* (1992), documents the story of a survivor through autobiographical art, and includes excerpts from interviews with Karl Stojka himself, it obviously does not give all the detail contained in his autobiography, which has not yet been translated into English. There are no works in the English language about literature concerning or by German-speaking Gypsies, and in this respect this volume is thus breaking completely new ground.

Structure and Themes of this Volume

Sinti and Roma: Gypsies in German-Speaking Society and Literature is the first work to be published in English which combines analysis of the social and political history of the persecution of the German Sinti and Roma leading to their genocide during the Nazi regime, the postwar rise of the Sinti and Roma civil rights movement, the relationship between the German and Romani languages, and articles on literature about and by German-speaking Gypsies. The aim is to introduce an English-speaking audience to a much-maligned minority group, about which misconceptions and prejudices abound, and to emphasise the diversity of experience and the expression of this heterogeneity in literature.

Chapter 1 provides an overview of the intersecting paths of the Sinti and Roma community and the majority of the German population over the centuries. The mirror-image of the wariness of the *Gadzo* towards the Gypsy is to be found in the suspicions harboured by the Gypsy towards the *Gadzo*.[21] In order to appreciate the later chapters, it is important to realise that pressure had been mounting on the Gypsies for over five centuries, and that the drawing up of demarcation lines between Gypsies and non-Gypsies was characterised by ignorance and ineptitude, which in turn bred suspicion and hostility. The chapter concludes with brief accounts of endeavours to counteract discrimination in the spheres of education and the arts.

Given the paucity of information available about the history of the Sinti and Roma, it is helpful to focus in depth on one particular group. In Chapter 2 Ludwig Eiber examines the experiences of Sinti and Roma in Munich. From the end of the nineteenth century Bavaria was in the forefront of discriminatory laws against the Gypsies, and during the Nazi regime there was an acceleration in the number of decrees and laws passed which restricted the freedom and rights of the Gypsies, despite the fact that the group was not posing a major threat to the majority population. The measures taken to rid the nation of what was perceived as the 'Gypsy Menace' culminated in atrocities such as compulsory sterilisation, maltreatment in labour camps, the use of human guinea-pigs for medical experiments, and the deportation of thousands of Sinti and Roma to concentration camps. Eiber concludes by presenting specific case-studies of Sinti and Roma individuals and families, in order to illustrate the ways in which innocent people were made victims of unjust laws.

Although some recent studies highlight the suffering of groups other than the Jews in the Holocaust,[22] very little has been written about discrimination in the postwar period. In Chapter 3 Sybil Milton draws attention to the continuity of anti-Gypsyism from 1945 to the 1990s. She highlights the problems faced by those seeking financial compensation for their suffering and loss of earnings during the Nazi period, and looks at the ways in which lawyers, police and bureaucrats were frequently the very same people who had persecuted the group during the Nazi period. The refusal to acknowledge the genocide of the Gypsies is charted alongside the repeated attempts to bring the rights of the Sinti and Roma to public notice. Parallels are drawn between the treatment of the Gypsies and that of the Jews, but differences between the experiences of different types of victim should not be minimised. A whole section of Holocaust victims should not disappear into a mass of anonymous statistics and be subsumed into the history of the Jewish people.

It would be wrong to see the Sinti and Roma merely as victims. In Chapter 4 Yaron Matras charts and analyses the various postwar campaigns conducted by the Sinti and Roma community in Germany. He identifies four key phases; first, the early postwar endeavours to gain compensation for suffering under the Nazis; second, the increasingly vocal public protests including hunger strikes and marches to government buildings; third, the formation of associations and the evolution of a collective awareness, and finally the constitutional debates and the embedding of the civil rights movement in an international context. The impact of such activity has been gradual, and it is only in the late 1980s and 1990s that government bodies are finally acknowledging the genocide of the Gypsies and recognising the need to compensate families of victims and survivors. As the number of those eligible to bring claims dwindles, attention is moving to the more general issue of achieving official recognition of the Sinti and Roma as an ethnic minority with clearly defined human rights.

In Chapter 5, which forms the bridge between the socio-political section of the volume and the analysis of the representation of this reality in literature, the connections between the German and Romani languages are explored. Linguist Anthony Grant discusses the interaction of German and Romani, beginning by examining the nature of Romani as a cluster of languages. The dispersal of German-speaking communities in central and eastern Europe means that several Romani dialects came into contact with varieties of German (as demonstrated by the presence of loan-words). Owing to several centuries of close contact and functional bilin-gualism among the Sinti, German has influenced Romani far more than has happened in the other direction, and this influence shows up in syntax as well as in lexicon. German is also important as the premier language of Romani scholarship over the centuries, and the most significant one (with English) at the present time. Grant highlights the difficult relationship between Romani and German as political entities: the persecutions which culminated in the atrocities of the Hitler regime have reinforced the social role of Romani as a secret language, and there is an unwillingness in Germany to concede any official status either to Sinto or to any other dialect of a language which has been spoken on German soil for almost six centuries.

The following chapters evaluate images and self-images of the Sinti and Roma in German-language literature. In Chapter 6 Daniel Strauß looks at the hitherto largely neglected image of the *Zigeuner* in German society and literature, showing how it is impossible to judge one without referring to the other. Over the centuries the central image has been one of a criminal, uncultured and primitive people. Even the supposedly positive, popular, romantic image of the musical, dancing, sensual Gypsy is riddled with stereotypical features, and it is rare to find any elements of differentiation within the portrayal of the whole ethnic group. The tendency to generalise has been reinforced by the collections of so-called *Zigeunermärchen* (Gypsy fairy tales), in which German collectors appropriate the group's culture and highlight those elements which they feel the German reader will expect to encounter. Clichés cannot be blamed on the 'eternally constant nature of the Gypsy' but have their origins in the continuing interest of the majority community in perpetuating such images.

In Chapter 7 Wilhelm Solms traces the ethnic demonising of the Jews and the Gypsies back to the Middle Ages, and focuses on the similarities between the image of the Jew and the image of the Gypsy in fairy tales, taking most of his examples from tales collected and published in the nineteenth century. He looks at the traditional *Volksmärchen* and *Kinder- und Hausmärchen* collected by the Brothers Grimm, and then at *Kunstmärchen*, including works by Brentano, Tieck, Arnim and Storm, and finally at the image of the Gypsy in the so-called *Zigeunermärchen*. Whereas it is traditionally accepted that the images of the Gypsy in the Romantic movement are generally positive, and that negative images dominate in the post-Romantic *Kunstmärchen*, Solms points out that even in the *Zigeunermärchen* the images contribute to the demonising of the Gypsy. Drawing on a wide selection of tales, he proves how invidious the images of Gypsies are, especially when presented within the framework of a farcical tale, and shows how falsification of history can contribute to moulding negative images of the minority group in the minds of the majority population, particularly when readers are at a formative age.

Works written for young people are also investigated by Michail Krausnick, himself a children's writer. In Chapter 8 he analyses contemporary images of Sinti and Roma in German schoolbooks and children's and teenage fiction. He draws on a wide range of examples to show how even seemingly sympathetic portrayals of the group frequently display a lack of understanding, and distort the image of the Sinti and Roma, who seem more subject to slander, misrepresentation and virulent prejudices than any other ethnic group. Krausnick examines the intentions of the author, the effect of the images on the reader and the implications this form of representation has for the ethnic group itself. Traditionally there are three stereotypical images, the Gypsy child who has to be tamed and integrated, the dancing Gypsy child who is seen as fantastic, erotic or romantic, and the Gypsy child who is respected. Krausnick concludes that this division into stereotypes is less useful than a distinction between works in which the characters are seen as mythical figures, and those in which they are real characters, but that it is extremely rare to find realistic, differentiated images.

In Chapter 9 the spotlight is on the representation of contemporary aspects of the life of Sinti and Roma in the German-speaking world, looking at both images and self-images in post-1980 German-language literature. Austrian writer Erich Hackl's meticulously researched 1989 *Erzählung* entitled *Abschied von Sidonie* (Farewell Sidonia) breaks new ground in that it has as its theme the genocide of the Roma in the Holocaust. Since Romani is an oral language and there are very, very few works in Romani accessible to German readers, it is important to examine in detail the few autobiographical works which were written in German after 1980 by writers from the Sinti and Roma minority in Germany and Austria. Here *Vergangenheitsbewältigung* (the coming to terms with the past) plays an important role, and there are far more reflections of a socially critical and political nature than in contemporary English-language works by Gypsies and Travellers. The works in German have been written by German and Austrian Romanies, including Alfred Lessing, Ceija Stoika and her brother Karl, and emphasise the ethnic identity of the Sinti and Roma. The analysis of literary images and self-images concludes with a brief look at how eastern European Roma portray their impressions of life in Germany and reflect on the discrimination they experience on grounds of ethnicity.

Notes

1. See M. Markefka, *Vorurteile — Minderheiten — Diskriminierung*, 7th rev. edn, Neuwied, Kriftel, Berlin, Luchterhand, 1995.
2. 'Gypsy' is a term denoting ethnic affiliation, and is thus written throughout with a capital letter.
3. See A. Fraser's substantial volume *The Gypsies*, 2nd edn, Oxford, Cambridge (Mass.), Blackwell, 1995, for an excellent general survey of Gypsies throughout Europe. Fraser examines the semantic nuances of the term 'Gypsy' in his introduction.
4. The offensive use of terms relating to ethnic affiliation is discussed later in the chapter.
5. R. Gilsenbach, *Oh Django, sing deinen Zorn!: Sinti und Roma unter den Deutschen*, Berlin, BasisDruck, 1993, p.275.

ZIGEUNERSTEAK

Markkleeberg. Ich esse im Hotel 'Forsthaus Raschwitz' zu Mittag. Am Nebentisch nehmen sechs Männer Platz. [...] Der Ober zückt den Notizblock. Die sechs einigen sich auf ein und dasselbe Gericht: 'Zigeunersteak.' Also sechs Zigeuner?' fragt der Ober zurück.

Ich schaue auf die Speisenkarte. Dort finde ich: 'Steak nach Zigeunerart.'

Die Gäste nicken. Einer bekräftigt: 'Sechs Zigeuner.'

Nehmen wir an, die Bestellung hätte gelautet: 'Sechs Niggersteak.'

Also sechs Nigger?' [...]

Sechs Zigeunersteak.' / 'Also sechs Zigeuner?' [...]

Da wird der Ober bemüht und nicht der Staatsanwalt. Da schmeckt's den sechs.

6. As has been shown, it would be misleading to polarise the Sinti and Roma on the one hand and the Germans on the other, since the two groups overlap.

7. G. Wahrig, *Deutsches Wörterbuch*, Gütersloh, Berlin, Munich, Vienna, Bertelsmann, 1972, p.4,104.

8. See Markefka, *Vorurteile — Minderheiten — Diskriminierung*, pp.35-43, for a wider range of examples of how words can be important indicators of different types of racial prejudice.

9. J. Bischoff, 'Den Minderheitenschutz gesetzlich regeln', *IG Medien Nord*, Hamburg, 1995, pp.4-5.

10. L. Rinser, *Wer wirft den Stein?: Zigeuner sein in Deutschland; Eine Anklage*, Stuttgart, Edition Weitbrecht, 1985.

11. Throughout Europe Roma/Gypsies encounter similar prejudices, which are anchored in the language of everyday use. In Britain, for example, an old skipping-rhyme goes: 'My mother said that I never should / Play with the gypsies in the wood; / If I did, she would say, / Naughty girl to disobey', and is taken from the poem 'Come Hither' by Walter de la Mare, 1922, listed in *A Dictionary of Famous Quotations*, ed. by R. Hyman, London, Pan, 1967, p.236.

12. Abridged from a table based on information from the Gypsy Research Centre in Paris in 1994, published in J-P. Liégeois and N. Gheorghe's *Roma/Gypsies: A European Minority*, London, Minority Rights Group, 1995, p.7. The figures are roughly similar to those cited by P. Köpf in *Stichwort: Sinti und Roma*, Munich, Heyne, 1994, except that Köpf puts the figure for Switzerland at about five thousand.

13. Liégeois and Gheorghe, *Roma/Gypsies*, p.10.

14. I. Hancock, 'Introduction', in *The Gypsies of Eastern Europe*, ed. by D. Crowe and J. Kolsti, New York, London, M.E. Sharpe, 1991, p.8.

15. Liégeois and Gheorghe, *Roma/Gypsies*, p.12.

16. See Liégeois and Gheorghe, *Roma/Gypsies*, for a detailed account of current initiatives.

17. Fraser, *The Gypsies*, pp.252-253.

18. See G. Baumgärtner, 'Sinti und Roma in Österreich' in *pogrom*, 130/1987, ed. by Gesellschaft für bedrohte Völker, pp.47-50, for a more detailed account.

19. Fraser, *The Gypsies*.

20. I. Fonseca, *Bury Me Standing*, London, Chatto & Windus, 1995, p.225 and p.227.

21. Since 'Gadzo' represents an attempt to transcribe the Romani word for a non-Gypsy, a number of alternative spellings exist in English, ranging from the most common 'Gorgio' to 'Gadjo' and 'Gadgie'.

22. See C. Supple, *From Prejudice to Genocide: Learning about the Holocaust*, Stoke-on-Trent, Trentham Books, 1993. A whole chapter is devoted to 'The Gypsies of Europe 1400-1928', but references to the treatment of Gypsies during the Nazi period and in the postwar period are scattered throughout the rest of the book rather than forming a discrete unit.

Dedicated to my Mother

CHAPTER 1

Piecing Together the Jigsaw: The History of the Sinti and Roma in Germany

Susan Tebbutt

Lines of Demarcation and Discrimination

Hostility to Gypsies is not merely a twentieth century phenomenon, but is a recurring element during some five hundred years of European history, with persecution and discriminatory laws in many countries including Germany, Austria, Switzerland, France, the Netherlands, Spain, Portugal and Britain. From the first arrival of Gypsies in western Europe it has been common practice for local dignitaries, and later even governments, to draw up demarcation lines between the indigenous population and the Gypsies, under the clear understanding that the lines did not represent a neutral, objective division but facilitated the perception of those classified as Gypsies as inferior, in a hierarchy established (initially implicitly, later explicitly) by those in positions of power.

The official record of a donation being given to 'Tartars' (most probably Gypsies) in Hildesheim in 1407 marks the start of the relationship between Gypsies and non-Gypsies in Germany. The willingness to give support to a group of people fleeing persecution in their home country was soon accompanied by a more cautious approach. Only a decade later the same municipal authorities in Hildesheim, while again giving alms to the Gypsies, also set a guard over them. Seen in Germany by the guilds as representing competition, by the Church as unwelcome heathens, and by the ruling powers as an unpredictable, potential threat to law and order, the Gypsies were soon subject to discriminatory measures. From 1449 onwards the town of Frankfurt am Main often forcibly ejected them. Other towns soon followed suit, using different strategies to achieve the same end, namely a type of apartheid. Bribery in the form of presents was the tactic used in 1463 by the people of Bamberg, who were only prepared to tolerate the Gypsies who were camping by the town walls if they did not come into the centre of the town. At the end of the fifteenth century the Imperial Diet issued edicts revoking Emperor Sigismund's writ granting the Gypsies safe conduct. The Gypsies were outlawed. Why?

Suspected of moving around the country as spies for the Turks, the Gypsies were stigmatised and refused entrance at the frontiers on account of their darker skin colour, their language and their different customs. It was believed that they brought epidemics in their wake, and that they represented a threat to the indigenous sedentary population. In 1571 a young Gypsy was stabbed in Frankfurt am Main. The court ruled that the perpetrator, a non-Gypsy, should be acquitted, on the grounds that since Gypsies were not to be tolerated in Germany, the man was justified in taking the law into his own hands.[1] This blatant condoning of a criminal offence highlights the dual standards operating in terms of the behaviour expected of the Gypsies and the non-Gypsies.

The official state sanction for killing a Gypsy was given by Elector John George II of Saxony, who in 1661 imposed the death penalty for any Gypsies found on his territory, a practice which today would be described as 'ethnic cleansing'. The volume of anti-Gypsy legislation was growing rapidly, with over 120 laws being passed in the two hundred years between 1551 and 1751. In 1710, for example, Prince Adolph Frederick of Mecklenburg-Strelitz sharpened up sanctions in the principality of Ratzeburg, ordering that:

> ... when no criminal charges could be substantiated against Gypsies captured there, older males not capable of being put to work and women over 25 were to be flogged, branded and expelled in small groups by different routes, and executed if they came back; younger females, and youths not fit for heavy work, were similarly to be ejected; while healthy males faced life confinement with forced labour. Children under 10, however, were to be taken away and handed over to good Christian people to be given a proper upbringing.[2]

The decree differentiates very clearly between those considered to be good people, represented by the Germans, and those who are perceived as bad, the Gypsies, and makes value judgements about the Gypsy way of life in the reference to the 'proper upbringing' which it was felt Gypsies could not provide. The 'good Christian people' were, however, ready to subject the Gypsies to flogging, branding, mutilation (cutting off ears), torture, beheading, death on the wheel, and being hung, drawn and quartered for no crime other than belonging to the Gypsy minority. In the same way that signs banning Jews were erected in parks, restaurants and shops during the Third Reich, wooden blocks depicting the whipping and hanging of Gypsies were erected by authorities in the eighteenth century at the entrances to towns and villages to act as a deterrent and reminder of the punishments Gypsies might face if caught.[3]

Efforts to Enforce Assimilation

During the reign of Empress Maria Theresa (1740–1780) and that of her son Joseph II, a number of radical measures were taken, precipitated in part by economic and demographic factors such as the need for more men to form part of the work-force and the army, following the ravages of the Habsburg/Turkish conflicts, which had led to Hungary being underpopulated. Historian Angus Fraser describes Joseph II's regulations of 1783, which were more restrictive than any which had gone before and included the following new elements:

> ... no changing of names; houses to be numbered; monthly reports on way of life; nomadism forbidden: settled Gypsies allowed to visit fairs only in cases of special need; smithery banned except when certified as necessary by the authorities; numbers of musicians restricted; begging prohibited; Gypsies not to be settlers in their own right, but to be put into the service of others; Gypsy children, from the age of four upwards, to be distributed at least every two years among the neighbouring districts.[4]

These measures were designed to enforce the immobilisation and assimilation of Gypsies, and were felt most in the Burgenland area (which at that time formed part of Hungary). The policy of containment and assimilation was also applied by Frederick the Great of Prussia, who ordered the founding of special villages for Gypsies, the first being set up in Friedrichslohra in Saxony at the end of the eighteenth century. By 1828 the Evangelical Missionary

Society of Naumburg and District was responsible for over fifty Gypsies living there. Wilhelm Blankenburg, a teacher from Berlin, was put in charge of their education. The humanist ideal of continually improving the world and its citizens was tinged with a colonialist-like desire to remould the Gypsies in the image of the majority population. The aim of the Church mission was not only to convert the supposedly 'heathen' Gypsies and their children to Christianity, but to persuade them of the desirability of leading a sedentary way of life. The Gypsies were to learn to read and write, but were also encouraged to give up practising their traditional skills such as basket-making, carving and fortune-telling, and take up activities which were considered more socially acceptable. By the mid-1830s the task of educating some hundred Gypsies became too much for Blankenburg and his wife alone, particularly since the local population was not prepared to support the project. The local government authorities in Magdeburg withdrew their support and resettled the adult Gypsies, as though they were convicts, in workhouses, and moved their children to orphanages, bringing to an end the most striking example in Germany of the policy of attempting to assimilate the Gypsies.

Registration and Exclusion Strategies

By the end of the nineteenth century the authorities were increasingly bent on tightening their control over the life of the Gypsies. The most extensive and systematic programme of registration was that of the Bavarian Police, under Alfred Dillmann, who set up a headquarters in Munich in 1899 specifically to register the presence of Gypsies in each district, record those passing through, and note any infringements of the law. In 1905 Dillmann produced a so-called *Zigeuner-Buch* (Gypsy Register) to record the information which had been collected on over three thousand Gypsies and Travellers. The directive on *Bekämpfung der Zigeunerplage* (Fighting the Gypsy Plague), issued in 1906 by the Prussian Minister of the Interior in collaboration with nine neighbouring states, was intended both to make the bureaucratic requirements for a licence to practise an itinerant trade so complex as to act as a deterrent, and at the same time to forbid Gypsies from remaining in towns. By 1911 Gypsies were being fingerprinted, and the number of files on Gypsies was growing rapidly, but the quantitative increase in documentation was not accompanied by a qualitative increase in understanding of the ethnic minority group, which was seen as a homogeneous mass rather than as a collection of individuals. This tunnel vision paved the way for Hitler's racist policies towards 'the Gypsies'.

The case of Johann 'Gypsy' Trollmann from Hanover is symptomatic of the racist over-reliance on categorisation to enforce discrimination. In 1932 Trollmann was one of the most successful boxers in Germany, praised by both the general public and the boxing fraternity for his style, nimbleness, speed and intelligence. Praised, that is, until Hitler came to power. By March 1933 Erich Seelig, the German champion, had been stripped of his title for no reason other than that he was a Jew. Trollmann was the favourite to win the title. Worried that an already embarrassing situation might be exacerbated by a 'Gypsy' gaining the title, the boxing association set a stronger, heavier boxer, Adolf Witt, to fight him. Trollmann emerged nevertheless as the clear winner, but the referee declared the fight a draw. After much vociferous protest from the fans, Trollmann was officially declared the German champion. Inflamed by the success of the 'Gypsy', the authorities set about denouncing him as an oily clown, describing what had previously been praised as his agility as 'Gypsy-like unpredictability'. Eight days later Trollmann, like Seelig before him, was stripped of his title. On 21 July 1933 he took his revenge in the ring. He dyed his black hair blonde, and radically altered his boxing technique. Instead of skipping round light-footedly, Trollmann parodied the racist cliché by remaining rooted to the spot in the middle of the ring like the solid German oak tree, holding out resolutely till his final defeat in the fifth round. Like so many German Sinti, Trollmann was called up in 1939 and served in Russia in the infantry. In 1942 he was arrested by the Gestapo and then sent to Neuengamme concentration camp near Hamburg, where he was forced to do heavy labour, but even here the humiliation was not over, because occasionally SS officers 'invited' him to box. Due to his weakened state and the fact that the SS always chose the strongest of his guards as opponents, Trollmann always lost. Despite the great emphasis in Germany on registering and recording the activities of the Gypsies, accurate documentation of the fate of the Gypsies is not a feature of the concentration camp archive material. Witnesses report that Trollman was shot. The death certificate, however, merely states: 'The worker Johann Trollmann passed away on 9 February 1943 at 6 am in Hamburg-Neuengamme, Hausdeich 60'.[5]

Marginalisation, Segregation and Maltreatment

The Nuremberg Race Laws passed in 1935 deprived not only Jews but also Gypsies of the right to vote, and prevented intermarriage or sexual relationships between Gypsies, (mistakenly considered not to be 'Aryan') and non-Gypsies. The classification of Gypsies and Travellers into *Zigeuner* (Gypsy), *Zigeunermischling* (part-Gypsy) and *Nichtzigeuner* (non-Gypsy) was of crucial importance to their fate.[6] Sinti and Roma were banned from speaking Romani, not allowed to travel by tram, or go to the cinema. Children were withdrawn from normal schooling or sent to schools for children with special needs, for no reason other than that they were of Gypsy origin, and were forbidden to talk to German children.

November 1936 saw the opening in Berlin of the Rassen-hygienische und Bevölkerungsbiologische Forschungsstelle (Racial Hygiene and Demographic Biology Research Unit) under Dr Robert Ritter. He and his aide, Eva Justin, visited the Gypsy camps and conducted interviews with the Gypsies, and took countless photos of men, women and children from all angles with a view to establishing the supposed link between heredity and criminality using data such as fingerprints, family trees and anthropometric measurements. The fact that Eva Justin befriended the Gypsies, even learning some of the Romani language, made it even more bitter that the evidence collected by the Research Unit facilitated the rapid location and deportation of the Sinti and Roma to the concentration camps.

Despite the expansion of the bureaucratic system of recording the presence and movements of Gypsies, it is important to point out that the registration system was deeply flawed. Given the increasing number of Gypsies who were leading a sedentary life, the old distinctions between Gypsies and non-Gypsies were no longer water-tight, and the authorities begin to make mistakes in drawing their demarcation lines. Near Soest, for example, there were many sedentary Gypsies descended from those who had settled at the Gypsy colony in Berleburg, and there were also a number of Gypsies working in the north of the area engaged in work such as mending kettles, sharpening scissors, making baskets and mending umbrellas, travelling round in the summer months to neighbouring markets, but always returning to their homes in Soest. An official record of 17 July 1937 states, however, that no Gypsies were recorded in the area at all, despite the presence of the two above-mentioned groups, whereas on 18 February 1938 the statement that: 'Every year the District of Soest is plagued with Gypsies when the cattle markets are taking place there',[7] indicates that a clear distinction is made between the seasonal arrival of nomadic Gypsies and the rest of the majority population. Even in the late twentieth century the majority population is thus singularly slow to acknowledge the existence of those Sinti and Roma who do not attract public attention because of their (usually enforced) mobility.

Even before Gypsies were deported to the concentration camps, the terrible injustices and crimes against humanity perpetrated against the ethnic group had begun with programmes of destruction through work.[8] Between 1935 and 1939 a number of individual towns took strict measures to limit the activities of the Sinti and Roma, by compulsorily resettling them in guarded camps, with barbed wire fences round the perimeter.[9] This interim patchwork of parallel local decrees provided the prototype for the synchronisation and radicalisation of measures against Sinti and Roma throughout the Reich after 1935. Although states and provinces had lost their original autonomy under Nazi rule, they were retained as administrative units and could implement policies on their own initiative as long as they did not contravene national policy. Thus, these local measures cumulatively imposed greater police surveillance and arbitrary intimidation on German Sinti and Roma, intensified restrictions on their freedom of movement, and limited their employment. After 1935, several municipal governments and local welfare offices pressured the German police to confine a growing number of German Gypsies in newly created municipal Gypsy camps, closely coordinated by the German Association of Cities. These camps were in essence SS-*Sonderlager*, special internment camps combining elements of protective custody concentration camps and embryonic ghettos; they held full families including women and young children. Usually located on the outskirts of cities, these camps were guarded by the SS, the gendarmerie, or the uniformed city police. They became reserve depots for forced labour, genealogical registration, and compulsory sterilisation. Between 1935 and 1939, Gypsy camps were created in Cologne, Düsseldorf, Essen, Frankfurt, Hamburg, Magdeburg, Pölitz near Stettin and other German cities. These camps evolved after 1939 from municipal internment camps into *Sammellager* (assembly centres) for systematic deportation to concentration camps, ghettos and killing centres. The inmates of these camps were stripped of their permits to practise a trade and forced to do heavy manual labour. They had to turn out each day for *Appell* (roll-call) and women had to do the same heavy work as the men, often for twelve to fifteen hours a day. The higher the productivity rate, the higher the death-rate, but if any Gypsy missed a day's work they were reported as 'work-shy' or 'asocial' and sent off to the concentration camps.

Paradoxically, the municipal authorities frequently used the argument that existing Gypsy camps were unhygienic and dilapidated as an excuse to close them down and resettle the Gypsies, but the new camps themselves were characterised by atrocious living conditions. After the closing of the huge, sprawling, infamous Heinefeld 'shanty-town' in Düsseldorf in 1933, the Town Council divided those living there into three groups, firstly those *Volksgenossen* (NS term — national comrade) who had conducted themselves impeccably and who were to be given homes, secondly those 'elements' who could still be reformed, who were to be given the equivalent of council flats, and finally those irrevocably 'asocial' inhabitants and Gypsies who were to be re-housed. By 1937 almost all the Sinti and Roma in Düsseldorf were rounded up (the caravans they left behind were set on fire by the SS) and herded into the camp in the Höherweg, where the barracks had bars across the windows and iron doors which were bolted from the outside, where children were even forbidden from playing ball, and where all inmates were strictly forbidden from being out after ten o'clock at night.[10]

In preparation for the Olympic Games in 1936, the authorities in Berlin endeavoured to make the city 'Gypsy-free'. On 16 July 1936 six hundred Sinti and Roma were rounded up and detained and taken to the camp in nearby Marzahn. There were about 130 caravans and barracks for some 800 to 1,000 people, and there was such inadequate shelter that some people even had to sleep under the vans, with only blankets and rags to shelter them from the cold and wind. There were only two toilet blocks for up to a thousand people and illness was rife and the mortality rate high.[11]

In Frankfurt the city council agreed to round up all the Gypsies in a camp in the Dieselstraße in the north-east of the city, spending 16,200 *Reichsmark* on building the camp, including providing fencing, the entrance gate, a house for the camp commandant, earth closets, electricity and a standpipe for water. In 1937 some 55 Sinti men women and children were brought to the camp, which was about eighty metres long by twenty metres wide. They had to sleep crammed together in empty furniture vans, and by May

1941 there were some 300 Sinti living on the site. A Sinti woman remembers what life was like in the camp:

> Even the children had to work; an eight-year-old child had to help to unload bricks, this child jumped down from the van and was run over. We all screamed for help. In response to his question [the supervisor's] we explained to him that the child had been run over, and his answer was: 'He's only a Gypsy child, our German soldiers at the Front are also dying'.[12]

In the winter of 1941/1942 the failure of the German army's tactics in the Soviet Union meant that efforts were intensified in the munitions industry. Most of the labour camps connected to German industries and munitions production were part (satellites and subcamps) of the concentration camp system under the jurisdiction of the Reich Security Central Office (the RSHA). Forced and slave labour were an integral part of the concentration camp system after 1937/1938. Labour camps and forced labour conscription in industry preceded deportation in some cases, but were usually linked to the growing network of concentration camps and their satellites after 1938.

> In the following years [from winter 1941/1942 onwards] up until the end of the war many Sinti and Roma were also taken from the concentration camps and their labour squads to work as forced labour in munitions firms which were essential to the war effort. Among them were such prestigious firms as the aeroplane construction firm Messerschmitt and Heinkel, the electrical firms of Siemens and AEG, automobile-producers Daimler-Benz and BMW, armourers Krupp and Rheinmetall, or the chemical company I. G. Farben (today Hoechst, Bayer, BASF et al.), to name but a few of the large industrial firms. In addition there were also a substantial number of less well-known firms, who were for instance involved in producing munitions or were producing attachments and replacement parts for planes, tanks, submarines and other items of the machinery of war.[13]

Gypsies also worked in quarries, coal-mines and in the construction of motorways and military installations, and cleared rubble off the streets after bombing raids. The inhuman treatment of the Sinti and Roma was not recognised for a long time as qualifying them for any compensation, as will be explained in detail in Chapter 4.

Sinti and Roma in Concentration Camps

From 1938 Gypsies from Germany and Austria were sent to concentration camps, including Dachau, Buchenwald, Mauthausen,

Sachsenhausen, Neuengamme, Flossenbürg, Ravensbrück, Natz-weiler, Lackenbach and Auschwitz, and aspects of the experiences of Sinti and Roma are dealt with in later chapters, including Chapter 9.

On 16 December 1942 Himmler's Auschwitz decree led to the deportation of 22,000 Sinti and Roma from Europe to the concentration camp at Auschwitz-Birkenau to the section known from March 1943 as the *Zigeunerlager* (Gypsy Camp). It was about 600 metres long by 120 metres wide, with 32 accommodation blocks, each originally meant for stabling a maximum of 52 horses. Some five hundred Gypsies were housed in each of the barracks. Inmates slept in three-tiered wooden bunks. There were no windows, and the only light came from some skylights in the roof. Even at night the prisoners were frightened of the brutality of the SS, who would come in drunk to the barracks and wake the sleeping prisoners, beat them and take female Gypsies into their quarters and sexually abuse them. By April 1943 there were some 12,000 prisoners in the 'Gypsy Camp', of whom just over half were women.[14] In Auschwitz Dr Mengele was particularly interested in identical twins, whom he misused, conducting medical experiments and then dissecting the bodies. An eye-witness reports: 'A Sinti boy who survived the camp told us in an eye-witness interview how he and his brother were instructed by Dr Mengele to carry glass containers from the sick-block to a waiting car. The containers were filled with liquid in which human organs were floating.'[15] Almost half of the internees in the camps died of starvation, the effects of typhoid epidemics, noma (a cancer-like disease), or of abuse by the guards.

In the night of the 2/3 August 1944 the camp was liquidated and the remaining 2,897 Sinti and Roma, men, women and children, were sent to the gas chambers and murdered in one night. On the morning of 3 August the 'Gypsy camp' was silent and deserted. In total, half a million European Romanies died in the Holocaust, but their fate has been largely neglected by historians.

Postwar Discrimination

Evidence of the continuity of discrimination against Sinti and Roma in the postwar period is presented in Chapters 3 and 4. In this brief overview one recent example illustrates the continuity of the discrimination against the Sinti and Roma. Of the 438,191 people seeking political asylum in Germany in 1992, almost 100,000 were Roma, many of them fugitives from pogroms in Romania and other central European countries, but the German government again refused to acknowledge that they were political refugees, for whom a return to their homeland could well mean loss of freedom, or life.[16] In *The Gypsies* Angus Fraser sums up the German response:

> In Germany – the prime destination for many – xenophobic attacks erupted and vigilante groups launched defensive action against camps and hostels for Gypsies and other refugees and immigrant workers. Pressure mounted for also expelling those who had arrived years before without having official rights of residence, and for amendment of the country's constitution and tightening of its law on asylum. In 1992 the German government struck a repatriation deal with Romania. (p.291)

This deportation of Roma between November 1992 and February 1993 was referred to by the Chairman of the Roma National Congress (RNC) in Hamburg as a 'modern form of ethnic cleansing',[17] and the RNC accuses the government of making the Roma into scapegoats for problems associated with unification, such as the arson attacks on refugee hostels.

Given the discrimination and persecution over the centuries, it is hardly surprising that the Sinti and Roma community is wary of researchers and suspicious of their motives. At the end of the twentieth century efforts are finally being made to present documentary evidence from Sinti and Roma about their experiences, but there is still much apprehension about how this evidence will be presented and evaluated. For this reason many Sinti and Roma understandably request anonymity, particularly those who had previously coexisted harmoniously for decades if not centuries with their German fellow citizens, in order to minimise the possible danger of xenophobic attacks.

There is a need to heighten awareness of anti-Gypsyism,[18] in the same way that anti-Semitism has long been acknowledged as a social phenomenon. In 1995 German television screened Michail Krausnick's award-winning film *Auf Wiedersehen im Himmel* (Until We Meet Again in Heaven), which portrays the deportation to Auschwitz of Gypsy children from the St Joseph's Children's Home in Mulfingen in Germany. The fact that both Krausnick's film and Austrian television's film version of Erich Hackl's novel *Abschied von Sidonie* (Farewell Sidonia), based on the true story of the deportation of Austrian Roma Sidonie Adlersburg to Auschwitz, have struck a chord with the public is a hopeful sign that German-speaking society is finally starting to see the Holocaust in its totality rather than solely in terms of anti-Semitism. Half a century after the end of the Second World War, memorials are finally being erected in Germany which acknowledge the death of Sinti and Roma in the Holocaust. Professor Ian Hancock, President of the International Romani Union, highlights the need to redress the balance:

> That attitudes are beginning to change and that awareness is beginning to grow, was evidenced at the 26th Scholars' Conference on the Holocaust and the Churches held in Minneapolis in March, 1996, entitled 'A Mandate for the 21st Century'. Here, Yehuda Bauer initiated a public statement in the name of the Conference, issued to the media accompanied by twelve pages of signatures supporting it, and officially deploring the anti-gypsyism which is escalating throughout Europe. It read: 'Fifty years after the end of World War II, one of the most terrible genocide acts of the Nazi regime, the mass destruction of the Romani (Gypsy) people, is still being ignored. Their continued victification, discrimination and persecution on racist grounds, reminiscent of Nazi attitudes, has not ceased, especially in the countries of Europe. It is the sense of the following scholars who participated at the 26th Annual Scholars' Conference on the Holocaust and the Churches, that it is appropriate for democratic governments, religious organizations, academic and civil bodies, to call upon governments and political parties in the countries mentioned to act forcefully against anti-Romani policies, which, if continued, may well create another political genocidal situation.'[19]

Breaking Down Barriers and Fostering Understanding

A number of steps have been taken to improve the educational opportunities of the Sinti and Roma in Germany, such as the project near Ravensburg, which involve working together with the Sinti and Roma community rather than pushing them down the path of assimilation.[20] Courses have been set up in Hamburg to help Sinti and Roma with literacy and with the theoretical part of the driving test. Cultural initiatives are also springing up in individual cities and areas, with greater efforts being made in the 1980s and 1990s not only to integrate Romani children into German schools, but also to encourage events at which the Romani culture is celebrated, such as the creation of a cultural meeting place in Hamm, where young Sinti and Roma can learn to make music and sing traditional songs.

Initiatives to promote the culture of the ethnic group are important, given that the image of the Roma/Gypsy in art, like that in literature, tends to oscillate between romantic, sensuous images of nomadic people living close to nature, and images of squalor and disorder. Few artists have captured the essence of individuals, an exception being the artist Otto Pankok, who befriended, lived with and painted many members of the Gypsy community in Düsseldorf in the early 1930s.[21] Karl Stojka, an Austrian Roma born in 1931 near Vienna, has broken through into the Gadzo-dominated world of art, and is now an internationally famous artist, who has had exhibitions in Vienna, Washington D.C., London, Auschwitz, the Netherlands and Japan. He was deported to Auschwitz together with his family and after years of travelling he returned to Vienna. He claims: 'When I paint a picture, I am not only painting the house, the flowers, the fields or the tree, no, I paint what is in my body, what my heart, my blood and my soul say, because it is only if you believe in a soul and if you believe that there really is another life after this one that you can paint these pictures'. Some forty years after the end of the war Stojka still has frequent nightmares about his experiences in Auschwitz. Whether it is his portrayal of his father dangling limply on the electrically charged barbed-wire fence having committed suicide (in reality, his father was beaten to death, although he ostensibly died from a heart attack), or the evocation of the gassing of 2,897 Sinti and Roma on that fateful night in August 1943, his art conveys the intensity of his emotions and the horrendous nature of the Holocaust, and has a highly political dimension. Each painting bears not only Stojka's signature, but the number tattooed permanently on his arm, Z5742, and some of the concentration camp prisoners he depicts are wearing the Z cloth triangle on their blue striped overalls, thus standing out as stigmatised Gypsies, whose ethnic identity is the root cause of their suffering. Stojka writes: 'I was born for a short stay on this earth. I brought nothing with me and will also take nothing with me. God determined that I was born a Gypsy and I thank God for that; I am always proud to be a Gypsy'.[22]

The establishment of the Documentation and Cultural Centre of the Central Council of the German Sinti and Roma in Heidelberg now provides valuable opportunities for contact between Sinti and Roma and the *Mehrheitsbevölkerung* (majority population) and is intended to foster greater appreciation of the contribution of the minority group to the cultural life of Germany and to give the group facilities for promoting and celebrating their own culture. The *Sinti Werkstatt* (Sinti Craft Workshop) near

Landau in Baden-Württemberg, the first and only one of its kind in Germany, promotes the concept of pride in being a member of the Gypsy ethnic group, and also offers facilities for the display and practice of the traditional crafts of carving in wood and stone, basket-making, painting and decorative art, while at the same time heightening the majority population's awareness of the achievements of the minority group.

These educational and cultural initiatives are important, in that a framework is being established within which it is possible to acknowledge the presence of the Sinti and Roma community and their contribution to the social and cultural life of German-speaking countries today. Rather than drawing artificial demarcation lines or enforcing assimilation, marginalisation or exclusion of the Sinti and Roma, it is essential to work towards intercultural initiatives designed to lead to a better mutual understanding of the Gypsies and the Gadzos.

Notes

1. Information taken from J. S. Hohmann, *Geschichte der Zigeunerverfolgung in Deutschland*, rev. edn, Frankfurt am Main, Campus, 1988, pp.17-18.
2. A. Fraser, *The Gypsies*, 2nd edn, Oxford, Cambridge (Mass), Blackwell, 1995, p.150.
3. See Hohmann, *Geschichte der Zigeunerverfolgung in Deutschland*, pp.7-47, for a detailed account of repressive measures against the Gypsies from the fifteenth to eighteenth century.
4. Fraser, *The Gypsies*, p.159.
5. All the information about Trollmann is summarised and translated from the account in M. Krausnick, *Wo sind sie hingekommen?*, Gerlingen, Bleicher, 1995, pp.73-79.
6. See D. Kenrick and G. Puxon, *Gypsies under the Swastika*, Hatfield, University of Hertfordshire Press, 1995, for further information on the refinement in 1941 of the earlier classification criteria of the *Zigeuner*, p.37.
7. M. Brand, 'Die vergessene Verfolgung: Der Zigeunerbeauftragte aus Soest und seine Opfer', *Soester Zeitschrift*, 107/1995, pp.105-106. 'Eine Zigeunerplage tritt im Kreis Soest in jedem Jahr anläßlich der stattfindenden Viehmärkte auf'.
8. See R. Rose and W. Weiss, *Sinti und Roma im 'Dritten Reich'*, Göttingen, Lamuv, 1991.
9. The catalogue written by K. Fings and F. Sparing, *Nur wenige kamen zurück*, Cologne, Selbstverlag, 1990, contains a number of photographs from the archives in Koblenz of Sinti and Roma in the camps. See also S. Milton 'Antechamber to Birkenau: The Zigeunerlager after 1933', in *Die Normalität des Verbrechens: Bilanz und Perspektiven der Forschung zu den nationalsozialistischen Gewaltverbrechen; Festschrift für Wolfgang Scheffler zum 65. Geburtstag*, ed. by H. Grabitz, K. Bästlein, J. Tuchel et al., Berlin, Hentrich, 1994, pp.241–259, and expanded in German, S. Milton, 'Der Weg zur "Endlösung der Zigeunerfrage": Von der Ausgrenzung zur Ermordung der Sinti und Roma', in E. Bamberger and A. Ehmann, eds, *Kinder und Jugendliche als Opfer des Holocaust*, Heidelberg, Dokumentationszentrum Deutscher Sinti und Roma, 1995, pp.25–49.

10. See K. Fings and F. Sparing, '*z.Zt. Zigeunerlager*', Cologne,Volksblatt, 1992, for an account of the history of political and administrative approaches to dealing with Sinti and Roma in Düsseldorf in the Nazi period based on a wide range of archive material and interviews with survivors.

11. See W. Benz, *Feindbild und Vorurteil*, Munich, dtv, 1996, Chapter 7, pp.139-169 for an account of the Marzahn camp in Berlin.

12. Eye-witness quoted in E. von Hase-Mihalik and D. Kreuzkamp, *Du kriegst auch einen schönen Wohnwagen*, Frankfurt am Main, Brandes & Apsel, 1990, p.54. 'Selbst die Kinder mußten arbeiten, ein 8-jähriger Junge mußte helfen, Backsteine abzuladen, dies Kind sprang vom Wagen herunter und wurde überfahren. Wir schrien alle um Hilfe. Auf seine Frage [...] erklärten wir ihm, das Kind ist überfahren worden, seine Antwort war: "Es ist ja nur ein Zigeunerkind, unsere deutschen Soldaten sterben auch an der Front"'.

13. Rose and Weiss, *Sinti und Roma im 'Dritten Reich'*, pp.15-16. 'In den folgenden Jahren bis zum Kriegsende wurden aus den Konzentrationslagern und ihren Arbeitskommandos auch viele Sinti und Roma zur Zwangsarbeit in kriegswichtigen Rüstungsbetrieben abgestellt. Darunter waren so namhafte Unternehmen wie die Flugzeugwerke Messerschmitt und Heinkel, die Elektrokonzerne Siemens und AEG, die Automobilhersteller Daimler-Benz und BMW, die Waffenschmiede Krupp und Rheinmetall oder der Chemiekonzern I.G. Farben (heute Hoechst, Bayer, BASF u.a.), um nur einige der großen Industrieunternehmen zu nennen. Daneben gab es auch eine stattliche Anzahl von weniger bekannten Unternehmen, die etwa mit der Munitionsherstellung beschäftigt waren oder die Ersatz- und Zubehörteile für Flugzeuge, Panzer, Unterseeboote und anderes Kriegsgerät produzierten.'

14. See Verband der Roma in Polen, ed. *Das Schicksal der Sinti und Roma im KL Auschwitz-Birkenau*, Warsaw, Kanzlei des Sejm, 1994, for detailed reports, photos and statistics relating to Sinti and Roma in Auschwitz.

15. Bamberger and Ehmann, eds, *Kinder und Jugendliche als Opfer des Holocaust*, p.82. 'Ein überlebender Sinti-Junge hat uns in einem Zeitzeugengespräch berichtet, wie er gemeinsam mit seinem Bruder von Dr. Mengele angewiesen wurde, mit Flüssigkeit gefüllte Glasbehälter, in denen menschliche Organe schwammen, vom Krankenbau in einen bereitstehenden Wagen zu tragen'. The volume highlights the racist nature of Nazi policies towards the Sinti and Roma minority.

16. In December 1990 some 200 Roma refugees took refuge in the *Stiftskirche* in the centre of Tübingen. The presence of the Roma in the church stirred up a hornets' nest among the population, with racist comments being directed at those involved in helping the refugees. See 'Antirassistische Arbeit — Linksradikaler Anspruch und realpolitische Praxis' in *'Ein Herrenvolk von Untertanen'*, ed. by A. Foitzik et al., Duisburg, DISS, 1992, pp.185-198, for an account of the work of the support group, including a discussion of the problems some of the feminist helpers had in developing links with the Romani women, who they felt were locked into a patriarchal system.

17. P. Köpf, *Stichwort: Sinti und Roma*, Munich, Heyne, 1994. Quoted in the section on the question of asylum-seekers, pp.80-82.

18. The first conference on anti-Gypsyism was held in Heidelberg and included prominent historians and scholars from Germany and the United States.

19. I. Hancock, 'Responses to the Porrajmos (The Romani Holocaust)', in *Is the Holocaust Unique?*, ed. by A. S. Rosenbaum, Colorado, Oxford, Westview Press, 1996, pp.63-64.

20. See F. Lindemann, *Die Sinti aus dem Ummenwinkel*, Weinheim, Basel, Beltz, 1991, for an account of how conditions in the Ummenwinkel estate were improved. At the end of the 1970s a ringroad was to be built right through the old Gypsy camp and the council

decided to provide new housing for the Sinti and Roma. The programme involved the provision of a Kindergarten, afternoon activities and a youth club for the over-thirteens.

21. Pankok's paintings of Gypsies were first shown in 1932 in the Düsseldorf *Kunsthalle*. After the opening of the major exhibition of some 650 works considered to be examples of 'Degenerate art' in Munich in 1937, including one of Pankok's lithographs, 'Hoto II' (1932), his work was banned by Hitler because of its overtly political message. It was not until 1947 that Pankok was again allowed to show his work.

22. K. Stojka, *Ein Kind in Birkenau*, Vienna, Eigenverlag, 1995. The pages of the catalogue are not numbered. See also S. Milton, ed. and transl. *The Story of Karl Stojka: A Childhood in Birkenau*, Washington, D.C., United States Holocaust Memorial Museum, 1992.

CHAPTER 2

The Persecution of the Sinti and Roma in Munich 1933–1945*

Ludwig Eiber

On the morning of 8 March 1943 the police in Munich conducted a wide-scale series of arrests of Sinti and Roma families, as did police in other places in the Reich. Josef H., a Sinto from Munich, remembers the occasion:

> At five o'clock in the morning six men from the Gestapo were suddenly standing in front of the door of my flat. They ordered us all to get dressed immediately. My wife and six children were supposed to go too; the youngest was only three years old. The Gestapo apologised, claiming that it was an urgent matter, because we were to be resettled somewhere. When they felt we weren't going fast enough, the men got rough with us. When we went out of the house we saw a lorry. Some of my relatives were already sitting on it.[1]

The 141 people detained in Munich, from the baby who was only a few months old to the seventy-nine-year-old woman, were deported on 13 March 1943 to the extermination camp in Auschwitz. Only a very few survived the genocide and returned to Munich.

The date 8 March 1943 marks the climax of a development which lasted about fifty years, which led from the discrimination and marginalisation of the Sinti and Roma to their ghettoisation, to plans for their deportation, and finally to the genocide of a whole people. Munich and Bavaria played a special role here, in that the government and police in Bavaria had been at the forefront of this policy since the end of the nineteenth century.

* Translated by Susan Tebbutt

Having said this, the number of Sinti and Roma living or residing temporarily in Bavaria had never been very high in comparison with other *Länder* of the Reich and the families who were resident in Bavaria had been living there for generations, many of them for centuries, as the research conducted by the National Socialist racial researchers shows. According to statistics from the police headquarters in Munich issued on 29 May 1925 there were fifty-eight 'Gypsies and vagrants' registered in the administrative region of Upper Bavaria in April/May of that year, and in the whole of Bavaria east of the Rhine there were 272 in the same period of time. References to Sinti and Roma for the town of Munich are only available from the end of the 1920s, because the relevant files are missing for the period before this. There is mention of families in residence or families passing through in reports from the neighbouring villages and villages such as Riem, Perlach and Freimann, which were later incorporated into the city. There was a marked influx of Sinti and Roma into the cities in the 1920s in Germany.

We know very little about the life of the Sinti (and occasionally Roma) families in the Munich area in the 1920s and 1930s. After the passing of the 'Bavarian Law to Combat Gypsies, Travellers and the Workshy' in 1926 many families moved away to Berlin. Up until the end of the 1920s apparently only very few families actually had a permanent place of residence within the municipal area of Munich. But time and time again groups of various sizes made a stop there, especially in winter. In Munich the 1930s saw a steep increase in the numbers, so that by the outbreak of war between two hundred and two hundred and fifty Sinti and Roma were resident there. It seems likely that this is connected to the increase in discrimination and persecution based on racial grounds from 1935 onwards, which had more impact in flat districts (since it was easier there to discourage people from being itinerant). A further factor was that opportunities to travel were being more and more severely limited after 1935, and by 1939 were completely stopped by the *Festsetzungserlaß* (decree prohibiting changes of residence) which prohibited Gypsies from travelling anywhere.

The great majority of the Sinti and the twenty or so Roma in Munich belonged to a small limited number of family groups, such as the H., M., Ki. and Ste. Families.[2] Some of them practised traditional Sinti trades such as peddling, whilst others worked as violin-makers or musicians. Thus the newspaper report from the

year 1931 which states that almost all Gypsies in Upper Bavaria
are musicians,[3] is somewhat exaggerated. Others, for example, like
several members of the H. family, which owned a small house in
Deisenhofen Street, worked as haulage contractors. They
transported gravel, foodstuffs and other goods in their horse-drawn
vehicles. The parts of town in which the Munich Sinti lived were
concentrated particularly in the east, especially in the districts of
Giesing, Au, Haidhausen and Ramersdorf. They mostly lived in
houses, but some of them lived in sheds or caravans on allotments.
In general the Sinti in Munich led a secluded life and seem hardly
to have been noticed by the rest of the population. The police in
Munich did not set up camps, as they did in Berlin, Cologne,
Frankfurt and other cities.

Since the end of the nineteenth century racist ways of thinking
had become widespread among the Bavarian police as well as in
other parts of the administrative machinery, and as a result of
this Bavaria was in the vanguard of an extreme policy of discrimination, marginalisation and persecution. From about 1870
onwards it is possible to see a change in police regulations.
Whereas they previously classified people moving from place to
place on the highways (such as puppeteers, beggars and fairground people) according to social and occupational criteria,
which meant that the Sinti were not mentioned by name, they
were now referred to by the racist classification 'Gypsy'.
Furthermore, the Gypsies were explicitly taken out of the
complex tangle of 'people on the move' and kept under special
police supervision and observation. Ethnic affiliation rather than
criminal behaviour was the trigger for the supervision and
persecution. Thus a Department responsible for Gypsy matters
was set up by the police authorities in Munich in 1890 to which all
information about Gypsies staying in Bavaria, or breaking the law
there, was to be reported. In 1905 their director, Detective Super-
intendent Alfred Dillmann, published a 'Gypsy Register' which
listed all itinerant Sinti who had been registered by the police.
Before the First World War and during the Weimar Republic
there had been attempts to create a uniform set of police
regulations and prohibitions, along the lines of the Bavarian
model, which would be applicable throughout the Reich, but
these fell through because of the resistance of the Parliaments,
despite the willingness of the police in the other Länder. Nevertheless in the 1920s the Munich Police Gypsy Department
became the central institution in the Reich, and all reports were

gathered there. The Central Office to Combat the Gypsy Menace became the headquarters of a national data bank on Gypsies and remained in Munich until 1938, when the department was moved to Berlin.

During the First World War the freedom of movement of the travelling Sinti was considerably restricted by the military authorities, and the penalties for infringements were drastically increased. These regulations continued to operate after the war and on 16 July 1926 the Bavarian State Parliament passed the 'Law to Combat Gypsies, Travellers and the Workshy', which was based on those regulations. The rules for its implementation explained what a 'Gypsy' was, stating that the term 'Gypsy' was in common currency and did not require any further explanation, and that racial science would provide information about who was to be perceived to be a Gypsy.

The law contained wide-reaching prohibitive and punitive regulations, and thus subjected the Sinti to the most severe discrimination and persecution.

Article 1
Gypsies and persons who roam about in the manner of Gypsies — 'travellers' — may only itinerate with wagons and caravans if they have permission from the police authorities responsible.
    This permission may only be granted for a maximum of one calendar year and is revocable at all times.
    The licence permitting them to do so is to be presented on demand to the (police) officers responsible.

Article 2
Gypsies and travellers may not itinerate with school-age children. Exceptions may be granted by the responsible police authorities, if adequate provision has been made for the education of the children.

Article 3
Gypsies and travellers can only itinerate with horses, dogs and animals which serve commercial functions if they possess a licence to do so from the responsible police authorities ...

Article 4
Gypsies and travellers may not possess firearms or ammunition unless they have been expressly permitted to do by the responsible police authorities.

Article 5
Gypsies and travellers may not roam about or camp in bands. The association of several single persons or several families, and the association of single persons with a family to which they do not belong, is to be regarded as constituting a band. A group of persons living together like a family is also to be regarded as a band.

Article 6
Gypsies and travellers may only encamp or park their wagons and caravans on open-air sites designated by the local police authorities, and only for a period of time specified by the local police authorities.

Article 9
Gypsies and travellers over sixteen years of age who are unable to prove regular employment may be sent to workhouses for up to two years by the responsible police authorities on the grounds of public security.[4]

Over and above this there were further restrictions imposed on travelling. The permit to 'travel around with a caravan' was 'never' to be issued to foreign Gypsies and vagrants, and 'where possible' was not to be granted to stateless people. As a rule it was only to be issued to such people who were authorised to practise an itinerant trade for the year in question, and Gypsies had to register with the local police authority of the place where they were spending the night and prove their identity. In the case of 'Gypsies and vagrants' with a criminal record, the authorities could lay down set routes, ban them from staying in certain parishes or districts, or allocate them a specific town where they had to stay. The authorities could send away people without Bavarian nationality on the grounds that they posed a threat to public safety, and could send away foreign or stateless Gypsies without having to state any particular grounds for doing so.

The plethora of permits required for travelling around was enough to provoke people to infringe the rules, and those people were then always threatened with prison sentences. Dr Wilhelm Hoegner, the Social Democrat MP in the Bavarian government and later President of Bavaria, criticised this practice (which was to become commonplace under the Nazi regime) as follows: 'In this way administrative organs facilitated an insupportable modification of judicial decrees'.[5] Other critics pointed unsuccessfully to racist elements of the law which contravened the constitution of the Reich.

After the Nationalist Socialists came to power in 1933, the Bavarian authorities demanded an even tighter application of the law, while the regulations themselves were considered adequate. When Heinrich Himmler took over control of the whole German police force in 1936 as 'Reichsführer SS and Head of the German Police' the Bavarian policy was extended to the whole Reich. Himmler originated from Munich, and had previously been in charge of the political police in Bavaria, together with his adjutant Reinhard Heydrich. After the move to Berlin a number of officials from the Bavarian Police Force took over the important posts in the Gestapo Headquarters and in the Reich Criminal Investigation Department.

With the introduction of the NS Race Laws in 1935 the already existing racist element in the persecution measures against Sinti and Roma became even more marked. Admittedly the Sinti and Roma were not mentioned explicitly in the Nuremberg Laws, and were furthermore unambiguously of 'Aryan' descent, but Stuckart and Globke concluded in their commentary on the Racial Laws, that alien blood was all blood which was not German blood and not related to German blood. The only people who were of alien blood in Europe were generally Jews ... and Gypsies.[6] One of the first visible consequences of the now openly racially motivated persecution was the Decree of 6 June 1936 issued by the Minister of the Interior for the Reich and Prussia with recommendations on how to combat the 'Gypsy Menace'. It was directed explicitly against the 'foreign Gypsy people who are inimical to German national traditions'. Whereas the emphasis in Bavaria had previously been particularly on deterrents and expulsion, the authorities now strove to 'make people sedentary', and this drive was accompanied by numerous regulations which limited freedom of movement.

Determining the 'racial' affiliation of the 'Gypsies' was, however, not a straightforward matter. Even when defining 'Racial Jews' the criterion of religious affiliation had been used! There was not anything comparable in the case of the Sinti and Roma. In general they had assumed the religion of the place they were living in, and were Christian. To sort out this matter the Reich Department of Health, on Himmler's instructions, set up a Racial Hygiene and Demographic Biology Research Unit (henceforth referred to as 'Research Unit') under the directorship of Professor Robert Ritter. Its task was to register all Gypsies living within the boundaries of the Reich and categorise them according to 'racial' characteristics. This meant that it also rendered visible as Gypsies those Sinti and Roma who had chosen a sedentary way of life and had become assimilated. Professor Ritter and his colleagues, including Eva Justin, Dr Adolf Würth, Sophie Ehrhardt and Ruth Kellermann, evaluated archives and registry office documents and interrogated Sinti and Roma in their homes, on caravan sites and even in concentration camps, about their origins. They systematically recorded their physical characteristics on a 'Racial Data Evaluation Form' (published by the Anthropological Institute in Munich) and drew up family trees, many of which were several metres long and included well over a hundred people. For people unwilling to provide information there was the threat of the police and the concentration camp. In Bavaria the registering did not start until 1939, probably under Eva Justin.

Personal data, genealogical links between relatives, and physical characteristics, (even down to the length of ear-lobes) were registered, as the Racial Data Form for the fifteen-year-old Roma girl Hulda Ste. from Munich shows. The collected data then formed the basis from which the Research Unit drew up family trees (the H. family tree goes right back to 1795) and set up a 'eugenic file' for each individual person. In this they differentiated between 'genuine Gypsies' (Z), 'part-Gypsies' (ZM) and 'non-Gypsies' (NZ). The Criminal Police Department in Munich recorded the receipt of 876 reports for Bavaria for the period up to 1 April 1942, of which 54 were 'Z' and 485 'ZM'.

In order to improve the coordination of police supervision the Central Police Department responsible for 'Gypsies' in Munich came under the aegis of the Reich Criminal Police Headquarters in Berlin with effect from 1 October 1938 and was called the 'Reich Central Office to Combat the Gypsy Menace'. In a report on 25 April 1938 it had proposed this step itself, pointing to its extensive stocks of files:

> In this respect it is to be noted that the Central Police Department in Munich responsible for 'Gypsies' has files enabling the official identification of eighty to ninety percent of all Gypsies in Germany, including both sedentary and itinerant Gypsies, part-Gypsies, and other people travelling round Gypsy-style. There are some 18,000 files on families or individuals in existence. The total number of registered people amounts to 33,524 people, of whom 17,210 are male and 16,314 female. Of these 18,138 are classified as Gypsy or part-Gypsy, 10,788 as Gypsy-style travellers, and 4,598 as other itinerant workers or sedentary people employed in work which involved travelling.[7]

Registration was conducted from the start with the deliberate intent of eliminating the 'Gypsies' from the 'German national body'. Even if this still referred in the early years to ghettoisation in camps or expulsion from the Reich, in March 1936 there was already the first mention of 'introducing the total solution to the Gypsy problem on either a national or international level' in a memorandum prepared for State Secretary Hans Pfundtner of the Reich Ministry of the Interior. In the following years the discussion between those concerned (the Racial Hygiene and Demographic Biology Research Unit, the Reich Chief Medical Officer and

Himmler's Central Office for Reich Security) still only revolved around the actual methods to be used in the 'Final Solution', whether they be internment, sterilisation, deportation or annihilation. After Ritter had substantially concluded the process of registration he proposed the following with reference to the long-planned 'Gypsy Law':

> Everything will now depend on this law coming into force soon and on people getting down to work immediately in a uniform and uncompromising way. The Gypsy question can only be considered solved when the bulk of asocial and good-for-nothing part-Gypsies are gathered together in large camps for migrant workers and encouraged to work, and when the further reproduction of this population of half-breeds is finally stopped.[8]

At the same time, from 1938 onwards, procedures against the Sinti and Roma were tightened up even further. A special tax was imposed on Sinti and Roma and in October 1939 they were removed from wherever they happened to be and taken into 'compulsory residence'; those fit for work were compulsorily signed on by the Employment Offices to work on construction sites or in the munitions industry.

Dr Catto, the head of the Criminal Investigation Department Central Office in Munich, gave his view of the present situation and future of the Munich Sinti and Roma in a note written on 29 October 1941:

> The situation in Munich at present is that about 200 Gypsies are distributed over the whole municipal area of the city, some living in flats, some in caravans. They are almost all in work and are being supervised by the Gypsy Department. It seems pointless to gather them together into a camp, since experiences (for example in Austria) have shown that when they are brought together in a camp their urge to travel is stimulated afresh, and there have been numerous instances of people leaving the place where they were being kept. Therefore until the Gypsies are totally eradicated it would seem advisable not to do anything further unless there are new directives from the Central Office for Reich Security.[9]

The expression 'totally eradicated' points to the fact that the genocide of the Sinti and Roma was already decided, as far as the top police officials were concerned. After the genocide of the Sinti and Roma had begun in summer 1941 in parts of the Soviet areas, the final decision to annihilate the Sinti and Roma within the boundaries of the Reich was taken, and in December 1942 Himmler ordered their deportation to the extermination camp Auschwitz-Birkenau. March 1943 marked the start of the great transports of deportees out of the Reich and the occupied areas to

Auschwitz. On 14 March 1943 141 Sinti/Roma adults and children were deported from Munich in cattle trucks. In the *Zigeunerlager* in Auschwitz most of them died of hunger and exhaustion or were murdered by the SS. At the start of August 1944 when the camp was dissolved only 4,500 of the 23,000 taken there were still alive. Approximately 1,500 people who were still fit to work were taken to concentration camps within the Reich and deployed as slave labour, and almost 3,000 people who were unfit to work (including the sick, the weak, old people and children) were murdered that same day in the gas chambers.

Among those who survived Auschwitz there were a few solitary members of Munich families. Their suffering was, however, not yet over. In the concentration camp at Ravensbrück, to which women and children had been taken, women and girls were brutally subjected to compulsory sterilisation. Prisoners, like for example Rosa M., who had been deported from Munich, were hired out by the SS to munitions firms as forced labour. In March 1945 a transport of women and children, including several from Munich, such as Sofie H. and two of her sons, was deported to the concentration camp at Mauthausen near Linz, in Austria, which was regarded as an extermination camp, and were sent on from there to Bergen-Belsen. Here they were liberated in mid-April 1945 by British troops.

Sinti who had been categorised as 'genuine' Gypsies by the Research Unit and who were assimilated into mainstream society were able to avoid being deported to Auschwitz in 1943 if they allowed themselves to be sterilised. This happened to several members of Munich families, whilst others, like for example Thomas H., who refused to allow the sterilisation, were deported to Auschwitz.

The concentration camp near Munich, Dachau, was involved in the persecution of Sinti and Roma in a number of ways. From as early as 1933 individual Sinti and Roma had been involuntarily incarcerated in the camp, and a fairly large number were arrested and brought to the camp during the massive campaigns to arrest the so-called 'workshy' and 'asocial' in 1937/1938. In June 1939 several hundred Austrian Sinti and Roma arrived in Dachau after mass arrests in Austria. Regardless of how they were justified, every deportation to a concentration camp, an institution of terror and arbitrariness, was an act of injustice.

Numerous Sinti and Roma were among the prisoners in the concentration camp at Dachau upon whom doctors conducted medical experiments, some of which had a fatal outcome. Similar experiments were carried out in the concentration camps at Auschwitz, Ravensbrück and Natzweiler. On behalf of the Technological Department of the Luftwaffe doctors began experiments in July/August 1944 aimed at making sea water drinkable. The reason for these experiments was the Luftwaffe's interest in providing pilots who had crashed at sea with drinking water. There were two methods to choose between for making sea water drinkable. The first method involved neutralising the salt by chemical processes with the help of silver nitrate. In the second, called the Berka Process after its inventor, the salt stayed in the sea water and only its taste was neutralised. The high cost of the first method was bemoaned, and doubts were expressed about the effectiveness of the Berka Process. In order to clear up the controversy which arose between the Technological Department and the Medical Inspectorate of the Luftwaffe, an experimental programme was devised at the initiative of Professor Eppinger of the University of Vienna, with Eppinger's Chief Medical Officer, Dr Wilhelm Beiglböck, in charge. It was at the recommendation of Dr Becker-Freyseng (the expert on aeronautical medicine in the Medical Inspectorate) that Himmler had forty concentration camp prisoners sent there to take part in the experiments, and these Sinti and Roma who had been brought from Auschwitz to the concentration camp in Buchenwald were selected and transported to Dachau on 7 August 1944. Among them were several from Munich who had survived Auschwitz.

In Dachau they were accommodated in the sick bay. First they were all given pilots' rations for ten days and then Beiglböck had them divided up into four groups as follows. There was one group which was to go hungry and thirsty, one group which got pure sea water and one group which was supposed to drink sea water with the Berka supplement, and in this group some got 500 ccm and some 1,000 ccm of the supplement per day. A control group which was supposed to receive a normal amount to drink did, however, then get the aforementioned water which had been desalinated. The whole experiment was designed to run for twelve days, but for the individual prisoners it lasted somewhere between six and ten days. For the prisoners whose only nourishment was pure sea water or sea water with chemicals, the twelve days were a murderous torture; one prisoner went mad. Even if there were apparently no fatalities during the course of the experiments, this does not automatically mean that no-one died of the after-effects, but at the very least it was extremely probable that they suffered physical and psychological damage.

In April 1945 between twenty and fifty Sinti arrived in Dachau with a transport from the concentration camp in Natzweiler and were taken from there to the annexe of the concentration camp in Munich-Riem. One of them, Sylvester L., reports on what happened to him:

> I was imprisoned by the Gestapo in Wiesbaden on 9 March 1943 on racial-political grounds and committed to the concentration camp in Auschwitz. At that time my father was already dead. At the same time my mother and my brother were imprisoned too. Both died in the concentration camp. From Auschwitz I was taken to the so-called 'experimental ward' in Natzweiler where every possible sort of experiment was conducted on us. Of the ninety or so people who were transferred there at that time, at most five or six men survived these experiments. Most died there and then. The others died later gradually of the after-effects. After that I spent about six months in Neckar-Elz near Heidelberg. From there we then had to flee the Americans, who were getting closer, and we ended up in Dachau. From the main camp in Dachau I was then taken immediately to the annexe in Munich-Riem.[10]

All of the approximately fifteen hundred prisoners were crammed together in the stables of the SS Central Riding School. They had to work on the airport compound where they were to repair bomb damage to the runways and buildings. The prisoners had to fill in the holes left by bombs and level them out. The work was supervised by German civilian labourers, probably employed by construction firms who worked for the organisation Todt (OT). According to reports the prisoners were not beaten during the work.

The prisoners slept on straw in the empty stables, with some twenty or thirty men to a box. There were also some two or three-storey wooden benches with straw on them. The food was inadequate, not only in terms of the quantity but also in terms of quality. In the mornings an indefinable drink was dished out, which was described as tea or coffee. At midday the prisoners got a thin potato or turnip soup and in the evenings they got their bread ration, which was initially one loaf for four people and later one loaf for ten people.

Sick prisoners were maltreated, unless it emerged that they had a temperature of at least 39 degrees. According to the reports there was no sick bay and no treatment for the sick. Many prisoners were so weak that they collapsed on the trek of some two kilometres to their place of work. Former prisoners reported that these people, who were at the end of their strength, were killed by the SS guards.

There was no protection in the camp from air-raids. If there was an air-raid warning the SS opened the gate to the camp and the prisoners were ordered to fan out into the compound and hide. At the same time the SS threatened to shoot anyone who did not come back immediately the alarm was over. Many prisoners used the opportunity to get something edible from the fields or to beg for food from the farmers in the vicinity. If the SS caught them doing so, they were shot. A prisoner who was accused by a woman in the town of having stolen a loaf was first locked in an air-raid shelter, and then shot three days later in front of the assembled prisoners at roll call. Prisoners were often denounced by people from the nearby town and surrounding farms, and this always led to the execution of the accused. In another case twenty Russian prisoners are said to have been shot in the back of the neck in February or March 1945. According to the reports of former prisoners, during the period the camp was in existence some fifty prisoners were executed in this way on the roll call square, many by Trenkle. On 9 April 1945 the airport was heavily bombed and according to air-raid reports at least 41 prisoners lost their lives, and about forty were wounded. Those wounded were taken back to the main camp in Dachau. Despite the air-raid warning the concentration camp prisoners had not been permitted to leave the runway. When the Allied troops were approaching at the end of April 1945, the SS, in order to prevent the liberation, forced the prisoners to set off on evacuation marches, which proved for many to be fatal.

Of the 141 Sinti and Roma deported from Munich it is only possible to establish the fate of a few. It is to be assumed that by far the great majority lost their lives in Auschwitz or died later in Ravensbrück, Mauthausen, Bergen-Belsen or other concentration camps. For this reason only a few cases are cited here.

Josef H.'s family

Josef H. was born on 15 March 1904 in Retzbach in Upper Franconia and his wife Sofie was born on 11 April 1913 in Walderode near Lüneburg. They were married in a registry office on 28 April 1932. Their six children, daughters Emma and Rosemarie and sons Hugo, Manfred, Rigo and Peter were born between 1929 and 1939, four of them in Munich.

Since about 1932 the family had been resident in Munich, where Josef H. ran his own haulage business. The whole family was arrested on 8 March 1943 and deported to Auschwitz. It is presumed that the whole family was taken to Ravensbrück in July/August 1944 in a fairly large transport and then split up and housed separately in the women's and men's camps. The compulsory sterilisation was carried out in Ravensbrück. Josef H. signed on for the 'Dirlewanger Unit'[11] after it had been agreed that his family would then be set free. The oldest son Manfred was sent with him to Sachsenhausen and managed to escape from there while on the evacuation march in April 1945. His wife and other children did not manage to escape. Instead they were taken away on 10 March 1945 on a transport to Mauthausen (in total there were 447 Sinti/Roma women and children), where they only stayed for two weeks. Then they set off on an eight-day journey to Bergen-Belsen, where the members of the family, sick and at the end of their strength, were liberated by the English.

Konrad H.'s family

Konrad H. was born on 28 March 1901 in Kitzingen. His wife 'Notschga' Alma was born on 21 March 1902 in Scheßel near Rottenburg. They married in a registry office in 1927 and had five children, sons Ludwig and Johann Baptist and daughters Maria, Anna and Werna, who were born between 1929 and 1938. They had been living in Munich since 1931, where Konrad H. ran a haulage business. In 1941 Konrad H. was called up for military service, and in 1942 was dismissed because he was a Gypsy. On 8 March 1943 the whole family was arrested and deported to Auschwitz. The mother was one of the first to die. In July/August 1944 the survivors were transported to Ravensbrück and the children were sterilised there. Ludwig and his father were taken to Sachsenhausen concentration camp, where Konrad H. signed up for the new 'Dirlewanger Storm Brigade' in order to get his family released. He was sent to serve on the Eastern Front and from there ended up being taken prisoner by the Russians. He returned in 1946. Ludwig H. remained in Sachsenhausen and managed to escape with three cousins during the evacuation march. The sisters and the younger brother Johann Baptist stayed in Ravensbrück, and it is thought that they were taken from there on the above-mentioned transport via Mauthausen to Bergen-Belsen. Ludwig H., who came back to Munich after the liberation, went with relatives to Bergen-Belsen and found his brother in the hospital there suffering from tuberculosis and half-starved. He brought him back to Munich.

Franz S.'s family

Franz S. was born on 27 April 1905 in Wernfeld, and his wife Veronika was born on 7 May 1899 in Viernheim. They had five daughters, Margarete, Emilie, Frieda, Gerda and Brunhilde, who came into the world between 1924 and 1934. The family had been living in Munich since the beginning of the 1930s where Franz S. had a haulage firm. In 1940–1941 he was called up for military service and in 1942 was dismissed like all other Sinti and Roma. Franz S. was arrested on 5 September 1942 because he had not denounced his nephew, Eduard He. (who had gone into hiding), to the police. Eduard He., who had carried out several break-ins on garden sheds to get food for himself, was sentenced to death and executed. For the same crime the special court in Munich sentenced S., together with his wife, to three months in prison. After serving his sentence Franz S. was released on 10 December 1942. The state attorney agreed to postpone Veronika S.'s sentence until 1 May 1943. The whole family was arrested on 8 March 1943, with the exception of Franz S., who had at first managed to escape being arrested because his brother Michael He., Eduard's father, had given him a tip-off. Nevertheless he went to the police voluntarily because he did not want to abandon his family. Nobody returned. All members of the S. family perished in Auschwitz.

Fridolin K.

Fridolin K. was a violin-maker. In the middle of the 1920s he went to Munich from the Württemberg area and settled here. It was there that he met his future wife Maria. She was not a Sintezza. They had five children. Fridolin K. had turned away from the traditional Sinti way of life and lived totally assimilated into the community. He was not deported in

March 1943, but had to subject himself to compulsory sterilisation. On 3 October 1943 he, his eldest son, his brother and Peter H. were sterilised in the Surgical Clinic in Munich. Maria K. reports that her husband and her son suffered for the rest of their lives from this degradation. Both died early, the son at the age of forty-one.

Rosa F.

Rosa F. was born in 1924 and lived with her parents and brothers and sisters in Vienna and was admitted to the Gypsy camp in Lackenbach in Burgenland as part of a campaign of arrests. After a few months when her family were supposed to be deported to Litzmannstadt (Lodz) with a large transport, Rosa F. went to Munich, where three months later she was arrested again. Back in the camp in Lackenbach she was punished, but a few weeks later managed to escape again to Munich. Once again she was arrested and first taken to Villach, then to the hospital in Klagenfurt because of illness. When she regained her health she escaped to Munich yet again, where she lived in hiding for about a year and a half with her fiancé and later husband Johann M. in Ungsteiner Street. On the birth of her first son her false identity was discovered and she was imprisoned yet again. Her husband succeeded in persuading Detective Officer Zeiser to set free the baby, which was only a few weeks old, by appealing to his love for his own children. Rosa F. was deported to Auschwitz and sent from there to Ravensbrück and on from there to a subsidiary camp in Wolkenburg on the river Mulde. Here she missed her child so much that she escaped, but was arrested again. On returning to the camp she was severely physically abused. In the process one of her arms was broken. She was locked in the air-raid shelter without any clothes for eight days, and was further punished by being thrashed twenty-five times. During the evacuation transport to Dachau Rosa F. managed to flee again by hiding by some willow trees, and this last time it was for good. Her parents and brothers and sisters died in the section of the ghetto in Lodz where Gypsies were housed.

These personal histories stand for many. The suffering and terror are only documented in the memories of the survivors.

It is estimated that about 25,000 German Sinti and Roma and some 500,000 Sinti and Roma in Europe perished as a result of the persecution during the Nazi regime. Of the Munich Sinti and Roma who were deported only very few came back. Whole families were destroyed, and in other cases only a few family members survived. Thus the social network, which was based on families and family groupings, and in which the old people carried out important functions, was largely destroyed, and the survival of the Sinti and Roma as an ethnic community was put in jeopardy. Like all concentration camp prisoners the survivors were marked for life by the physical deprivations and suffering and by the indelible memories of the terror. This was the background against which survivors founded the 'Committee of German Gypsies' in 1946 in Munich. They demanded authorisation to represent the German Gypsies, a prosecuting counsel at the Nuremberg Trials, recognition as victims of persecution during the Nazi regime and compensation. They also demanded to be recognised as an ethnic minority, with the right to be treated equally in economic and cultural terms. Their attempt to rehabilitate the persecuted Sinti and Roma was, however, to no avail.

In fact, the opposite was the case. The discrimination on the part of the police and authorities continued uninterrupted. The old law concerning the Gypsies and the work-shy was still in force and it was not until 1947 that it was repealed by the U.S. military government, on the grounds that it was not in accordance with legal principles. Thereupon the police began to work out a new draft bill, and employees of the former National Socialist Police Gypsy Department were put in overall charge. The 'Vagrants Law' which was finally passed by the Bavarian State Parliament in 1953 was essentially modelled on the old law. The practices of register-ing and discriminating were continued and Nazi files continued to be used. It was not until 1970 that the law was finally repealed and not replaced.

The Sinti had to fight for a long time, often in vain, to receive compensation and to be vindicated. The persecution of the Sinti and Roma on racial grounds was denied for a long time or was limited to the period after the deportation to Auschwitz in 1943. In many cases compensation was refused. The judgement of the Bavarian High Court in Munich was one of the most restrictive and set the standards for the others. When the courts finally got round to accepting that racial persecution had been taking place from 1938 onwards it was too late for many people. Attempts on the part of individuals to put up a fight against this treatment remained unsuccessful. The Sintezza Rosa M., for example, who had been refused compensation for having been deported to Auschwitz, had to go through the experience of having the police officer who had given the order for her deportation facing her in court as the expert witness from the police authorities.

It was not until 1979/1980 that the civil rights movement had its first successes thanks to the initiative of the Verband der Sinti (Association of Sinti) and the Society for Endangered Peoples. A memorial event in Bergen-Belsen reminded people of the genocide of the Sinti and Roma. At the concentration camp memorial site in Dachau the hunger strike of a number of Sinti campaigning against the further utilisation of the Nazi files by Bavarian police caused an international sensation. As a consequence there was a certain amount of recognition in the Federal Republic of the Sinti and Roma as victims of the Nazi regime. It is symptomatic of this changed situation, for example, that at the commemoration of the fiftieth anniversary of the liberation of the concentration camp in Flossenbürg in April 1995 the Sinto Hugo H. spoke as the representative of the Sinti and Roma. At the age of ten he had been deported from Munich to Auschwitz on 13 March 1943.

Notes

1. L. Eiber, ed., 'Ich wußte, es wird schlimm', Munich, Buchendorfer, 1993, p.100.
2. All surnames are omitted to preserve the privacy of survivors, in accordance with data protection regulations.
3. Newspaper report dated 7 June 1931, quoted in Eiber, 'Ich wußte, es wird schlimm', p.30.
4. I have used the translation into English given in M. Burleigh and W. Wippermann, *The Racial State: Germany 1933–1945*, Cambridge, New York, Port Chester, Melbourne, Sydney, CUP, 1991, pp.114–115.
5. Quoted in Eiber, 'Ich wußte, es wird schlimm', p.41.
6. See W. Stuckart and H. Globke, *Kommentar zur deutschen Rassengesetzgebung*, Vol. 1, Munich, 1936, pp.55f.
7. Quoted in Eiber, 'Ich wußte, es wird schlimm', p.51.
8. Ibid. p.59 and p.62.
9. Ibid. p.72.
10. Ibid. p.89.
11. The first 'Dirlewanger Unit' was a battalion consisting of convicted criminals with sharpshooting talents. After 1943 the SS 'Dirlewanger Storm Brigade' included ostensible volunteers and sometimes also concentration camp prisoners desperate to survive, who thought they might be able to escape or surrender to the enemy. This latter brigade served on the eastern front and became notorious for excessive brutality.

CHAPTER 3

Persecuting the Survivors: The Continuity of 'Anti-Gypsyism' in Postwar Germany and Austria

Sybil Milton

Today, fifty years after the end of the great slaughter in Nazi-occupied Europe and almost a decade after the collapse of Communism, the old ethnic and racial hatreds, which we had thought banished, seem to have reappeared throughout Europe. In the former Yugoslavia, Serbs and Croats are once again locked in battle. In the Caucasus, Armenians are once again fighting for their survival. In German streets, bullies with swastikas are once again burning and killing. In Russia, men like Zhirinovsky are once again peddling the defamatory myth of a Jewish world conspiracy. And throughout Europe, the Roma and Sinti (usually referred to as Gypsies) — Europe's largest racial minority — are once again, as they did fifty years ago under Nazi tyranny, facing destruction at the hands of their European neighbours.

The traditional term 'Gypsy', and its equivalent European versions, like *Zigeuner* in German, is a designation given by outsiders. The primary definition in the second edition of *The Oxford English Dictionary* of 1989 is still racial, classifying Gypsies as 'a wandering race of Hindu origin', and describing them as people with 'dark tawny skin and black hair' — whereas the term 'Swedes' in that same dictionary does not mention their fair complexions. The traditional term 'Gypsy' has other derogatory contemporary connotations, making Sinti and Roma collective scapegoats for social, political, and economic dislocations in postwar Europe. The marginalisation of Sinti and Roma is usually based on institutionalised discrimination tied to popular prejudices and exclusionary nationalism. The virulent anti-Roma prejudices that culminated in the Nazi Holocaust have returned in the 1990s as physical attacks on Roma in Austria, the Czech and Slovak Republics, Romania, Poland, Bulgaria, and the former Soviet Union; and also as social engineering schemes involving sterilisation and denaturalisation in both eastern and western Europe.

Discrimination against Sinti and Roma did not cease with the collapse of Nazi Germany in 1945. During the immediate postwar years, harassment by German and Austrian police, housing, health, and welfare authorities was routine. In Germany, Gypsy registration files created during the Nazi era were transferred to postwar successor agencies; these compromising files disappeared or were destroyed when public disclosure of their existence proved embarrassing. Thus, for example, from the early 1950s to the mid-1970s, the Landfahrerzentrale (Vagrant Department) of the Bavarian police retained the 'Gypsy' records of the Zentralstelle zur Bekämpfung des Zigeunerunwesens (Central Office to Combat the Gypsy Menace), which after 1936 had its headquarters in Munich. These records disappeared and were allegedly destroyed in the 1970s, when the nascent Sinti and Roma civil rights movement initiated inquiries about them.[1]

Although Control Council Law No. 1, the first order of the Allied occupation government in Germany, provided for the repeal of 'laws of a political or discriminatory nature upon which the Nazi regime rested', it did not specifically itemise Nazi anti-Gypsy decrees and administrative regulations. Contravening the intent if not the explicit letter of this Allied law, the city of Cologne in 1949 explicitly stipulated the continued validity of the 8 December 1938 Heinrich Himmler directive for 'Fighting the Gypsy Plague'. The Cologne police issued a circular on 12 March 1949 entitled *Bekämpfung des Zigeunerunwesens* (Combating the Gypsy Menace), revealing the continuity of attitudes to Himmler's May 1938 order that named the Munich police bureau of Gypsy affairs as the Reichszentrale zur Bekämpfung des Zigeunerunwesens. Moreover, these 1949 Cologne regulations continued Nazi restrictions on issuing licenses for Gypsies with itinerant trades (musicians, craftsmen, and travelling vendors) and mandated the registration and surveillance of all local Gypsy employment.[2] Similar repressive regulations were also issued by local authorities in Düsseldorf.

In both Cologne and Düsseldorf, local governments compelled Sinti and Roma survivors to return to the dilapidated housing and marginal sanitation of Nazi municipal Gypsy internment camps and were empowered to evict and prosecute returning survivors and refugees found residing in other unapproved sites regulated by city councils.[3] In the early 1950s, the Düsseldorf artist Otto Pankok described the hostility of local authorities and the marginal living conditions imposed on Sinti survivors in the Höherweg Gypsy camp:

> In my town, they once again directed them [Sinti survivors] to housing in barracks surrounded by barbed wire, where they had previously been incarcerated by the Nazis. Today they still live with the filth and most primitive conditions of that camp. Hitler did not complete the extermination of the Gypsies, but this is taking place slowly and steadily today in what one imagines as a new, more civilized era.[4]

Prior to the 1980s, few archives and scholars were interested in documenting Nazi crimes against Roma and Sinti. The fragmentation and dispersion of German records during and after the Second World War hampered early recognition of the importance of the partial files of Dr Robert Ritter's Rassenhygienische und Bevölkerungsbiologische Forschungsstelle des Reichsgesundheitsamtes (Racial Hygiene and Demographic Biology Research Unit) located in the research files of his associate, Professor Sophie Ehrhardt, at Tübingen University. Ritter was the so-called race scientist, trained as a child psychiatrist and physician, who had directed Nazi governmental research in the classification and registration of Roma and Sinti; in 1941, Ritter had become chief of the Kriminalbiologisches Institut der Sicherheitspolizei (Criminal Biological Institute of the Security Police) located within the Reichssicherheitshauptamt (RSHA) (Central Office for Reich Security). Ritter's team of younger racial scientists and researchers included Sophie Ehrhardt, a zoologist and anthropologist, whose research had focused on East Prussian Gypsies and on Jews and Gypsies in the Lodz ghetto and in the Dachau and Sachsenhausen concentration camps. Ehrhardt was appointed Professor of Anthropology at Tübingen University in 1942. Ritter's team accumulated and classified data about thirty thousand Gypsies, creating genealogical charts accompanied by case histories with photographs, official documents (including registration lists of Gypsy internees in Nazi special internment camps), measurements, and other physical evidence. In order to justify their policies, the Nazi regime had co-opted Ritter's research to assist in the identification and classification of Gypsies. The postwar privatisation of these official records of Nazi governmental agencies, housed with the same researchers who had once created this data, impaired postwar analysis of these records to assist survivors with restitution claims and delayed for more than three decades serious academic understanding of the racial nature of Nazi beliefs and policies toward Roma and Sinti. Moreover, it took several years to catalogue these records after they were finally transferred in 1981 to the German Federal archives in Koblenz.[5]

In addition, German bureaucrats encouraged the emphasis on Jewish victimisation in Holocaust historiography, since the excesses of anti-Semitism could be blamed on the pathology of Hitler and his SS followers; whereas, the murder of German nationals in the so-called euthanasia killings and the killing of Sinti and Roma, both carried out by 'ordinary' German bureaucrats, scientists, and policemen, implicated a far larger segment of the German population. Moreover, the focus on Nazi anti-Semitism also prevented discussion of how deeply the German scientific community was involved in the killing operations against Jews as well as against Gypsies and the handicapped, the three groups deemed 'alien' and 'other' in Nazi German policy.

And finally, German postwar restitution legislation and its implementation excluded most Sinti and Roma survivors, subjecting them to arbitrary and repetitive bureaucratic humiliations. Most Gypsy survivors were initially disqualified from receiving compensation as racial victims for imprisonment prior to the March 1943 Auschwitz decree. Although this date was later changed to December 1938, both dates excluded restitution for incarceration in early internment camps such as Marzahn near Berlin or Lackenbach in Burgenland, ignored deportation to ghettos such as Radom or Bialystok after May 1940, restricted claims for health disabilities caused by involuntary sterilisation and medical experiments, and required minimum periods of involuntary detention in certain officially recognised camps and ghettos to qualify for meagre settlements. Claims filed by Sinti and Roma survivors for homes and businesses impounded at deportation were invariably disallowed, often after investigation by the same policemen who had previously arrested them in the Nazi era. Health claims for physical and psychological trauma were similarly disregarded. This failure of empathy with Sinti and

Roma survivors was rationalised using the language of Nazi stereotypes and of Ritter's research team that had once defined the victims as 'asocial and criminal'.

Despite minor improvements in both legislation and court decisions by the 1980s, hostile practices such as the involuntary denaturalisation of many German Sinti survivors and the reduction of modest restitution settlements by deducting any prior welfare assistance established a flagrant pattern of official dissembling and hostility.[6] Former Nazi functionaries or guards who had served in the Salzburg-Maxglan and Lackenbach internment, labour, and transit camps appeared as expert witnesses before Austrian and German courts against Roma survivors seeking restitution for damage to their health in these camps. Despite their bias and complicity, these Nazi veterans were deemed credible in Leni Riefenstahl's court case to censor a documentary film that revealed her role in using Roma forced labour from Maxglan in making her film *Tiefland*.[7]

Identity papers and passports of most deported German Sinti and Roma had been confiscated. Although Allied occupation authorities issued new identity papers to returning survivors, German authorities frequently confiscated these documents, claiming that Gypsy survivors lacked proof of German nationality and were therefore stateless. In fact, however, papers authenticating their citizenship claims could often be found in local German restitution and finance departments where receipts signed after 1940 for the transfer of property and possessions confiscated from Gypsies were also located. This denial of citizenship to Sinti survivors also meant the loss of civil rights, including the right to vote in German elections. For stateless Sinti, passports had to be renewed every two years for a fee of about 40 Marks and they were compelled to pay for visas when they travelled outside Germany (whereas German nationals received free passports for a period of ten years). These Sinti survivors faced the omnipresent threat of expulsion. For example, between 1950 and 1967, the city of Cologne deported many Sinti whose prewar identity cards confirming their German citizenship were available in local police files.[8]

One case from Bavaria was truly bizarre. The Sinto Andreas Kaufmann, Jr, born in 1927 in Simmerberg, in the Landau-Bodensee district, was declared stateless by Bavarian authorities in the early 1970s, because his ancestors had in 1819 illegally moved to Bavaria from the Kingdom of Württemberg. His genealogical records revealed more than two hundred years of unbroken ancestral residences in various Württemberg and Bavarian towns. Although German constitutional law prohibits discrimination on the basis of race, and exceptional laws against Gypsies are prohibited, the city of Munich ruled in September 1971 that Kaufmann's citizenship claims could not be recognised 'since he had inadequate proof required for citizenship'. In 1979, after multiple appeals by the plaintiff, the Bavarian constitutional court finally awarded Kaufmann German citizenship.[9]

Despite democratisation and economic recovery, de-Nazification in postwar Germany and Austria remained incomplete. West German political culture included widespread amnesia with regard to the continuities of personnel in government and academia. These continuities exemplified one aspect of the collective failure to assume political responsibility for the Nazi murder of Sinti and Roma. For example, the staff of the Racial Hygiene and Demographic Biology Research Unit in Berlin-Dahlem had little difficulty in securing employment after 1945 and they eluded all penalties during postwar judicial proceedings. Robert Ritter taught criminal biology at the University of Tübingen from late 1944 to 1946, and was hired in December 1947 as a pediatrician by the Frankfurt Health Office. Once again, Ritter hired Dr Eva Justin to work with him; she was employed as a psychologist at the Frankfurt Health Office. After brief investigations, judicial proceedings against Ritter and Justin as accessories in the murder of German Gypsies were discontinued.[10] Dr Sophie Ehrhardt continued her research and teaching as a professor of anthropology at Tübingen University, where she used the plaster casts of Gypsy heads and fingerprint data from the records of the Racial Hygiene Unit entrusted to her after the war. Judicial proceedings against her were dropped in 1985.[11] Dr Adolf Würth became an official in the Bureau of Statistics in Baden-Württemberg from 1951 to 1970. Würth was never tried as an accessory to murder, since judicial investigations of his career were discontinued. Many perpetrators were never placed on trial; for example, the physician and anthropologist Professor Otmar Freiherr von Verschuer, who had supervised and subsidised many of Josef Mengele's notorious experiments on Gypsy and Jewish twins at Auschwitz, was never indicted or investigated. After the war, he established the Human Genetics Institute at the University of Münster in 1951 and was appointed a professor at Münster in 1953.[12] Verschuer also wrote the introduction to a biologically deterministic study on 'hereditary vagrancy' published under the auspices and support of the Public Health Department of the German Federal Ministry of the Interior.[13] Moreover, similar postwar research about Roma and Sinti continued to be funded by the Deutsche Forschungs-gemeinschaft (German Research Foundation), the same agency that had subsidised Robert Ritter's research team during the Nazi era.[14]

Anatomical, anthropometrical, and linguistic research data gathered during the Nazi era continued to be routinely used in postwar German and Austrian academic publications. Several case studies illustrate this lack of remorse and sensitivity. In 1952, Heinrich Hufmann's dissertation about 'Exterior Pelvic Measure-ments and the Sexual Development of Female Gypsies' was accepted by the Düsseldorf Academy of Medicine. Hufmann's involuntary subjects had been Roma women living on the outskirts of Kragujevic (Serbia), where Hufmann had been stationed as an army physician; these women had survived the *Wehrmacht* massacre of two hundred male Roma and more than seven thousand Serbs in late October 1941. His dissertation never mentions these details, although he disingenuously notes that he had encountered difficulties in securing anatomical measurements: 'The technical aspects of this investigation were difficult. It was not easy to get the women to undress completely'. Hufmann also wrote about the 'primitive and instinctual nature of Gypsy behaviour ... including thievery and licentiousness', frequently quoting from Gerhard Stein's 1938 doctoral dissertation, which had been supervised by Otmar von Verschuer and had been based on anthropological measurements of Roma and Sinti prisoners in the internment camp at Berlin-Marzahn.[15]

Johann Knobloch's 1953 publication of 'Romani texts from Burgenland' acknowledged that his linguistic research was based on field research at the Lackenbach internment camp for Roma during two weeks in early 1943. Roma prisoners were retained at Lackenbach until Knobloch submitted his dissertation to the University of Vienna and they were then deported to Auschwitz-Birkenau, where most were killed. Knobloch's visit had been arranged after correspondence between the University of Vienna and the Stiftung Ahnenerbe (Reich Genealogical Research Foundation) of the SS, and Robert Ritter's Criminal Biological Institute of the Security Police (then Office V of the RSHA). Sinti and Roma prisoners were used as involuntary research subjects by

German academics, although they obviously concealed any connection between their research and Nazi genocide in their postwar publications. Thus, Knobloch minimises the deadly result of internment at Lackenbach and his descriptions were consequently quoted by even such reputable scholars as Donald Kenrick and Grattan Puxon, who were unaware of Knobloch's complicity.[16]

Postwar police careers revealed a similar lack of consequences for involvement in the deportation and killing of Sinti and Roma. Thus, Josef Eichberger, who had been responsible for Gypsy deportations in the RSHA, became head of the 'Gypsy' department of the Bavarian State Police; Leo Karsten became head of the Landfahrer (Migrants) Department of the Baden State Police in Karlsruhe; and Hans Maly, a senior officer in Department VA2 (preventive measures against asocials, prostitutes, and Gypsies) of the RSHA from January to late September 1943, was hired as head of the Bonn detective forces after 1945. Judicial proceedings were dropped against these policemen.[17] From 1969 to 1971, during the trial of Otto Bovensiepen, the former chief of the Berlin Gestapo, the statute of limitations had expired on all crimes of the Nazi period except murder. Bovensiepen was indicted for 'knowingly and with base motives assisting in the deportation and killing of at least 35,000 Berlin Jews and 252 Gypsies'. The trial was suspended in 1971, since Bovensiepen had suffered a heart attack and his physician testified that he would never be able to live through the trial.[18] Recently, after a forty-three month trial, the Siegen District Court sentenced Ernst August König on 24 January 1991 to life imprisonment for murders he had committed as SS Blockführer in the Gypsy camp BIIe at Auschwitz-Birkenau.[19]

Allied tribunals of the four postwar occupation armies and the successor states (the Federal Republic of Germany, the German Democratic Republic, and the Republic of Austria) tried large numbers of Nazi criminals for crimes committed during the Second World War; usually specific crimes against Sinti and Roma were part of larger indictments for participation in the *Einsatzkommandos* or crimes committed in the concentration camps.[20] It is uncommon to find explicit acknowledgment of Sinti and Roma victims in many European postwar Holocaust memorials. Their tragic fate is belatedly recognised in recent monuments on Museumplein in Amsterdam, at the former Gypsy camps in Salzburg and Lackenbach, in concentration camp memorials at Bergen-Belsen, Buchenwald, Mauthausen, and

Auschwitz-Birkenau, and in new memorials at the children's home in Mulfingen, as well as at the sites of their deportation in Heidelberg and Wiesbaden.[21]

German unification and changes in the former Soviet bloc since 1990 have altered the political map of Europe. These changes are, however, still incomplete and it is therefore too early for any final analysis. Nevertheless, recent developments do show that the administration of memorials in the countries of Eastern Europe and in reunited Germany will at best transform and at worst diminish the status of most Holocaust memorials. Growing popular resentment against Jews and Gypsies, hatred of outsiders, as well as the emergence of local fascist and neo-Nazi groups also bode ill for the future.[22]

The belated recognition of the Roma and Sinti Holocaust is still incomplete in current historiography. During the 1980s new sources and research have produced interpretations that correct many of the old imbalances by pointing to the connections between the murder of the Jews and that of the Gypsies and the disabled. These new analyses have, however, been unable so far to alter the older interpretation; prejudice and the habits of forty years cannot be reversed overnight.

In late November 1995, *Stern* magazine printed a vignette showing the pernicious continuities of 'anti-Gypsyism' among government officials. One senior staff member at the Bundestag, Wolfgang Dexheimer, met with American exchange fellows, and told them: 'Previously we could say "Gypsies", now we have to say Sinti and Roma… They lack personal hygiene and are thieves… The word "Gypsy" is after all found in *Duden*…' This remarkable speech included the sentence: 'You Americans feel just the same about Mexicans'. The *Stern* reporter stated that the outraged American visitors prompted the decision to prohibit Dexheimer from addressing academic exchange fellows in the future.[23] Similarly verbal callousness has proliferated in central Europe. Thus, Chancellor Vranitzky of Austria publicly censored statements by a Bolzano city councillor who 'advocated the gassing of Gypsies'.[24] The Hungarian skinhead band 'Gypsy Destroyer Guard Regiment' has produced a very popular song with the title 'Gypsy Free Zone', advocating the 'extermination of Gypsies, whether child, woman, or man'.[25]

Renewed verbal assaults against Sinti and Roma have coincided with increased physical violence against Gypsies in virtually every country of central and eastern Europe and police harassment has increased against many Roma communities. The press has blamed all Roma for the recent increase of crime, although in fact most of the actual offenses committed by Roma are subsistence thefts for food staples. In Germany, where Sinti and Roma have resided for more than five hundred years, they were denied ethnic minority group status, which would protect their linguistic and cultural rights, although this group status was acknowledged much earlier for Sorbs, Wends, and Frisians living in Germany. Discrimination, violence, and loss of rights have become common pan-European phenomena for Roma and Sinti since 1990. Their visibility and increased vulnerability require more than local human rights solutions.

It must be noted that these prejudicial stereotypes are also found in the United States. The *Chevy Chase Village Crier* of February 1996 carried a notice entitled 'Residents Beware' in the Police Beat section; this brief article warned suburban residents of a 'Gypsy scam'. A similar story 'Watch Out for Gypsies' had appeared in the July-August 1993 issue and contained a paragraph on 'How to Recognize Gypsies'. Hostile local authorities and ethnic prejudices are not only found in Europe. The quarterly magazine *o Drom*, published by the Lau Mazirel Association in Amsterdam, stated in its inaugural September 1994 issue: 'We are not a problem, we have problems'. This maxim may provide the basis for a more constructive dialogue for protecting Romani cultural heritage and civil rights. Alternating policies of assimilation and rejection in Europe, both East and West, have led to a new awareness of the tragic situation confronting almost eight million European Roma. The legacy of the Holocaust requires the rejection of anti-Gypsyism as part of an international commitment to dignity and tolerance.

Notes

1. See L. Eiber, Ed., '*Ich wußte, es wird schlimm': Die Verfolgung der Sinti und Roma in München 1933–1945*, Munich, Buchendorfer, 1993, pp. 10–11 and pp.132–136; and E. Thurner, *Nationalsozialismus und Zigeuner in Österreich*, Vienna, Salzburg, Geyer Edition, 1983, appendix XXVIII, facsimile of 29 September 1948 notice from the Austrian Federal Ministry of the Interior to all police departments recommending expulsion for 'the increasing Gypsy nuisance'. See also K. Fings and F. Sparing, 'Regelung der Zigeunerfrage', *Konkret* 11/1993, pp.26–29; idem, 'Vertuscht, verleugnet, versteckt: Akten zur NS-Verfolgung von Sinti und Roma', *Beiträge zur nationalsozialistischen Gesundheits- und Sozialpolitik* 12/1995, pp. 181–201; and M. Schenk, *Rassismus gegen Sinti und Roma*, Frankfurt, Berlin, Bern, New York, Peter Lang, 1994.

2. Control Council Law No. 1 (29 October 1945), *Control Council for Germany* (the Official Gazette of the Control Council for Germany), pp.3–4; Runderlaß des Reichsführer SS und Chef der Deutschen Polizei im Ministerium des Innern, 8 December 1938, betr. 'Bekämpfung der Zigeunerplage', *Ministerialblatt des Reichs- und Preußischen Ministeriums des Innern* 51/1938, pp.2105–10; and K. Fings and F. Sparing, 'Das Zigeuner-Lager in Köln-Bickendorf, 1935–1958', *1999: Zeitschrift für Sozialgeschichte des 20. und 21. Jahrhunderts* 6, 3/1991, p.35.

3. Fings and Sparing, 'Das Zigeuner-Lager in Köln-Bickendorf', pp.34–38; and idem, '*z. Zt. Zigeunerlager': Die Verfolgung der Düsseldorfer Sinti und Roma im Nationalsozialismus*, Cologne, Volksblatt, 1992, pp.81–88. For the history of Nazi municipal Gypsy internment camps, see S. Milton, 'Der Weg zur "Endlösung der Zigeunerfrage": Von der Ausgrenzung zur Ermordung der Sinti und Roma', in E. Bamberger and A. Ehmann, eds, *Kinder und Jugendliche als Opfer des Holocaust*, Heidelberg: Dokumentationszentrum Deutscher Sinti und Roma, 1995, pp.29–49.

4. Otto Pankok Archive, Hünxe-Drevenack, Germany: Otto Pankok, 'Die Zigeuner im heutigen Deutschland', undated manuscript (ca. 1952). This text is excerpted in the exhibition catalogue of the Mahn- und Gedenkstätte Düsseldorf, *'Ach Freunde, wohin seid Ihr verweht?': Otto Pankok und die Düsseldorfer Sinti*, Düsseldorf, Stadtdruckerei, 1993, p.26.

5. See Eiber, '*Ich wußte, es wird schlimm'*, pp.136–138; R. Rose, *Bürgerrechte für Sinti und Roma: Das Buch zum Rassismus in Deutschland*, Heidelberg, Zentralrat Deutscher Sinti und Roma, 1987, pp.122–130; and J. Henke, 'Quellenschicksale und Bewertungsfragen: Archivische Probleme bei der Überlieferungsbildung zur Verfolgung der Sinti und Roma im Dritten Reich', *Vierteljahrshefte für Zeitgeschichte* 41, 1/1993, pp.61–77.

The belated fuller understanding of Ritter's research is only now reflected in new scholarly literature, such as H. Friedlander, *The Origins of Nazi Genocide: From Euthanasia to the Final Solution*, Chapel Hill, London, University of North Carolina Press, 1995, pp.246–262 and Michael Zimmermann, *Rassenutopie und Genozid: Die nationalsozialistische 'Lösung der Zigeunerfrage'*, Hamburg, Christians, 1996.

6. See Rose, *Bürgerrechte für Sinti und Roma*, pp.46–67; A. Spitta, 'Entschädigung für Zigeuner?: Geschichte eines Vorurteils,' in *Wiedergutmachung in der Bundesrepublik Deutschland*, ed. by L. Herbst and C. Goschler, Munich, Oldenbourg, 1989, pp.385–401; C. Pross, *Wiedergutmachung: Der Kleinkrieg gegen die Opfer*, Frankfurt, Athenäum, 1988; and I. Müller, *Hitler's Justice: The Courts of the Third Reich*, transl. by D. L. Schneider, Cambridge, (Mass), Harvard University Press, 1991, pp.261–269. See also the script for the film by K. Seybold and M. Spitta, *Das falsche Wort: Wiedergutmachung an Zigeunern (Sinti) in Deutschland?*, Munich, Katrin Seybold Film Productions, 1980.

For Austria, see B. Bailer–Galanda, 'Verfolgt und vergessen: Die Diskriminierung einzelner Opfergruppen durch die Opferfürsorgegesetzgebung', *Dokumentationsarchiv des österreichischen Widerstandes Jahrbuch 1992*, pp.16–20.

7. N. Gladitz, *Zeit des Schweigens und der Dunkelheit*, WDR film, 1983; Documentation Archives of the Austrian Resistance, Vienna, File E 18518: Urteil Amtsgericht München, Privatklagesache Leni Riefenstahl gegen Helmut Kindler; and E. Thurner and B. Rieger, 'Nationalsozialistische Verfolgung, "Wiedergutmachungs"-Praxis und Lebensverhältnisse der Sinti und Roma', in *Roma: Das unbekannte Volk*, ed. by M. Heinschink and U. Hemetek, Vienna, Cologne, Weimar, Böhlau, 1994, pp.49–96.

8. T. Zülch, ed., *In Auschwitz vergast, bis heute verfolgt: Zur Situation der Roma und Sinti in Deutschland und Europa*, Reinbek bei Hamburg, Rowohlt, 1979, pp.237–240; and the exhibition catalogue of the Landesverband Deutscher Sinti und Roma NRW, Rom e.V. Köln, and Verein EL-DE-Haus, ed., *Nur wenige kamen zurück: Sinti und Roma im Nationalsozialismus*, Cologne, 1990, p.46.

9. Zülch, *In Auschwitz vergast*, pp.227–237.

10. Zentrale Stelle der Landesjustizverwaltungen, Ludwigsburg [hereafter ZStL], 415 AR 55/82: StA Frankfurt, Verfahren gegen [henceforth gg] (against) Robert Ritter u.a., 55 (3) Js 5582/48 (discontinued 28 August 1950); ibid., 402 AR 116/61: StA Frankfurt, Verfahren gg. Eva Justin u.a., 4 Js 220/59 (discontinued 27 April 1961); ibid., 415 AR 930/61: StA Frankfurt, Verfahren gg. Eva Justin, 4 Js 220/59 (discontinued 12 December 1960).

11. ZStL, 415 AR 314/81: StA Stuttgart, Verfahren gg. Sophie Ehrhardt u.a., 7 (19) Js 928/81 (discontinued 29 January 1982, reinstituted 15 March 1982, discontinued 21 November 1985).

12. C. Pross and G. Aly, eds, *The Value of the Human Being: Medicine in Nazi Germany, 1918–1945*, transl. by M. Iwand, Berlin, Ärztekammer Berlin and Edition Hentrich, 1991, p.38.

13. H. Arnold, *Vaganten, Komödianten, Fieranten und Briganten: Untersuchungen zum Vagantenproblem an vagierenden Bevölkerungsgruppen vorwiegend der Pfalz*, Number 9 in the 'Schriftenreihe aus dem Gebiete des öffentlichen Gesundheitswesens' of the Federal Ministry of the Interior, Stuttgart, Georg Thieme Verlag, 1958, p.(v).

14. M. Winter, 'Kontinuitäten in der deutschen Zigeunerforschung und Zigeunerpolitik', *Beiträge zur nationalsozialistischen Gesundheits- und Sozialpolitik* 6/1988, pp.135–152.

15. Heinrich Hufmann, *Äußere Beckenmaße und geschlechtliche Entwicklung bei Zigeunerinnen*, Düsseldorf, 1952, p.4; J. S. Hohmann, *Robert Ritter und die Erben der Kriminalbiologie: 'Zigeunerforschung' im Nationalsozialismus und in Westdeutschland im Zeichen des Rassismus*, Frankfurt, Bern, New York, Paris, Peter Lang, 1991, pp.307–310; and M. Schenk, *Rassismus*, pp.203–204. For data on Gerhard Stein, see Milton, 'Der Weg zur "Endlösung der Zigeunerfrage"', pp.37–38. For background on Kragujevic, see W. Mamoschek and H. Safrian, '717./117. ID: Eine Infanterie-Division auf dem Balkan', in H. Heer and K. Naumann, eds, *Vernichtungskrieg: Verbrechen der Wehrmacht 1941–1944*, Hamburg, Hamburger Edition, 1995, pp.363–365 and *Trials of War Criminals before the Nuremberg Military Tribunals under Control Council Law No. 10* [Green Series] (14 vols.; Washington, D.C., 1950–1952), *Vol. 11*, pp.980–983 (Nuremberg Document NOKW 387: Report of 20 October 1941 to the Chief of Staff, Commander Serbia, concerning execution of male civilians in Kragujevic in retaliation for the killing and wounding of German soldiers by the Serbian resistance, signed by Captain von Bischofhausen).

16. Hohmann, *Robert Ritter*, pp. 320–323; J. Knobloch, *Romani Texte aus dem Burgenland*, Eisenstadt, 1953; and J. Knobloch and I. Sudbrack, 'Zigeunerkundliche Forschungen', *Innsbrucker Beiträge zur Kulturwissenschaft*, Sonderheft 42/1977. See D. Kenrick and G. Puxon, *Gypsies under the Swastika*, Hatfield, University of Hertfordshire Press, 1995, p.53.

17. ZStL, 414 AR-Z 196/59: StA Frankenthal, Verfahren gg. Leo Karsten, 9 Js 686/57 abd 9 Js 153/59 (discontinued 30 July 1960); ibid., 415 AR 930/61: StA Cologne, Verfahren Hans Maly u.a., 24 Js 429/61, 24 Ks 1/64 (discontinued 13 May 1970).

18. StA Berlin, Verfahren gg. Otto Bovensiepen u.a., 1 Js 9/65; microfilm of the indictment at the Leo Baeck Institute Archives, New York.

19. Auschwitz-Birkenau State Museum and Documentation and Cultural Centre of the German Sinti and Roma, Heidelberg, ed., *Memorial Book: The Gypsies at Auschwitz-Birkenau*, 2 vols, Munich, London, New York, Paris, K.G. Saur, 1993, Vol. 2, p.1643. König committed suicide in prison.

20. Rose, *Bürgerrechte für Sinti und Roma*, pp.130–134; H. Friedlander, 'The Judiciary and Nazi Crimes in Postwar Germany', *Simon Wiesenthal Center Annual* 1/1984, pp.27–44; J. Weber and P. Steinbach, eds, *Vergangenheitsbewältigung durch Strafverfahren?: NS-Prozesse in der*

Bundesrepublik Deutschland, Munich, Günter Olzog Verlag, 1984; and H. Lichtenstein, *Im Namen des Volkes?: Eine persönliche Bilanz der NS-Prozesse*, Cologne, Bund, 1984.
For Austria, see K. Marschall, *Volksgerichtsbarkeit und Verfolgung von nationalsozialistischen Gewaltverbrechen in Österreich: Eine Dokumentation*, 2nd edn, Vienna, Bundesministerium für Justiz, 1987.

21. S. Milton (text) and I. Nowinski (photographs), *In Fitting Memory: The Art and Politics of Holocaust Memorials*, Detroit, Wayne State University Press, 1991.

22. See *Pogrom* 21, 154 /1990, pp.11–30, containing articles on Roma in Bulgaria, Czechoslovakia, Hungary, Romania, and the former German Democratic Republic.

23. This press clipping was sent to me by Professor Geoffrey Giles, University of Florida, Gainesville, December 1995.

24. FBIS-WEU-93-201, 20 October 1993, p.4.

25. *The New York Times*, 2 November 1992.

CHAPTER 4

The Development of the Romani Civil Rights Movement in Germany 1945-1996

Yaron Matras

This chapter deals with the emergence of political organisation structures and the shaping of political ideology in the Romani community of Germany, beginning in the early postwar years, and taking into consideration as most recent developments the participation of German-based Romani associations in international events in the mid-1990s. It is a brief introduction, rather than a thorough survey, but it attempts nevertheless to provide an analytical descriptive perspective. Based on the nature of the issues dealt with throughout the period under consideration, the identity of the clients served by the movement, the formation of networks and their structural typology, and the ideas and policies pursued, I have divided the development of the Romani civil rights movement in postwar Germany into four phases.

Phase 1 is defined as 'support of individual reintegration and early organisational attempts' in the years immediately following the war, and in the early years after the formation of the Federal Republic. Organised civil rights activities during this phase were predominantly oriented to the family or extended family, aiming at supporting, or indeed enabling the reintegration of individuals who had survived wartime persecutions.

Phase 1 gradually gave rise to Phase 2, which I define as 'the formation of associations and ideological consolidation'. The factors behind this gradual shift into a new stage were partly internal, as individuals working on behalf of relatives and personal acquaintances gathered expertise and knowledge and began representing the interests of an entire community, leading to the emergence of ethnic awareness and solid operational structures; in addition there were external factors, since ideological consolidation was stimulated first by the confrontation with repressive measures that constituted institutional, government-backed patterns, and was later inspired by ideologies of civil rights movements outside the Romani community. There was thus an overlap between activities in Phase 1 and the roots of Phase 2 during the mid-1950s and the 1960s, with the formation of associations and ideological consolidation reaching a peak during the late 1970s and early 1980s.

Phase 3, which began in the early 1980s and lasted until Romani civil rights issues became embedded, following the political transition in eastern Europe, in an international working context around 1992, was characterised by the prevalence of 'constitutional and ideological debates' among the associations. One of the central issues of controversy was the attitude assumed towards Romani immigrants, refugees, and asylum seekers who were not German nationals. Decentralisation of political activities over this and other issues was typical of Phase 3, contrasting with Phase 2, which was characterised by attempts at the centralisation of representation.

Finally, Phase 4 revolved around the 'embedding of civil rights activities in an international context' following the political transition in eastern Europe, the formation of dozens of Romani associations there, and the emergence of partnerships at the international level. Phase 4 coincided with the aftermath of German reunification, the termination of postwar reconciliatory thinking in Germany, the introduction of new restrictions on immigration and asylum, and rising racist violence. At the same time multilateral organisations such as the Council of Europe and the Conference/Organisation on Security and Cooperation in Europe (CSCE/OSCE), and international human rights organisations increased their involvement in Romani affairs significantly. A still ongoing chapter in the history of Romani civil rights activities, Phase 4 saw German-based Romani associations encountering new opportunities and responsibilities, and with them the need for strategic and ideological reorientation.

Phase 1: Support of Individual Reintegration and Early Organisational Attempts

In 1945 survivors of the Nazi persecution began returning to their prewar places of residence in Germany. Most had nowhere to live, no jobs, and in many cases were suffering from severe health problems caused by the abuse they had been exposed to during the war years. Romani survivors were not the only ones returning. They joined displaced persons and other survivors and victims of persecution, who in the years following the war had started to create a network of mutual support and assistance. Their offices had been set up in the occupation zones and were run by the victims and survivors themselves, and it was to such offices that Sinti and Roma turned for support in securing residence permits, housing, and medical aid, and later to claim reparations as victims of racial persecution. In some cases, the organisational forms adopted by Jewish survivors, Communists, and other groups persecuted by the Nazis were copied by Sinti and Roma, who began forming their own networks.

The issues dealt with in this phase were very specific material needs. The 'clients' were usually members of the extended family, on whose behalf applications were made by relatives for permits to settle in caravan sites on the fringe of German towns, or for welfare and reparations as victims of Nazi terror. Though regular offices did not yet exist, and funding for such community activities was also lacking, in the early 1950s some groups appeared to have already adopted labels identifying themselves as associations working on behalf of Sinti or Roma.

The establishment of the Federal Republic saw the gradual takeover of social and welfare responsibilities by local German authorities, who were now, in the place of victim support associations and the Allied administrations, in charge of processing applications and reparation claims. They rejected all claims filed by Sinti and Roma on a wholesale basis, refusing to recognise deliberate racial persecution of Gypsies during the Nazi era. At this stage, the first seeds of Phase 2 – the formation of associations and ideological consolidation – were sown, as Romani representatives sought legal advice and took legal action challenging administrative decisions. Legal actions required a partnership between Romani claimants, activists on their behalf, and legal professionals, in this case from outside the community, an organisational model which was to form the basis for the formation of civil rights associations during Phase 2.

The re-initiation in the early 1950s of centralised surveillance of Gypsies by the police, including the re-establishment of the *Landfahrerzentralen* (Central Police Registers of Vagrants) in places like Munich and Hamburg, provided evidence that the denial of victim status to Gypsies had a deep structural background in the political climate and identity of the newly emerged Federal Republic. This impression was reinforced by a court ruling by the *Bundesgerichtshof* (Federal Court) in Koblenz in 1956 in which Nazi persecution of Gypsies was defined as 'measures aimed at the prevention of criminality', thus justifying the wholesale denial of reparation claims. Further evidence was provided by the reluctance of German authorities to pursue complaints filed by Sinti and Roma against those responsible for the Nazi genocide on Gypsies, such as Robert Ritter, Eva Justin, or Sophie Ehrhardt, after testimonies by individual survivors had revealed their role in the systematic and organised persecution of Gypsies, and the failure of the judiciary to prosecute any of the persons involved.

Phase 1 had thus led to a growing awareness of the extent of the Holocaust, the difficulties of re-integration, postwar repression and unwillingness to assume responsibility for the atrocities of the past. The material problems with which individual Gypsies had been confronted, and for which they had sought solutions with the help of single community activists, had by now turned out to be a basic structural problem affecting the Romani community in postwar German society, one which could only be challenged by increasing internal community awareness and by seeking public support for a fundamental change in policy.

Phase 2: The Formation of Associations and Ideological Consolidation

Phase 2, the early beginnings of which went back to the mid-1950s and the challenging of legal and administrative restrictions, brought Romani activists a significant step beyond granting support and assistance on behalf of individuals seeking short-term solutions to specific material problems. Instead, activists began to challenge the image of Gypsies in German society and the policies that went with this. Phase 2 was thus characterised by the evolution of collective awareness among the Sinti and Roma as an ethnic minority, struggling to change the attitudes of the majority and its institutions. It saw the gradual development of a group of activists who had gained expertise and were now willing and seeking to implement it not only on behalf of individual family relations and friends, but of the entire community in their areas of residence, and later on a national scale. These representatives interacted and exchanged views, leading to what we could now call a gradually emerging civil rights movement undergoing ideological consolidation.

It is difficult to assess the immediate implications of the First World Romani Congress, held in London in 1971, for the emergence of the Romani movement in Germany. Unlike the Congress and the International Romani Union which it formed, the German-based movement had not evolved out of an intellectual interest in Romani history or culture, but as a typical grassroots movement operating on behalf of individuals, later on behalf of a collective, on key issues of elementary freedoms of movement, security, justice, and material welfare. Indeed, fundamental issues around which much of the International Romani Union's activities continue to revolve to this day, such as the standardisation of a written Romani language, the creation of a Romani encyclopaedia, or symbols such as a national flag and a national anthem, are often regarded with mistrust and even contempt in parts of the Sinti community in Germany, which remains protective of its culture and reluctant to share it with outsiders. A key issue for the emerging movement in Germany during the 1970s was, in fact, resistance towards any form of either central registration as Gypsies or outside interference with Romani culture, including research, this attitude being at least in part a result of the traumatic experiences with 'racial biologists' and their role in shaping anti-Gypsy policy during the Nazi era.

It is nevertheless apparent that the 3rd World Romani Congress, hosted in Göttingen in 1981, played a significant role in boosting the self-awareness and public relations of the emerging civil rights movement of Sinti and Roma in Germany, though the initiative and the organisational effort which enabled the congress to take place in Göttingen seems to have come from outside the Romani community. The key to the development during that decade can be seen in the involvement of the Gesellschaft für bedrohte Völker (Society for Endangered Peoples), based in Göttingen. The Society had created a broad national basis of local groups whose interest was focused on public activities on behalf of non-autonomous, small nations around the world, mostly in the developing world, whose cultures were threatened by the pressure of post-colonial majority societies, and who were often the object of severe physical repression. The German-based Sinti and Roma seemed to match the criteria of a people worthy of the Society's protection and solidarity. By the end of Phase 1 in the development of their movement their activities were centred around two main demands: reintegration into German society through restitution of their citizens' rights in the aftermath of the Holocaust, and the right to organise their community life free of the restrictions imposed by the postwar Federal Republic.

The second element, the right to a particular community life, was for many activists of the Society for Endangered Peoples reminiscent of the struggle of small nations in the developing world to resist the contaminating influence of 'modern civilisation' and to preserve an authentic, pre-colonial life-style and social organisation. The romanticism associated with the Gypsy life-style was thus recognised by the Society as an important potential resource by means of which popular political support for Romani self-organisation could be obtained. Support by the Society of the first demand, reintegration and repatriation, appears to have had much to do with the personal touch of Tilmann Zülch, the Society's founder and long-term Secretary-General. Zülch, himself an ethnic German native of East Prussia whose family had been forced to evacuate their native region in the aftermath of the war, is said to have had his first encounters with Gypsies who, though like himself natives of East Prussia, had been refused repatriation in the Federal Republic on the grounds that they were not ethnic Germans. Faced with a problem of fundamentals of nationhood and national identity, the Society adopted the cause of struggling for the recognition of Sinti and Roma as German nationals and of their community as an ethnic German community, in order to reverse the injustice done to their compatriots.

The partnership between the Verband Deutscher Sinti in Heidelberg and the Society for Endangered Peoples became the driving force behind the promotion of Romani civil rights activities in the late 1970s. At the structural level, the Society contributed by supporting media campaigns, such as challenging the use of the word 'Zigeuner' in the media and introducing 'Sinti and Roma' instead, emphasising ethnicity rather than life-style. It also supported public demonstrations such as the rally in Bergen-

Belsen in 1979 or the hunger-strike in Dachau in 1980. Here the symbolism of sites of former concentration camps was for the first time exploited in order to address, in a deliberately provocative manner, the continuity of repression and discrimination. It thus challenged the self-image of the Federal Republic as a state and society which claimed to have broken with its Nazi past.

Above all, the Society's contribution may be seen in the formation of an organisational network of Romani civil rights associations, where it has left a clear imprint. Hosting the 3rd World Romani Congress in Göttingen drew the public attention necessary to announce the formation of a federal organisational form, led by the Society's partner, the Verband Deutscher Sinti in Heidelberg. The name for the new institution – the Zentralrat Deutscher Sinti und Roma (Central Council of German Sinti and Roma) – was modelled on the Jewish representation, the Zentralrat der Juden in Deutschland (Central Council for Jews in Germany) though the word 'German' was chosen to figure more prominently here than in the name of the Jewish organisation, which merely includes 'in Germany', leaving the issue of origin and nationality/citizenship open. The *Zentralrat* of Sinti and Roma, it was decided, should emphasise the German nationality of its constituency. In addition, it recognised the partition of the Romani community into two groups, Sinti and Roma. At least two activists of the Society for Endangered Peoples joined the permanent staff of Romani Rose, who was elected President of the *Zentralrat*, thus institutionalising the Society's participation within the Romani civil rights movement.

Like the Jewish Central Council, the *Zentralrat*, based in Heidelberg, emerged as a federal head office, with regional offices in each of the *Bundesländer* or federal states (though the regional association in Hamburg never actually joined the *Zentralrat*'s federal model, and the participating association in Lower Saxony broke away some time after its formation). Thanks to the mediator role played by the Society for Endangered Peoples, it was possible to negotiate a scheme with Helmut Schmidt's Social Democratic Federal Government according to which the head office of the *Zentralrat* would receive political recognition and financial support. This was accompanied by a statement on the part of the Federal Government in which German responsibility for the Romani Holocaust was acknowledged. The scheme set a model for the operation of Romani offices in the *Länder*, most of which attained government recognition and financial support during the 1980s, and led to the formation of government-backed foundations in some *Länder* whose task was to settle reparation claims by Romani victims of Nazi persecution.

Phase 2, which culminated in the granting of political recognition to and structural support for the *Zentralrat*, may thus be summarised as follows: following earlier activities on behalf of individual clients seeking short-term solutions to specific material needs, the entire Romani community in Germany was now regarded as the client population of the associations, which in turn adopted the German scheme of registered societies based on fixed statutes and a monitored budget, and run by term-serving elected executives. These associations aimed at a medium-term improvement of the socio-political status of their communities in Germany, challenging both administrative measures and hostile public opinion. From individual case-oriented work they turned to broader public activism, using the symbolism of continuity of racial persecution to draw attention to structural repression. Public opinion was addressed overtly and provocatively. At the centre of the ideological consolidation process was the notion of a community of Sinti and Roma as an ethnic-cultural minority which was part of the German nation, and whose political claims were based on the injustice and racial persecution its members endured during the Nazi era. With the acknowledgement of this injustice in the 1982 Schmidt declaration and the attainment of government support for representative structures and associations, the Romani civil rights movement in Germany was able to show a significant and impressive achievement. The federal representation model, borrowed from the Jewish community, used the administrative partition as practised by the state and its institutions as its blueprint. This was a unique model unknown in Romani communities in other European countries; it later led to separation and political competition and rivalry during Phase 3.

Phase 3: Constitutional and Ideological Debates

Phase 3 emerged in the early 1980s with the independent political course pursued by the Hamburg-based Rom & Cinti Union, and the gradual formation of other associations, not aligned with the *Zentralrat*, in the Rhine area, Hessen, and elsewhere. In organisational terms this phase was characterised by decentralisation of structures and political issues, and a specialisation for certain groups of clients within the movement.

In the years from 1982 to 1984 Romani refugees, mostly from Yugoslavia, later from Poland, approached Romani organisations and asked for their support in preventing deportations to their country of origin and in attaining residence permits in Germany. The issue triggered debates within the *Zentralrat* and affiliated associations, which sharpened as the *Zentralrat* instructed its member associations not to support foreign Romani refugees, claiming that growing numbers of foreign Roma who 'abused their guest status in our country' might harm the image of German Sinti and Roma and so ruin much of the achievements of the German-based Romani movement. For the Rom & Cinti Union in Hamburg, led by Rudko Kawczynski, himself a stateless Rom, ignoring the issues facing refugees meant alienating part of the natural constituency to which the Romani civil rights movement owed its allegiance. Other support groups for Romani refugees from Yugoslavia and Poland also emerged elsewhere, leading in the late 1980s to the formation of independent Romani associations, led either by more veteran Romani immigrants from Yugoslavia, as in Cologne, Düsseldorf, or Stuttgart, or else by Roma of the Lovara tribe, as in Berlin, Krefeld, and Frankfurt. These joined regional and national campaigns aimed at drawing public attention to the plight of Romani refugees and negotiating settlement rights with regional (*Länder*) authorities.

In its campaign strategies, the refugee-support movement drew on the experience and symbolism of previous years, examples being the hunger-strike at the site of the former concentration camp Neuengamme near Hamburg in February 1989, or the seven-week camp erected as a sanctuary for over five hundred refugees at that site during the summer of 1989. Provocative action and demonstrations spread during 1990 to North-Rhine Westphalia, Baden-Württemberg, Bremen, and Berlin. While in Hamburg protest actions successfully led to the granting of residence permits to fifteen hundred Romani asylum seekers from Yugoslavia and Poland during 1990, public debate on the issue intensified with the arrival of thousands of Romani asylum seekers from Romania, and later from Bulgaria, via East Germany. The four-week march of some fifteen hundred Roma through the Ruhr district in January 1990 ended with a decree issued by the Minister of the Interior of North Rhine Westphalia, granting 'de facto stateless Roma' the right to apply for residence permits outside the formal framework of asylum or immigration procedures. The decree was later withdrawn, but it nevertheless represented a breakthrough in the extent to which the Romani movement could expect to challenge constitutional issues successfully on behalf of its non-German constituency.

Phase 3 thus represented a shift away, at least in parts of the established movement, as well as through the emergence of new associations, from the older constituency of clients, and with it a shift away from issues arising in the aftermath of the Holocaust and especially away from the emphasis of German origin and affiliation of the Romani community which had been central to the emergence and ideological consolidation of the *Zentralrat* and its member associations. In organisational terms, pressure through overt public actionism challenged government authorities to seek settlements in negotiations with representatives of specific Romani interest groups outside the *Zentralrat* framework. These representatives formed occasional strategic alliances, in effect creating an alternative model of representation to the centralised *Zentralrat*.

The changes in issues, clients, and organisational structure coincided with a change in ideological thinking and argumentation. The actions on behalf of Romani refugees and immigrants threatened by expulsion challenged constitutional issues that had been left outside the focus of the movement in its first two phases. They now combined the historical experience of the Holocaust with restrictive asylum and immigration policy in contemporary Germany, deriving their demand for a special residence status to be granted to contingents of Roma from a historical responsibility which they claimed Germany had towards the Romani people. As alliances were formed between Romani refugees from various countries and tribes, veteran immigrants, and German nationals among the Roma, the ideological common denominator became a pan-European Romani nationalism which crossed the traditional boundaries of clan-structure, tribal affiliation, and country of origin. This movement now sought outside intervention on the part of European, American, and Israeli politicians, international human rights organisations and multilateral institutions such as the Council of Europe and the United Nations, defining itself in opposition to state policy and even to some key constitutional concepts in Germany, such as the coupling of nationhood, citizenship and ethnicity, and breaking off from the inner-German conciliatory tone which had dominated *Zentralrat* activities so far.

In contrast with Phases 1 and 2, where the Romani movement aimed at having its constituency included into the constitutional framework of mainstream Germany, in Phase 3 the refugee movement demanded that Roma be exempted from the restrictions on immigration which the constitution imposed, arguing that there was no state in which Roma were granted protection. It was this ideological line which created a split between the refugee movement and the *Zentralrat*, which regarded the statelessness argumentation as a setback and a return to the undesirable image of Roma as 'homeless nomads', and as one which in effect challenged the reintegration ideology upon which the *Zentralrat* was founded.

Phase 3 was a turning point in the development of the Romani civil rights movement in Germany, for several reasons. First, it departed from its earlier tasks centred around the established families of German Sinti and Roma, as parts of the movement pursued political goals which led to the adoption of a pan-European perspective on Romani history and destiny. The founding of EUROM, an attempt to create a European Romani umbrella association, at a congress in Mühlheim/Ruhr in November 1990, was representative of this process. Second, it no longer copied other movements and organisational structures, but became itself a target for imitation by many local immigrant and minority associations in Germany. Romani leaders often assumed leading roles in multiethnic anti-racist alliances; in 1989 Rudko Kawczynski was nominated by the Green Party as its symbolic top candidate for the European elections. Finally, it succeeded in stimulating interest and action in Germany on behalf of Romani communities in eastern Europe, though this was an indirect and only marginally intentional outcome of its activities. Challenged by the Romani refugee movement, the traditional Romani leadership around the *Zentralrat* and government administration needed to demonstrate their support for Romani communities in the East.

Phase 4: Embedding of Civil Rights Activities in an International Context

The withdrawal of the Roma decree in North Rhine Westphalia was accompanied in 1991 by the announcement of a New Refugee Policy, later adopted under this label by the Federal

Government. The policy consisted of bilateral treaties with the countries of origin which extended German aid as well as token support for Romani-related development projects in return for uncomplicated 'processing' and admission of returnees. Such schemes emerged with Macedonia and later Romania, where the *Zentralrat* adopted one of the community projects. Indirectly, the struggle for settlement rights of Romani refugees was yielding at least some interest and attention to the fate of Romani communities in the East.

The transition from Phase 3 to Phase 4 was connected to the deadlock in the relations between the more militant parts of the Romani civil rights movement and German government institutions on the one hand, and the shift of interest from the national to the international or European level of politics and organisation forms on the other. One factor promoting this development which was internal to the movement was the emergence of a pan-European Romani nationalism in the context of refugee support campaigns in Germany. In this respect it is interesting to note that in Germany pan-European Romani nationalism did not emerge via the intellectual channel of the International Romani Union or the World Romani Congress in Göttingen in 1981, but ultimately through independent, local grassroots work with refugees. Other decisive factors can be seen in the overall political development in Germany in the early 1990s, as well as in the context of the eastern European political transition.

In Germany, the end of the postwar era was announced in connection with reunification of the two German states. In terms relevant to the Romani civil rights movement, the termination of the postwar era meant the termination of reconciliatory thinking in Germany, from which the movement had drawn much of its public legitimation arguments. The revised Aliens Act of 1992 saw the removal of legislative and negotiation powers on immigration and asylum issues from the *Länder* and their exclusive assignment to the Federal Government, while the constitutional right to political asylum was restricted by the first ever amendment to the postwar German constitution. Both developments were closely tied to the increasing movement of refugees, and to some extent of Romani refugees from the East. Overall the result was a deadlock in the prospect of negotiating any further specific settlements on behalf of Romani immigrants with German authorities.

In eastern Europe, the political transition led to the emergence of violent and extreme nationalism in many regions, and to increased hostilities against Roma. On the other hand, newly established Romani political organisations were quick to address the problems of their communities in international forums, drawing attention among other issues to restrictive government policies, as in the case of the citizenship laws of the Czech Republic, or of police harassment in Romania and Bulgaria. Such initiatives attracted the attention of international human rights associations such as Amnesty International and Helsinki Watch, which in turn encouraged multilateral organisations to take up the issue of Romani civil rights. Ultimately, it seemed that interest on the part of multilateral organisations was triggered foremost by the challenge imposed on Western governments by illegal immigration and continuing refugee movements of Roma from the East. Last but not least, the involvement of some bodies, such as the Council of Europe and the CSCE, in creating a new basis for Romani political participation was in part a result of direct lobbying on the part of Romani civil rights organisations, some of them based in Germany.

The adoption of resolutions in support of Romani rights by the CSCE in 1990, by the United Nations Human Rights Commission in 1992, and by the Council of Europe in 1993, and international events such as the European Union's Seville congress or the Council of Europe and CSCE joint seminar in Warsaw, both in 1994, showed a shift in the centre of Romani-related political discussion to the international arena. The Standing Conference of Romani Associations in Europe was established as a discussion forum in 1994, with the prospect of offering multilateral organisations and governments a united Romani representation as a partner in the area of Romani civil rights and cultural emancipation.

In Germany these developments met with much enthusiasm among the pan-European nationalist, 'militant' and pro-refugee associations. The *Zentralrat* on the other hand initially remained critical of many international initiatives. Overtly it rejected proposals for special protection measures for Roma as put forth by the Council of Europe and the CSCE High Commissioner for National Minorities, comparing them to Nazi 'Sondergesetze' (special laws) and discriminatory measures. Looking beyond the polemics, however, it appears that the *Zentralrat* was concerned that the embedding of Romani affairs in an international agenda would deprive it of its leading role as the sole, officially acknowledged representative of Sinti and Roma in Germany, and would reduce its status to that of one among many equal associations in the international arena. In addition, joining a discussion on pan-European Romani identity posed a fundamental ideological problem to the *Zentralrat*, which had originally embarked on a struggle to gain recognition as a minority which formed an integral part of the German nation.

The ideological debate around the minority and national status of the Roma in Europe became the central issue of discussion in Phase 4. Eager not to miss important developments, the *Zentralrat* reluctantly began participating in international events hosted by the Council of Europe and the CSCE in 1994. At its first such appearance at a meeting in Strasbourg, it presented a paper outlining its position on the Sinti and Roma as a 'deutsche Volksgruppe' (German ethnic minority). Contrasting with the *Zentralrat* position, the Rom & Cinti Union in Hamburg now renamed itself for international purposes as the Roma National Congress (RNC), seeking a militant Romani nationalist image while at the same time downplaying its German-based operational centre. Papers presented by the RNC at a CSCE consultation in The Hague in 1993 and at the Seville Congress called for a European Romani Rights Charter which would grant Roma political representation as a European nation.

The status debate, inspired partly by the opportunity to help shape documents and resolutions at the international level, thus centred around a long-term, pan-European perspective. It coincided with the shift from short- and medium-term actionism typical of Phases 2 and 3, to a cultivation of intellectual resources in the areas of information and education, where organisations such as Rom e.V. and the Roma National Congress drew on resources provided by multilateral organisations and private foundations operating outside Germany. Since many of these funds are available specifically as development aid to support activities in the area of civil liberties in eastern Europe, German-based associations came under pressure to adopt partner associations in the East and consolidate their pan-European orientation even further.

The relations with international and multilateral organisations in this phase were twofold: first, Romani civil rights associations sought to get attention from international bodies, to attain recognition as reliable Romani representatives and to gain access to funding and a part in development projects, as well as to become part of the decision-making process in Romani-related issues. Thus they recognised a shift of potential decision-making processes away from national governments and on to international bodies. Moreover, international bodies were regarded and accepted as potentially useful mediators between Romani associations and governments, and were occasionally used to convey messages to governments. The dialogue between the Romani civil rights movement and the German Federal Government on a variety of issues can be said to have developed into such an indirect dialogue, mediated by the activities of international bodies. On the other hand, the increasing involvement of international bodies also led to occasional scepticism on the part of German-based Romani associations. Such was the reaction of both the *Zentralrat* and the Roma National Congress to the establishment of a Roma Advisory Council, comprised mostly of delegated government experts, at the Council of Europe in 1995. Participation in the international process was thus equally motivated by the need to monitor the activities of international bodies and ensure an overlap of interests.

While Phase 3 saw the Romani movement in Germany facing a dilemma as to whether and how to support non-German Romani refugees and immigrants, in Phase 4 it is the extent of their involvement in the ongoing ethnic and social conflicts around Romani communities in central and eastern Europe which will determine whether or not they will qualify as serious and reliable partners in an emerging European network of Romani associations.

CHAPTER 5

Aspects of the Linguistic Interface Between German and Romani

Anthony P. Grant

Introduction

A historical discussion of the contacts and influences of German and Romani is of necessity grounded in paradox. There are a number of Romani dialects spoken in Germany, as there have been for several centuries, yet although the one most typically associated with Germany is referred to as 'rómanes' (an adverb with the sense of speaking 'in the Romani fashion') by its speakers, they do not always describe themselves by using the term Roma. There are possibly as many speakers of non-German forms of Romani in Germany as there are of what we might call German Romani, and there are at least as many speakers of German Romani outside Germany as there are in the country. The first record of German Romani was made not in Germany but in the Netherlands. The greatest amount of activity in publishing *on* German Romani is to be found in France and Italy. Although there has been little publishing *in* German Romani in Germany itself in the past, more material in German Romani is being produced now, and there is some publishing in other forms of Romani (including those varieties from other parts of Europe which have only been used in Germany for the past couple of decades).

The best place to begin unravelling this skein of contradictions is with a brief description of the nature of Romani in general and German Romani in particular.

A Thumbnail Descriptive Sketch of Romani

The 'Gypsy languages' have been traditionally divided into three main dialect groupings: Domari, or Asiatic Romani spoken in Syria, Lomavren or Armenian Romani, spoken in Armenia, and Romani proper, or European Romani, spoken in Europe and beyond. This subdivision has been abandoned; and it is not now assumed *a priori* that they are the linguistic result of a single migration of speakers from India towards the West at some time in the first millennium. For example, though all three languages have borrowed words from Iranian, especially Farsi and Kurdish, they have borrowed very few of the same words.[1] This suggests that speakers of these languages emigrated from the same broad geographical area but at differing times. Any discussion of 'Romani' in this chapter henceforth relates to European Romani.

The Romani language is of New Indo-Aryan (or Indic) affiliation, and is a daughter-language of an unattested language very closely allied to Sanskrit, which is the only attested Old Indo-Aryan language. Although it is still a matter of debate when the Roma left India (modern opinion seems to favour the departure as occurring about a thousand years ago), most researchers would maintain that the route they took into Europe is fairly clear, and can be gauged from the sources and numbers of loan-words into Romani. The Romani lexicon consists largely of Central Indic morphemes, maybe eight hundred in all, to which have been added considerable numbers of Iranian (especially Farsi) and Byzantine Greek words (maybe seventy-five words from Iranian and nearly three hundred from Greek in various dialects), a few dozen words each from Armenian and South Slavic, and smaller accretions from Dardic (north-west India), Georgian, probably Mongolian and Burushaski, and possibly Syriac or some other Semitic language. In addition there are about ninety morphemes of unknown origin, from a basic stock of about fifteen hundred.

Romani is characterised by a phonological system in which voiceless aspirated stops and voiceless unaspirated stops contrast with voiced unaspirated stops (thus: *p t k č* contrast with *ph th kh čh* and *b d g dž*). The distinction between the single-flap *r* and the trilled *rr* is phonemic: *bar* 'stone' versus *barr* 'garden'. Romani has five vowels, and stress is non-predictable, but tends to be on the final syllable in uninflected words inherited from Indo-Aryan.

Word order is fairly free (though Subject-Verb-Object and Verb-Subject-Object are the most frequent patterns) and Romani has case-marking for subject and object: it has eight cases in all. Singular and plural are distinguished, as are feminine and masculine genders, and animacy is encoded in nouns. The verb has three past tenses – imperfect, perfect/aorist and pluperfect, and in most dialects present and future are not distinguished, although a short form of the present indicative is formally identical with the subjunctive, while the longer form of the present is used as a future by exaptation. There are second-person imperative forms, and also a past (and in many dialects also a present) participle.

The lexicon has been characterised above; Boretzky and Igla[2] discuss the incontrovertible fact that the vocabulary inherited by Romani from Indo-Aryan is unusually small, and that many concepts are expressed either by periphrases or by adopting words from other languages. In the case of Kalderash this means that the two thousand or more Romanian loans (many of which are rarely used) outnumber the inherited Indo-Aryan lexical elements by a ratio of four to one. In some dialects (including German Romani) the inherited lexicon is very productive, and word-formation using inherited materials is extensive. Many other dialects, for instance Kalderash, prefer to borrow lexicon rather than create neologisms from previously existing morphemes.

The Nature of Romani as a Unified Language

Two contrasting facts about Romani need to be understood from the outset. Firstly, it is almost certain that the Roma came into Europe in one great migration, following one route via the Hindu Kush, Persia, Asia Minor, Greece and Serbia, in the early centuries of this millennium. The fact that Romani dialects share greater or lesser numbers of the same loan-words from languages with which Roma would have come into contact makes this all but certain. Thus all European Romani dialects derive from a single ancestral language. Secondly, because of accelerated rates of linguistic change within Romani dialects, any picture of Common European Romani needs to be built up from the cumulative evidence of the dialects or languages into which it split.

This task is complicated by the fact that many forms of Romani have become what is known as Para-Romani varieties:[3] they survive as languages which contain a certain amount of Romani vocabulary but which have abandoned Romani grammatical structure; the Romani words (usually mixed in with words from other sources, including some which cannot be identified) are used in the grammatical framework of another language, for instance English (Angloromani), Spanish (Caló), Norwegian or Swedish (Scandoromani), and so on. In some cases we can relate these Para-Romani varieties to Romani dialects which preserve the grammatical structure, thus Angloromani is related to varieties of British Romani which include Welsh Romani, which preserves more of the grammar and lexicon – but this is not always the case. For instance, the extensive lexicon of Caló (less than half of which can be related to Romani and much of which is etymologically opaque) is essentially the only attestation of Iberian Romani, though there are scanty records of an inflected variety of Romani once used in Catalonia, and a non-inflected form used in the Basque Country. The nature of Iberian Romani data, being lexical rather than grammatical, does not permit us to be sure if its affiliations are with the Northern dialects or the Balkan ones.

There is a Para-Romani variety involving German structure: Romnish, spoken in Denmark, uses a grammatical structure which mixes Low German and High German elements, while employing a lexicon related more closely to Scandinavian Romani than to German Romani.[4]

It is emphatically not the case that the different forms of Romani differ simply by virtue of their taking over words from differing languages and adding them to an identical core of Romani structures and lexicon, and that by substituting Finnish words for Czech ones in a Czech Romani text, one is using Finnish Romani instead of Czech Romani. There are considerable phonological and structural differences between the Romani varieties, which allow us to subgroup them (with some difficulty due to dialectal interference) into branches. Because these dialects are often mutually unintelligible – speakers of Finnish Romani, Macedonian Arli and Hungarian Lovari, for instance, would be unable to understand one another – there are grounds for classifying them as separate languages rather than dialects, while simultaneously recognising their uniformity of origin. This is why

I have largely talked about 'varieties' of Romani in this article. As for the lexicon, no single Romani dialect (including those spoken in the Balkans) preserves more than about 75 percent of the stock of morphemes which the speech of the Roma possessed when they first emerged north from south-eastern Europe at the beginning of the fifteenth century.

Romani varieties are generally divided, because of shared innovations in phonology, structure and lexicon, into four branches. The Balkan branch includes most dialects spoken in Bulgaria, Macedonia and Greece, and also many of those in southern Italy, as well as the Ursari dialect in Romanian and the extinct dialect once used in Crimea. Vlax or Danubian dialects are spoken in Serbia, Romania, Western Ukraine, and much of Hungary, although there are speakers of Lovari and Kalderash, both of them varieties of Vlax, throughout much of the world. The Central division comprises most of the dialects used in Hungary, the Czech Republics and Slovakia, and also those of southern Poland. Northern dialects comprise the fourth division.

There are four branches of Northern dialects. They share innovations but differ as much among themselves as Balkan dialects from Vlax or Northern ones. Baltic dialects occur in the Baltic States, Poland, Belarus, Ukraine and Russia. Scandinavian Romani is spoken in Denmark, Norway, Sweden and Finland, but only in the last-named country is it more than a Para-Romani dialect; Finnish Romani contains as many loans from Swedish as there are inherited Romani morphemes, and it is becoming more and more influenced by Finnish. British Romani is spoken in Britain (and in its Para-Romani form, Angloromani, also in the United States, Australia and South Africa). The last dialect is that originally spoken in Germany, which is also found in the Netherlands and elsewhere in western Europe. The speakers of this dialect call themselves *Sinte* (a plural form; masculine *sinto*, feminine *sinti*), which purportedly (but erroneously) is said to indicate a historical connection with the Pakistani province of Sindh. The dialect is known as *i sinti čib*, 'the tongue of the Sinte', in which *čib*, a feminine noun, means 'tongue, language'. It will henceforth be referred to as Sinti.

Sinti is one of the Romani dialects with the greatest number of unique characteristics, and has lived in the shadow of German for several centuries. Much of the inherited Romani lexicon has been lost and has been replaced by German loans or by compounds. The old distinctions between *č/čh* and between *r/rr* have been lost

(Sinti has just *č* and *r*); unstressed vowels have been reduced to schwa or zero and have led to the contraction of syllables, stressed vowels have been lengthened, especially in open syllables, and final consonants have been devoiced.

The Sinti lexicon contains a number of items from Czech, French and Italian, in addition to stray loans from Lusatian and Hungarian, indicating the path which the Sinte took before reaching Germany, and a number of words peculiar to the dialect and of unknown etymology. The best dictionary of Sinti is by an Austrian, von Sowa (1898); the Sinti grammar by Finck (1903), one of the leading typologists and Celticists of the time, is reliable, but its lexicon is untrustworthy, since it contains many ghost-words and other inaccurate material plagiarised from earlier inaccurate sources (material about which von Sowa had already expressed doubts). Holzinger's *Das Rómanes* (1993), based on fieldwork largely in northern Germany, is the best available grammar, and his 'Rómanes (Sinte)' (1995) is a useful sketch.[5]

German Romani as a 'Geographical Expression'

Sinti has been the chief variety of Romani used in many parts of Germany for several centuries. It is assumed to have about fifty thousand speakers in Germany, while there are between 100,000 and 200,000 Sinte world-wide.[6] It has been strongly influenced by varieties of German and has been regarded as 'German Romani' *par excellence*, but it is not the only variety of Romani to have been used on German (or Germanophone) soil, especially in the present era.

It is possible to find speakers of most Romani dialects somewhere in Germany today, even if for pragmatic reasons many of them assert their nationality as citizens of a Balkan state more readily than their Romani ethnicity; one can be Serbian and a Rom. Most of these speech communities in Germany, for which figures are presently unavailable, are of recent origin and owe their presence to war and poverty in south-eastern Europe. Balkan dialects are spoken in Germany by thousands of Arlija and Dzambaze who have left former Yugoslavia (many of whom came along in the waves of migration from Yugoslavia in the 1960s and 1970s). Central dialects are spoken by a few Romungre, speakers of what was once the principal Romani variety in Hungary. Vlax dialects are spoken by Lovara who came to Germany from Hungary (and to Hungary from Romania) in the 1870s, by Gurbetis who left Bosnia and other parts of the former Yugoslavia in the early 1990s, and also by Kalderasha and others who have migrated from Romania and Russia for more than a century (indeed since the abolition of serfdom in the 1860s), but especially in the last decade. There are also speakers of Central (and probably Baltic) Romani dialects among Roma who have left Poland for Germany since 1989. Some speakers of Czech Sinti (known as *Lalere Sinte* – 'dumb Sinte', because their dialect was unintelligible to German Sinte) can also be found, not least in Austria.[7]

There were speakers of non-Sinti dialects in Germany long before the migrations of ex-serfs in the 1860s, *Gastarbeiter* in the 1970s and refugees from war and post-Communist political instability in the 1990s. The shape of some of the material in the dictionary compiled by the Thuringian judge Bischoff (1827), for instance, points to some contact on Bischoff's part with Romani speakers from Romania or Hungary, though most of the material is Sinti.[8]

The boundaries of Germany have fluctuated wildly in the present century, and not all the Roma of prewar Germany used Sinti. In the former German province of East Prussia there were speakers of a Baltic Romani dialect which contained loans from local varieties of German and also from Lithuanian and Polish. This was documented by Biester in his article 'Über die Zigeuner, besonders im Königreich Preußen' (1793). He drew on material collected by Friedrich Krauss and Pastor Martinus Zippel, a man notorious for his likening of Roma to 'vermin on a healthy body'.[9] It is likely (though unproven) that there have always been speakers of Roman, a variety of the Central Romani dialect Romungro in Burgenland, Austria, which was long a Magyar-speaking (rather than a Germanophone) area.

The converse is also true. By no means all speakers of Sinti live in Germany, Switzerland or Austria, although many do and belong to families which have not left German-speaking areas in six centuries. There may be 100,000 speakers of varieties of Sinti outside Germany. Until the migrations of the Kalderasha in the 1870s, Sinti was the most widely spoken Romani variety in Western Europe. Numerous Sinti speakers were to be found in the Netherlands (where the first sample of the language, a word list of fifty-three entries, was collected at Groningen and glossed in Dutch by the nobleman Johan van Ewsum, who died in 1570[10]), in Belgium and Luxembourg. Sinti speakers could also be found in most of France, including Alsace, where they were known as *Manouches* — pan-Romani *manuš* 'person', and Sinti was spoken in northern and central Italy. Despite the ravages of persecution and the Nazi era, this picture of speaker distribution is still valid.

There were Sinti speakers in western Poland, and some, known as *Sasitke Roma* or 'German Roma', passed through what is now Poland in the late eighteenth century, acquiring some Polish loans on the way, and settled with the Volga Germans near Saratov. There were Sinti speakers in Bohemia and possibly Moravia and Slovakia, and there are a few Sinte families in north-west Hungary and also in Prekmurje, Slovenia. Some speakers of Sinti have emigrated to the United States or Australia. Not all people who speak Sinti are themselves Sinte: the Jenische, non-Romano travellers, pedlars and basket-makers in Germany and the Netherlands, spoke *Rotwelsch* (see below) among themselves, but some knew Sinti, and much information on Sinti has come down from the Jenisch author Engelbert Wittich, who learned the language from his wife.

The Structural Interface between German and Romani

German and Romani have been in contact for at least six centuries. It should be remembered that the present-day German-speaking area is much reduced from that to be found in the Middle Ages, when much of Bohemia, for instance, was German speaking, and when there were communities of German speakers in most towns in Central and Eastern Europe. The opportunities for German to influence Romani have been great, while the linguistic purism which drove long-established colloquial German loans out of Czech, say, or Hungarian, was unknown before the late eighteenth century.

Consequently some German loans, which have come in directly from local German dialects or which have entered via a territorial language, are found in Romani dialects which are not spoken in Germany. There are a handful in Slovak Romani, mediated from the German dialect of Zips/Spiš through their occurrence in

Eastern Slovak dialects, one or two in Hungarian Lovari (for instance *anšlogo* 'impact, hammer-blow', from the Austrian dialectal pronunciation of *Einschlag*), and a few in Kalderash taken from 'Transylvanian Saxon', for instance *bírto* 'innkeeper', German *Wirt*. Doubtless there are recent German loans into the varieties of Balkan and other dialects now spoken in Germany and Austria, but these have not been investigated systematically.

More important than these are loans occurring in dialects which were once spoken in Germany before they reached their present locations, often in the sixteenth century. Finnish Romani *kentos* 'child' may be German or possibly Old Swedish; Finnish Romani derives from dialects whose speakers were transferred in the sixteenth century from Germany via Scotland to Norway and Sweden and thence to Finland. About a dozen words of High German origin (and more from Polish) are found in North Russian Romani, indicating an eastward migration; furthermore the use of the Romani preposition *kija* 'towards' to indicate 'very, too much', may be a calque on German *zu*, since there is no parallel in Russian or Polish. Some fifteen words of German origin, and a similar number from French, are found in the form of British Romani used in North Wales.[11] These include a couple of forms, *šumbaria* 'diluted beer' (from *Schaumbier*) and *tranšuris* 'plate' (originally from French *tranchoir*). These are found also in Finnish Romani, and the latter form also occurs in Czech Romani and Sinti. These provide evidence of mutual origin or influence.

Of course the dialect most strongly influenced by German is Sinti itself. 'Gypsies' were first noted in Hildesheim in 1407, and their presence in Germany has been constant ever since. Many speakers of Sinti, especially those in the centre of the country, have lived in contact with German for centuries. German has been the only other language which they have regularly encountered, and they have been unable to escape German influence on their language, and this influence, grammatical as well as lexical, has been visible since the first Sinti texts, dating from the mid-eighteenth century, were made widely available by Pott in *Die Zigeuner in Europa und Asien* (1844–1845).

Some changes in Sinti may be internally motivated and independent of German influence, for instance the change of /-v/ to /-p/ (by way of /-f/), thus *lap* for *lav* 'I take'. Others are more likely to be attributable to German influence, for instance the development of unstressed short vowels to schwa and their subsequent deletion. One should also mention the prevalence in

Sinti texts of placing the subject in the second slot in the sentence, a feature of Romani which predates German contact but which has been reinforced by contact with German, and the increased use of post-verbal (Romani-derived) third-person clitics. Yet others involve the adoption of German morphemes and are clearly the result of German influence.

A few examples will suffice. The eight-case system has been preserved in Sinti, but several case-endings have been reinforced by German prepositions. Thus the dative, ablative and instrumental are formed in Sinti by placing *fir, fon, mit* before the noun with the addition of dative, ablative or instrumental endings on the noun stem. The conjunction *thaj* 'and' is lost (although it occurred in eighteenth-century Sinti) and replaced by *unt*. Many other German conjunctions and adverbs have been borrowed into Sinti. German verbal prefixes, such as *ent-, mit-, aus-*, are productive and have been attached to Sinti verbs.[12] Negation in Sinti is formed by placing *gar* (from *gar* nicht) after the verb rather than placing *na* before the verb.

The form *gar* is typical of a small set of Sinti words deriving from German which have extended the use which they enjoyed in German, and have been taken over as characteristically Sinti forms. Others include *táperel* 'he hits', *šála* 'coffee-cup' (of Austrian origin), *hálauter* 'everyone' — these are fully integrated Sinti forms and are more frequently used than are the German *tappen, Schale* and *lauter*.

Nonetheless, it must be recognised that Sinti has been able to preserve several non-German features through several centuries, such as a phonemic distinction between initial /s-/ and /z-/, and the ability to integrate both the numerous German-derived nouns and verbs into its own morphological system by causing them to decline or conjugate fully like other nouns and verbs in Sinti.

Not surprisingly, Romani has not exerted a great deal of influence on German. One of the few German words of Romani origin, *Verbunkos* (a dance-rhythm popularised by the works of Josef Haydn), has come in from Hungarian Romani and itself derives from German *Werbung* 'recruitment' (while Czech Romani has *verbiris* 'dancer'). The German tramps' and vagrants' language (and erstwhile underworld vocabulary) *Rotwelsch* contains elements of Romani, but they are few, and are vastly outnumbered by words derived from Hebrew or metaphorical extensions of German roots. A survey of 339 entries in a *Rotwelsch* vocabulary (the letters for German glosses from M to Q in Puchner's *Sprechen Sie Rotwelsch*, published in 1975) showed precisely two forms derived from

Romani (both of them function words, *bi* 'without' and *tschi* 'something, anything') and a couple more which might derive from Romani.[13] On the other hand, local underworld languages, such as *Masematte* in Münster and especially *Manisch* in Giessen contain a high proportion of Romani-derived elements.

Historical and Political Consequences of Work on Sinti

The prevailing tenor of the relationship between the Romani and German languages is unfriendly, as it has long been, and there are sound historical reasons why this should be so. This is especially the case with Sinti. Because the descriptive work on Sinti, though often conducted in all innocence by people working with German Sinte, was used for nefarious purposes by German criminologists, and since German personnel with Nazi connections, such as Dr Robert Ritter, tried to gain the confidence of Sinte by learning some of their language, there is an unspoken understanding among some 'tsiganologues' (people who study Romano culture and language) that material in Sinti should not be published. A tacit ethical embargo on work on German Sinti has operated since 1945, although some researchers and some Sinte feel more strongly about this than others. The statements in this chapter derive from findings from older and more recent published materials, and do not infringe this embargo; I have not quoted from unpublished data. It is because of the misuse of Sinti data that there is restricted access, for example, to Sinti materials in the Romani Archives at the University of Texas, Austin. This aligns with the long-standing wish of many of the Sinte to reveal neither the language nor its existence to outsiders.

Apart from the descriptive work by Austrian Johann Knobloch[14] (who has been accused of collecting much of his data from inmates in Lackenbach concentration camp in the 1940s), and field research, firstly by Michael Reinhard,[15] and later by Daniel Holzinger of the University of Klagenfurt with speakers from Hameln and Hildesheim,[16] relatively little work has been carried out on German Sinti since the 1930s, because of the understandable reluctance of the Sinte to disclose details of their language to outsiders. Although it is known that there are regional dialects, and that Sinti shows the influence of the local forms of colloquial German, which is an everyday language of all Sinte, there is no published explicitly detailed discussion of dialectal variation within German Sinti.

Much of the available information on varieties of modern Sinti is perforce derived from the several fairly extensive descriptions of non-German varieties, which share much with German Sinti as it was recorded last century (including a large number of German loans), but which have been influenced by the languages spoken by the surrounding communities. Until recently there was more in print on non-German Sinti than on German Sinti. Varieties of French and Italian Sinti have been especially well covered. D. Jean's *Glossaire de gadškeno manuš* (1970)[17] is a handy description of a variety of Manouche spoken in Alsace, and influenced by French and Alsatian. Calvet and Formoso's *Lexique tsigane* (1987)[18] describes a form of Sinti spoken in Piedmont, and influenced by French, Provençal, Italian and Piedmontese. This dialect is also covered in the vocabulary collected by Senzera.[19] There are distinctive varieties of Sinti in Veneto, Lombardy and Istria.

Von Sowa's dictionary of 1898 extracted all that was valuable or reliable from the earlier sources on German Sinti, in addition to providing forms from his fieldwork in Westphalia. He was building on a centuries-old tradition of investigation of Sinti. If van Ewsum (whose work was unknown to von Sowa) was the first person to record Sinti, Ludolf,[20] one of the most learned men of his time, was the first German to document it, with a word list purporting to cast a critical light on the supposed African origins of the Roma by showing the difference between Romani and the Semitic Ge'ez (Old Ethiopic) language, knowledge of which he had reintroduced to the West.

German-language scholarship, and the generally patronising attitude which accompanied it, was to be in the forefront of Romani studies until well into the present century. Only the fact that scholars from further countries have researched the language over the past century means that German scholarship has lost the lead in the field. At the end of the eighteenth century Rüdiger and Grellmann helped establish the Indic affiliations of Romani in German-language works.[21] Rüdiger had conducted first-hand fieldwork on the language by collecting data from a Sinti woman in Leipzig, and comments movingly[22] upon the hardships which the Sinte faced, but Grellmann was possessed of a repugnance towards the Roma on a par with that of Zippel, was working away from German-speaking territory as a professor of economics in St

Petersburg. The works of Pott and of the Slovene Miklosich[23] were fundamental in establishing many of the Indo-Aryan etyma whose discovery has long been a major topic in Romani scholarship. Like Grellmann, these scholars worked at arm's length from the people they were studying. The received wisdom is that Pott never met a Gypsy in his life, while Miklosich is claimed to have learned Romani but did little fieldwork on the language himself, preferring to integrate others' research.

It would appear that many of the people who collected Romani data had hostile feelings toward their consultants, and one might see the germ of a development towards 'scientific' objectification of Romani (something of beauty and interest as a topic of investigation) as divorced from the inhuman and criminalising attitudes which the investigators entertained towards the people who spoke it. To such scholars the language was all, and the people who spoke it did not matter. This becomes even clearer in the case of the work by Jühling[24] which though of minimal value linguistically, is significant in making clear the newer attitudes which prompted research into Sinti. These attitudes were also prevalent in the work of the judge Bischoff[25] and the Thuringian magistrate Liebich,[26] who investigated Romani in order to understand the language of a group whom they saw as criminals.

German-language work on Romani continues, notably with the research of Norbert Boretzky and Birgit Igla on Romani varieties (such as Arli and Kalderash) which are spoken in south-eastern Europe.[27] One should also mention the work of other scholars writing in German, especially those who investigate varieties of Romani used in German-speaking areas. Notable among these are Dieter W. Halwachs, who has studied the Romani of Burgenland, Petra Cech, who has investigated the Romani dialect of a group of basket-makers from Izmir, and Daniel Holzinger, with his definitive work *Das Rómanes* (1993) on Sinti. (German and English are still the two languages in which the bulk of Romani research is published, with French, Italian, Russian and Romani following some way behind, and a reading knowledge of German is indispensable to *tsiganologues*).

Little has been published in any variety of Romani in Germany[29] for the use of Romani-speakers themselves, but there are exceptions. There is a recent translation (1994) by Holzinger of St Mark's Gospel into Sinti, and a translation of St John's Gospel into Lovari by Jaija Sattler, a Lovaro resident in Berlin, was published by the British and Foreign Bible Society in 1930.[30]

Previous to Holzinger's work the only book produced in Sinti was another, much poorer, translation of the Gospel of St Mark into South German Sinti by Urban and Wittich in 1912;[31] Wittich was a Jenisch pedlar from Brötzingen near Karlsruhe, who claimed to be a Sinto and who served as a resource person for Sinti language and customs. He had learned these from his wife who had been married to a Sinto, Joseph Denner. He worked for the criminologist Johannes Jühling in the early years of this century, but his usefulness to German criminologists did not save him from the same fate which befell Sattler, namely death in a concentration camp. Religious materials, including translations of Scriptural passages, were compiled in heavily Germanicised Sinti by the Lutheran seminarians Tielich and Frenckel, under the leadership of Wilhelm Blankenburg, for the 'model Gypsy colony' of Friedrichslohra, Saxony, in 1837.[32] They were not welcomed by the intended recipients of the theologians' zeal, since the group in question was Catholic by affiliation as well as being resentful of this crude attempt at social engineering.

After all that has been said, it will come as no surprise to the reader to learn that Romani has no official recognition at national or local level in Germany, and that it never has had.

It is impossible to predict the future of any minority language anywhere in the world. Nonetheless it is probable that because of cultural, religious and other differences from the German community (not the least of these being cleanliness taboos among all groups, the practice of Islam or Eastern Orthodoxy by many of the groups from the Balkan countries, and appalling poverty and squalid living conditions for very many of the Roma and Sinte in Germany), a sense of ethnic separateness, reinforced greatly by the hostile and ill-informed attitudes of the majority of the Germans, will enable Romani varieties – including Sinti – to remain in use in the family circle and among fellow speakers for a long time to come.

Notes

1. See I. F. Hancock, 'On the Migration and Affiliation of the Domba', *Romani in Contact*, ed. Y. Matras, Amsterdam, John Benjamins, 1995, pp.25–51.
2. N. Boretzky and B. Igla, 'Zum Erbwortschatz des Romani', *Zeitschrift für Phonetik, Sprachwissenschaft und Kommunikationsforschung* 45/1992, pp.227–251.
3. See P. Bakker and M. Cortiade, *In the Margin of Romani*, Amsterdam, 1991.
4. See J. Miskow and V. Brøndal, 'Sigøjnersprog I Danmark', *Danske Studier*, 1923, pp.97–145.

5. See R. von Sowa, *Wörterbuch des Dialekts der deutschen Zigeuner: Abhandlungen für die Kunde des Morgenlandes*, XI Band, I. Teil, Leipzig, Deutsche Morgenländische Gesellschaft, 1898, F.N. Finck, *Lehrbuch des Dialekts der deutschen Zigeuner*, Marburg, Elwert, 1903, and D. Holzinger, *Das Rómanes: Grammatik und Diskursanalyse der Sprache der Sinte*, Innsbrucker Beiträge zur Kulturwissenschaft, Sonderheft 85, Innsbruck: Institut für Sprachwissenschaft der Universität Innsbruck, 1993 and 'Romanes (Sinte)', *LINCOM-EUROPA Languages of the World: Materials, 105*, Munich, LINCOM-EUROPA, 1995

6. Holzinger, *Das Rómanes*, p.1.

7. The 'Lalere Sinti' described by B. Gilliat Smith in the *Journal of the Gypsy Lore Society* (2/1908–1909), encountered in the Rheinland-Pfalz, were actually Lovara.

8. F. Bischoff, *Deutsch-Zigeunerisches Wörterbuch*, Ilmenau, 1827.

9. See J. E. Biester, 'Über die Zigeuner, besonders im Königreich Preussen, II. Von ihrer Sprache', *Berlinische Monatsschrift* 21/1793, pp.108–168 and pp.360–393

10. This is published in A. Kluyver's 'Un glossaire tsigane du seizième siècle', in the *Journal of the Gypsy Lore Society*, 4/1910–1911.

11. See J. Sampson, *The Dialects of the Gypsies of Wales*, Oxford, Clarendon Press, 1926.

12. This is discussed in B. Igla's 'Entlehnung und Lehnübersetzung deutscher Präfixerben im Sinti', *Prinzipien des Sprachwandels*, ed. J. Erfurt, B. Jessing and M. Perl, Bochum, Brockmeyer, 1992, pp.38–55.

13. See G. Puchner, *Sprechen Sie Rotwelsch: 2446 Wörter und Redewendungen der deutschen Gaunersprache*, Munich, Heimaran, 1975.

14. See J. Knobloch, 'Volkskundliche Sinti-Texte', *Anthropos* 45/1950, pp.223–250.

15. See M. A. Reinhard, 'The formation of occupational terms in German Romani (Dialect of the Sinte)', *International Journal of the Sociology of Language* 19/1979, pp.19–32.

16. See in particular Holzinger, *Das Romanes*, and 'Romanes'.

17. D. Jean, 'Glossaire de gadskeno manus', *Etudes tsiganes*, 1/1970, pp.2–69.

18. G. Calvet and B. Formoso, *Lexique tsigane II: dialecte sinto piémontais*, Paris, Publications Orientalistes de France, 1987

19. L. Senzera, L. 'Il dialetto dei Sinti Piemontesi', *Lacio Drom* 22/1986.

20. J. Ludolf, *J. H. Ludolfi ad suam Historiam Aethiopicam antehac editam Commentarius*, Frankfurt am Main, 1691.

21. J.C.C. Rüdiger, *Von der Sprache und Herkunft der Zigeuner aus Indien*, Leipzig, 1782 and H. M. G. Grellmann, *Die Zigeuner: Ein historischer Versuch über die Lebensart und Verfassung, Sitten und Schicksahle dieses Volkes in Europa, nebst ihrem Ursprünge*, Dessau, Leipzig, 1783.

22. See Rüdiger, *Von der Sprache und Herkunft der Zigeuner aus Indien*, p.38.

23. See A. F. Pott, *Die Zigeuner in Europa und Asien*, Halle, Heynemann, 1844–1845, and F.X. R. von Miklosich, 'Über die Mundarten und die Wanderungen der Zigeuner Europas', *Denkschriften der kaiserlichen Akademie der Wissenschaften*, Philosophisch-historische Klasse, vols 21–31, Vienna, Karl Gerolds Sohn, 1872–1881.

24. J. Jühling, 'I. Kriminalisches. II. Alphabetisches Wörterverzeichnis der Zigeunersprache', *Archiv für Kriminal-Anthropologie und Kriminalistik*, vols 31–32, 1908–1909.

25. Bischoff, *Deutsch-Zigeunerisches Wörterbuch*.

26. R. Liebich, *Die Zigeuner in ihrem Wesen und in ihrer Sprache*, Leipzig, Brockhaus, 1863

27. See N. Boretzky, and B. Igla, 'Zum Erbwortschatz des Romani', *Zeitschrift für Phonetik, Sprachwissenschaft und Kommunikationsforschung* 45/1992, pp.227–251, and *Wörterbuch Romani-Deutsch-Englisch für den südosteuropäischen Raum*, Wiesbaden, Harrassowitz, 1994.

28. See D. W. Halwachs et al., 'Romani', *LINCOM-EUROPA Languages of the World: Materials 107*, Munich, LINCOM-EUROPA (forthcoming); P. Cech and M. F. Heinschink, 'Sepecides-Romani', *LINCOM-EUROPA Languages of the World: Materials 106*, Munich, LINCOM-EUROPA, 1996 and Holzinger, *Das Rómanes*.

29. Emigrants from Yugoslavia, missionary groups and political associations have been distributing Romani-language material such as magazines and church newsletters for many years, but this is not widely available. In Austria the position is somewhat better, and magazines, poetry and school textbooks have been published in at least three dialects (Lovari, Serbian Kalderash and Burgenland Romani) by Roma and for Roma in recent years.

30. See D. Holzinger, *O Latscho Lab o Jesus Christusester* (Gospel according to St Mark), 2nd edn, Florshain, 1994 (transl. D. Holzinger, though this is not mentioned in the title), and J. Sattler, ed. by Pastor F. Zeller. *O voyako-hiro katar o Jesusesko Christuskero banasgimmo ä Johannestar*, Berlin, British and Foreign Bible Society, 1930.

31. R. Urban, and E. Wittich, *O Evangelio Jezus Kristusesko pala Markus*, Berlin, British and Foreign Bible Society, 1912.

32. See Pott, *Die Zigeuner in Europa und Asien*, vol.1, pp.491–521.

CHAPTER 6

Anti-Gypsyism in German Society and Literature*

Daniel Strauß

Stereotypes, Anti-Semitism and Anti-Gypsyism

In view of the threats, riots and attacks on Sinti and Roma, particularly the murderous attacks in Oberwart in Austria in 1995, we must call a spade a spade as far as the specific hostility towards the Sinti and Roma is concerned. We are dealing with a racism which is partly overt, partly covert, which develops in structures of prejudice. The breeding ground out of which acts of violence grow is the anti-Gypsy stereotype, which has been rehearsed, learned and handed down in a manner rivalled only by the anti-Semitic stereotype. It delivers ammunition and material for reporting in the media which discriminates against Gypsies. In this context the focal term, anti-Gypsyism, makes it clear that the so-called 'hatred of the Gypsies' cannot be simply dismissed as a subsidiary form of hostility to foreigners, but must be appreciated as a second basic form of xenophobia alongside anti-Semitism.

By anti-Gypsyism we therefore mean both the opposition to Sinti and Roma in the framework of political movements with nationalist racist programmes, as well as the totality of the images and myths of the 'Gypsy', in particular the current clichés which

* *Translated by Susan Tebbutt*

have become part and parcel of the cultural heritage in literature, music and other areas of social activity.

Stereotypes give simple answers in a complicated world. They disregard the individual case and the variety within a group. They operate with sweeping statements and generalisations. They work out 'types' with characteristics which are set in stone once and for all. They do not wish to enter into any kind of relationship with their opposite number, but wish instead to satisfy the need for a clear concept of the enemy.

The 'types' we are dealing with here are the product of the collective imagination and extrapolation. They are, however, not just floating around in the heads of self-professed 'enemies of the Gypsies'. They have found their way into many forms of representation and texts which we do not recognise straight away as racist.

Before I move on to deal with some examples, and in particular to deal with the 'image of the Gypsy' in literature, the distorted image of the Gypsy in the world of administration, politics and Nazi propaganda, and contemporary discrimination in the media, I would like to try to make some distinctions. As I cannot call on any previous work in this field — anti-Gypsyism research does not yet exist at all as a discipline — the example of anti-Semitism is helpful here.

In literature about anti-Semitism, historical manifestations of hostility to Jews are normally divided into four categories:

1. the anti-Judaism of the Graeco-Roman world,
2. the Christian anti-Judaism revolving round the accusation of the murder of God,
3. the political anti-Semitism which started in the 1870s, in which the identification of the Jews with modernisation and capitalism was important as a reaction to emancipation and
4. the racially motivated anti-Semitism of National Socialism.

There is neither time nor space here to go into details, and therefore I would merely wish to point out that the categories are important, if we are not to adhere to an amorphous 'eternal' anti-Semitism. The durability and the intensity of the emotions involved should not tempt us to see and misinterpret the labyrinth of causes in a one-dimensional way. Let me give an example. It is possible to bring in Christian anti-Judaism to help explain the motivation and factors behind the medieval pogroms. It is, however, of no use as an explanation of the National Socialist Holocaust. Anyone who sees the genocide of Jews, Sinti and Roma as a large-scale pogrom has not understood that we are dealing here with a completely new type of persecution and murder. It is precisely for this reason that we have to view the term anti-Gypsyism in a differentiated way.

We must draw a clear and unambiguous distinction between the genesis of the prejudice in the early modern period, the attempts to achieve an enforced assimilation during the Absolutist period and the 'Gypsy policy' of Imperial Germany and the Weimar Republic on the one hand, and the policy of the Final Solution in the Third Reich on the other hand. That does not mean that the existence of precursors and continuities should be denied. It does, however, mean that the uniqueness of the crimes of the National Socialist genocide cannot be trivialised in order to facilitate a historicist approach which has been misunderstood. I therefore suggest that we ought to differentiate between 'traditional anti-Gypsyism' and 'racially motivated anti-Gypsyism'.

For centuries the word 'Gypsy' was associated with stereotypes, negative images and slander. Here traditional anti-Gypsyism is operating in a web of prejudices which can also be applied to other minority groups. It results in a handing down of similar images and clichés in different contexts. Once again the parallels between anti-Semitism and anti-Gypsyism are striking.

The stereotype of the 'eternal' wandering Jew has its counterpart in the apparently inborn *Wanderlust* of the Gypsy. The hair-raising accusations of child-stealing and child-violation are levelled against both minority groups. Accusing the Jews of responsibility for the murder of God has its counterpart in the legend of Gypsies refusing the Holy Family a bed for the night, in the legend of the Gypsy blacksmith who forged the nails used in the crucifixion, and in other religious stories.

In the case of the anti-Gypsy stereotype these similarities make it clear that we are dealing with a construct: it yields no insights into the history and culture of the Sinti and Roma. Conversely, however, if we look at it critically, it definitely allows us to draw conclusions about the way in which those people who use it view the world and other people.

It is in politics that the consequences and effects of anti-Gypsyism are the most tangible. If we go back in history, the persecution of the Sinti in Germany begins with a decree issued by Achilles, the Elector of Brandenburg. In 1482 he banned Sinti from staying in his country. The German Empire also followed this example with the Imperial Diets of Lindau and Freiburg in 1496,

1497 and 1498, and revoked Emperor Sigismund's letter of safe conduct and declared all Sinti to be outlawed. Anyone could hunt them, whip them, lock them up or kill them. Thanks to the proliferation of small German states these imperial laws were not applied consistently everywhere. It has been proven that from 1497 to 1774 there were a total of 146 such decrees.

It was not until the turmoil of the Thirty Years War that attention was diverted from the 'persecution of the Gypsies'. In the seventeenth and eighteenth centuries the persecution was continued in an undiminished form. Sinti were to be flogged, branded, expelled from the country or punished with death.

It was, however, not only in the sphere of politics, but also in the economic sphere that the mechanisms of exclusion were directly in evidence. The tightly organised guilds felt that the Sinti and Roma with their traditional craftsmen's trades were a threat, and refused to allow them to join their corporations. The Sinti were also banned from acquiring land, in the same way that the Jews were.

Political repression and marginalisation in the world of work are linked to another issue. Sinti and Roma were treated as scapegoats who were held responsible for the costs of progress. In other words, people projected their problems in dealing with the emerging work-orientated society onto this ethnic group. These fears and collective fantasies revolve around two groups of concepts which in turn are linked to contradictory emotions.

In the minds of the majority population the 'Gypsy' embodies either what people desire or what they curse, what they hanker after or what is forbidden. Thus the 'Gypsy' provides the raw material for both demonisation and romanticisation. Kirsten Martins-Heuß writes about this phenomenon in a study of the mythical character of the Gypsy:

> The Gypsy is a phantom that has had a hold on people's minds for centuries and has always kept true to the same type of creature. A Gypsy is a dark strange person, always travelling, work-shy, living for the day without any plans, indulging in sensual pleasures. He delights the population with his artistic offerings. A Gypsy can be someone to whom one or many of the listed characteristics applies. One Gypsy is like another. If you know one, you know them all.[1]

The 'Gypsy Myth' in Literature

In literature there is a particularly long tradition of cultivating the 'Gypsy myth'. In all literary genres people have been working away and are still working at a 'type' which has nothing in common with the reality of the ethnic group. Whether it is in fairy tales, sagas, folk-songs or high literature, the texts are riddled with anti-Gypsyism and grotesque clichés which turn the original narrative tradition of the Sinti and Roma upside down. In other words, the self-images are completely submerged by images created by others. These images created by others are of course frequently incredibly hostile images.

The literary critic Wilhelm Solms has conducted an exemplary investigation into the aspect of the demonisation of 'Gypsies' and Jews in fairy tales and legends, and comes to the following conclusion:

> Both the Christian legends and the aetiological fairy tales which were allegedly narrated by Romanies are deliberate falsifications of history, in that they smuggle Sinti and Roma into the history of the Jewish people. And both serve a dual purpose: they serve to apportion blame to the Jews and transfer this blame to the Sinti and Roma, and thus at the same time they serve to justify their expulsion, which marked the beginning of their joint history of suffering.[2]

In a comparative study about collections of sagas, Ines Köhler-Zülch, a literary historian who worked on the *Encyclopaedia of Fairy Tales* in Göttingen, comes to the conclusion: 'The so-called Gypsy literature transports clichés in a pseudo-scientific way and hands them down over the centuries. In the collections of sagas the real living conditions of the Sinti and Roma are rarely or never thematised'.[3]

An examination of the story published in 1988 by Wolfdietrich Schnurre entitled 'Gypsy Ballad' shows that the transmission of anti-Gypsy images is by no means a thing of the past. The reverse is the case. To this very day writers (often well-meaning ones) represent Sinti and Roma in an exaggerated way or use them to make an ideological point.

According to the publisher's blurb, the 'Gypsy Ballad' is a book which pulls no punches, but is full of tolerance and brotherly love, and does not exclude a certain amount of unsentimental melancholy, because the Sinti and Roma way of viewing life is, according to the publishers, provocatively anachronistic. What is particularly anachronistic and really outmoded, though, is Schnurre's technique of trying to win the tolerance of the reader with a colourful succession of romantic images. Anyone who appeals to the yearnings of readers in such a transparent sort of way, who uses a certain amount of taste, has something very different in mind in objective terms – the sales-promoting presentation of the 'Gypsy' is not compatible with the true elucidation of a subject.

The Roots of Modern Anti-Gypsyism in Germany

If we work from Raul Hilberg's sequence of 'registering, selecting, annihilating', as roughly marking the stages of the route which led to Auschwitz, then we must trace the start of modern anti-Gypsyism back to the year 1899. The modern persecution of, and discrimination against, the Sinti and Roma began with the setting up of the 'Information Service for the Security Police with Reference to Gypsies' by the Bavarian State Police Headquarters in Munich in March 1899. Here for the first time the comprehensive registration and control of a whole group of the population was planned and organised. The climax of the anti-Gypsy measures of the pre-Nazi period was the special registration covering the whole of the Reich, with fingerprinting being undertaken in the year 1927.

Even before the National Socialists came to power in 1933, they began to collate information and devoted themselves to the registering of both Jews and Sinti and Roma. And even before the National Socialists declared in the 'Nuremberg Race Laws' that it was only possible for a person to be a 'citizen of the Reich' if he was of 'German or similar related blood', the racial ideological objectives of the NSDAP had already gone down in the statute books of the Third Reich, and underpinned the law for re-establishing the professional civil servant status of 7 April 1933 and the law for the prevention of genetically sick offspring of 14 July 1933. From the start the crucial element here is that the extermination of further generations of Sinti and Roma was demanded, and set in motion by means of compulsory sterilisation.

Dr Achim Gercke, head of the Office for Kinship Research within the Ministry of the Interior, maintains in his statement about his position on the planned Nuremberg Laws that the sole purpose of such a law is to 'draw a line between the pure Germans on the one hand, and on the other hand people living in Germany who come from countries outside Europe, or perhaps occasionally from countries within Europe'.[4] In their commentary on the

Nuremberg Laws Stuckart and Globke laid down that only Jews and Gypsies were to be regularly considered as alien and as a strange race from outside Europe.

With these early legal norms, definitions and administrative criteria it becomes clear that racial hatred formed the basis for anti-Semitism and anti-Gypsyism in the consciousness of the National Socialists right from the start. This meant that Sinti and Roma, just like the Jews, were no longer merely 'to blame' for a deplorable state of affairs, but had to suffer as scapegoats. Their mere existence was the ultimate disgrace. They were not to be expelled or re-educated to be 'better' citizens of the state. No. Their very physical existence itself was to be obliterated.

The new 'racially motivated anti-Gypsyism' was thus based on a theoretically different foundation. The final solution and mass annihilation – the dreadful practice of racial ideology – were not exactly modelled on the old methods of fanning anti-Semitic or anti-Gypsy prejudice, such as those used in the so-called 'gutter racism' of the *Stürmer*. The National Socialist crimes of genocide were in fact based on the ascribing of a scientific basis to traditional prejudices. To put it bluntly: the Nazis' biological concept of race, which had been elevated to a general maxim for action of all 'comrades', made possible the incomprehensible sudden swing away from the traditional persecution of and discrimination against minorities to the atrocities of the Holocaust. This indicates a further difference between racially motivated and traditional anti-Gypsyism.

The racial policy of the Nazis was determined centrally from above and was controlled and kept running by a massive propaganda machinery. Compared to this, the generally 'anti-Gypsy' attitude of the population as a whole (however this may be evaluated and assessed in individual cases) was absolutely secondary.

With Hitler's decree to strengthen the concept of *Volkstum* (the German national identity) of 7 October 1939, Reichsführer SS Heinrich Himmler was given the task of 'getting rid of harmful influences on the part of sections of the population hostile to the nation'. Within the framework of this programme, which was based on a command from the Führer, which later became infamous as the 'Final Solution', two groups of the population, the Jews and the Sinti and Roma, were condemned as 'alien to the nation and harmful' and left to the mercy of the concentration camps.

Anti-Gypsyism in Postwar German Society and Culture

There is indisputable evidence that anti-Gypsyism did not disappear from Germany in the year of 1945 after the Nazi Holocaust against more than 500,000 Sinti and Roma. In the years immediately after the war additional registration measures by the police and discrimination by federal and regional authorities were by no means isolated phenomena. Thus the discriminatory Law to Combat the Gypsy Menace remained in force in Hessen from 1929 to 1957. On 22 December 1953 the Bavarian State Parliament passed a so-called 'Vagrant Law'. Finally, the scandalous verdict of the Federal Court in 1954, in which it was denied that Sinti and Roma had been persecuted for racial reasons, is symptomatic of the anti-Gypsy climate of this period of time.

On probing into why National Socialist ways of thinking lived on, one inevitably comes up against the problem of the continuity of the staff working in the civil service and holding top positions in scientific and other institutions. The postwar careers of SS members, detectives and scientists who were involved in the registering, deporting and murder of the Sinti and Roma reveal this continuity of anti-Gypsyism particularly clearly.

Thus Josef Eichberger, who worked in Office V of the Central Office for Reich Security and was in charge of the deportations, became head of the 'Vagrant Department' of the Bavarian Regional Police Headquarters. The staff of the Racial Hygiene and Demographic Biology Research Unit also had no difficulties after 1945 in continuing to work and hold important posts. Dr Robert Ritter taught criminal biology at the University of Tübingen from 1944 to 1946 and was then taken on as a pediatrician at the Frankfurt Health Authority in December 1947. Once again Ritter worked there together with Eva Justin, who was employed as a psychologist at the same place. It was a similar story with Dr Sophie Ehrhardt, Dr Adolf Würth, the doctor and geneticist Professor Otmar Verschuer and Dr Hermann Arnold. It would not be difficult to cite more examples.

The racist way in which allusions are made to the ethnic affiliation of members of our (Sinti) minority group, where there is no actual reason for mentioning this, is a further instance of the continuity of anti-Gypsyism in the post-1945 period. In a democratic state individual citizens are responsible for themselves alone in the case of a false step. The completely irrelevant reference to skin colour or ethnic or religious affiliation in a report is more than just a misuse of the freedom of the press. Seen objectively, this practice has the effect of being incendiary, stirring up prejudices and spurring people on to racial hatred. I limit myself here to one example from the media.

In 1991 the Südwestfunk broadcast the film *Children of the Wind*, which contains excessively racist passages. Simon Wiesenthal considered the performance to be disparaging to the survivors of the Holocaust. Professor Franz Hamburger of the University of Mainz wrote in an official review: 'This series reflects the dominant structure of prejudices against the Sinti and Roma and can therefore evoke nothing else in the viewer but the confirmation of his fantasies which are governed by fear, hatred or misconceptions'.[5] In a court hearing the Heidelberg District Court accused the Südwestfunk of 'uninhibited and undifferentiated sweeping generalisations'.[6]

The result of this and other widespread media practices is that according to the latest questionnaire of the EMNID Institute in March 1994 (commissioned by the American Jewish Committee) 68 percent of the German population, in other words a two-thirds majority, openly express hatred and prejudice towards the Sinti and Roma.[7] The great mass of newspaper readers, film and television viewers do not, however, have any personal acquaintanceship with members of our ethnic group. That is, there are no personal experiences here. We are dealing with a stigmatisation which is manipulated by the media.

In the German media there is almost no mention at all of the real life of Sinti and Roma in Germany, who, as German citizens, are no different to the majority population in their careers or their social involvement in clubs and institutions. 'Normal' Sinti and Roma hardly ever feature in newspaper reports, pictures on state television channels or private television companies' programmes. Time and time again what is shown is the distorted picture of our ethnic group. That must stop once and for all.

If this chapter can heighten awareness of the fact that the compulsion to perpetuate clichés cannot be blamed on the 'eternally constant nature of the Gypsy', but has its origins in the continuing interest in the preservation of a socially determined image of an enemy, an important step has been taken towards improving Sinto-German relationships.

Notes

1. K. Martins-Heuß, *Zur mythischen Figur des Zigeuners*, Frankfurt am Main, 1983, p.93.
2. W. Solms, 'Zur Dämonisierung der Juden und Zigeuner im Märchen', in *Zigeunerbilder in der deutschsprachigen Literatur*, ed. D. Strauß and W. Solms, Heidelberg, 1995, pp.89f.
3. I. Köhler-Zülch, 'Die Figur des Zigeuners in deutschsprachigen Sagen', in *Zigeunerbilder in der deutschsprachigen Literatur*, ed. Strauß and Solms, p.16.
4. *Gesetz zum Schutz des deutschen Blutes und der deutschen Ehre* (Law for the Protection of German Blood and German Honour) of 15 September 1935, I. p.1146f.
5. Unpublished report submitted to the *Zentralrat Deutscher Sinti und Roma* in Heidelberg.
6. Quoted in *Rhein-Neckar-Zeitung*, 6 February 1992, p.7.
7. The EMNID Institute conducts demographic research.

CHAPTER 7

On the Demonising of Jews and Gypsies in Fairy Tales

Wilhelm Solms

Introduction

The title of the chapter is designed to make us think, both as Europeans and as connoisseurs of the fairy tale. It places on a par two ethnic groups which have both lived as minority groups in our midst, and of which only a few have survived, but who apart from this common fate are totally different in terms of origins, language and culture. According to the title, what they have in common is extremely negative, namely that they were seen by the majority population not as human beings but as non-human creatures. The title also presupposes that this perception not only reigned in the late Middle Ages at the time of the Inquisition, but has been passed on and is still being passed down via fairy tales right up to the present day, without having met with any objections or resistance from researchers into and connoisseurs of fairy tales.

I would like to prove this hypothesis by examining a field with which everyone is familiar, but which has been hardly explored at all from this particular angle, namely the *Volksmärchen*, which were formerly passed on by word of mouth, the *Kunstmärchen* (invented

* Translated by Susan Tebbutt

fairy tales) and the so-called *Zigeunermärchen* (Gypsy fairy tales), which go back to the oral narratives of the Sinti and Roma. Other genres of folk literature, such as sagas, legends, farce, mystery plays, jokes and songs have also contributed to the demonising of Jews and 'Gypsies'. It is of course not possible to cover this immense range of material in a few pages, but perhaps this chapter can help draw attention to the need for further academic research in the field.

Background

Although the ethnic demonising of the Jews and Gypsies in the Middle Ages will be familiar from the many publications in recent years about belief in the devil and witches, I would nevertheless like to focus briefly on this phenomenon.

In the Middle Ages Jews were considered to be people who helped the devil in his work, if not the children of the devil. Legends had it that Jews and the Antichrist were in league, and even that the Antichrist originated from a relationship between a Jewish woman and the devil. The Jews were said to owe their financial successes to the fact that they were friends with or related to the devil.

When the Sinti and Roma came to Europe at the beginning of the fifteenth century people took them to be the descendants of Cain and made them subject to the death penalty, citing Cain's words: 'and it shall come to pass, that every one that findeth me shall slay me'.[1] Alternatively, people maintained that the Gypsies, like the Tartars, originated from the Underworld. In a legend which circulated through the whole of Europe, the Sinti and Roma, together with the Jews, were held jointly responsible for the crucifixion of Christ. It was believed that not only the places where Jews gathered, but also Gypsy camps were the sites of the devil.

In the year 1492 the Spanish royals, Ferdinand and Isabella, even banned Jews and Moors, including *gitanos*, the Spanish Gypsies, from their country. At the start of the seventeenth century all sorcerers, soothsayers and magicians in France were hunted down, whereby those who called themselves 'Bohemians', that is the Roma who had emigrated from the East, were particularly singled out.

The Image of the Jew in Fairy Tales

Gypsy Fairy Tales

The fact that there were originally no links and later only a very limited number of points of similarity between the Gypsies and the Jews is shown by their fairy tales. In Jewish myths and fairy tales the figure of the Gypsy does not, to the best of my knowledge, feature at all, and in the *Zigeunermärchen* the figure of the Jew appears very rarely and does not have any uniform set of characteristics.

On one occasion a Jew acts as a money-lender who even demands back from a dead man the money he has lent.[2] On another occasion a Jew steals a peasant's money.[3] Both these tales are, however, in common circulation among the host nations. In two fairy tales the Jew appears as a hero, which is something I have not found either in Grimms' *Kinder- und Hausmärchen* (Nursery and Household Tales) or in the fairy tales of the host nations. In one of these two fairy tales the stupid son of a poor Jew wins the daughter of the King of the Turks[4] – the Jew plays the same role here as the Gypsy does in other fairy tales – and in the other[5] he acts as the trusty friend of a young nobleman. Although cleverer than the latter, he does not use his brains to trick him, but conquers a beautiful daughter of a king for him. In the tales of the Sinti and Roma it is thus not possible to detect any anti-Jewish tendency.

Other Volksmärchen and the Fairy Tales of the Brothers Grimm

Here I base my case on comprehensive research by Leander Petzold. In the fairy tales of different ethnic groups – Petzold included in his survey the four-volume collection entitled *Donauschwaben erzählen* (Swabians from the Danube area narrate their stories) – we encounter the Jew in two main types of job, either as a wealthy merchant who sometimes also offers credit to people, or as a poor rag-and-bone man and scrap dealer who travels from village to village. In the role of the stingy, greedy merchant, the Jew is usually swindled, and in the role of the rag-and-bone man he is sometimes mocked, sometimes pitied, and sometimes even helped. Taking the picture as a whole, the Jew is faced with contempt but not with aggression.

In the *Kinder- und Hausmärchen* a Jew appears on four occasions, namely in 'Der gute Handel' (The Good Deal),[6] 'Der gute Lappen'

(The Good Rag),[7] 'Die klare Sonne bringt es an den Tag' (The Clear Sun brings it to the Light of Day)[8] and 'Der Jude im Dorn' (The Jew in the Thorns).[9] In the first he is beaten many times with a stick, in the second and third he is beaten to death, once when he is guilty and on the other occasion through no fault of his own, and in the fourth he is sentenced to death and hanged. The Jew is thus always the victim. Petzold comes to the general conclusion that: 'In the folk narratives Jews are mostly characterised as standing outside the law, as suffering people, as losers'. The following observation may also be added to that: the mishandling and killing of the Jew meets with the approval of the narrator in all but one case, and for a long time also met with the approval of the listeners or readers. When the Jew in the thorns acknowledges at the end that the knave had 'earned the money honestly', which he had gained from him with the help of the magic fiddle, this is not in fact the truth. Anyone who still feels that his being sentenced to death is his just desserts must be obsessed with the prejudice that a Jew is always in the wrong.

Despite such anti-Jewish evidence, Petzold is of the opinion that the image of the Jew in folk literature shows 'fewer aggressively negative traits than that of the contemporary anti- Jewish propaganda literature of the educated classes'. This verdict does not unfortunately apply only to bourgeois 'propaganda literature' but also to many works of high literature and even to some *Kunstmärchen*.

Kunstmärchen

In recent years, thanks to government funding, the image of the Jew in German history and German literary history, unlike the image of the 'Gypsy', has been investigated on many occasions. The German *Kunstmärchen* were, however, seemingly overlooked. For example, anyone looking through the list of names for Brentano, the writer of fairy tales, would search in vain.

Disturbing texts about Jews and 'Gypsies' are already in evidence in the collection of folk songs and poems by Arnim and Brentano, 'Des Knaben Wunderhorn' (The Boy's Magic Horn). After the first volume appeared in 1806, Brentano devised the plan of also publishing children's fairy tales and commissioned the Brothers Grimm to collect fairy tales for him. The fifty-three texts which the Brothers Grimm sent him in September 1810 not only form the original manuscript version of the *Kinder- und*

Hausmärchen, but also the most important source of Brentano's 'Märchen vom Rhein' (Rhine fairy tales) which were composed in 1812. In the fourth and last, the 'Märchen vom Schneider Siebentodt auf einen Schlag' (Tale of the Tailor Seven-dead-at-one-blow) Brentano merged elements from two tales, 'Das tapfere Schneiderlein' (The Brave Little Tailor) and 'Daumerlings Wanderschaft' (Daumerling's Travels), and embellished them with 'Schneider-Lieder' (Tailors' Songs) from the second volume of the *Wunderhorn*, and figments of his own imagination. The key element which differentiates Brentano's fairy tale from its sources the instant you look at it is not, however, mentioned in the commentaries. The first half of it represents a terrifying example of anti-Jewish literature.

In her historical critical edition Brigitte Schillbach sees the tale as 'a satire on tailors', but overlooks the satire on the Jews, although the tailors appear here in the positive role of heroes and the Jews appear in the role of adversaries or, to be more accurate, as victims. The fairy tale is about the battle of the tailors against the Jews. Before the beginning of the battle the question of guilt is clarified, as it is in real life. 'One morning in Amsterdam it looked as if day was never going to dawn'. Thus begins the tale. Because the Jews in the Jews' town observe the 'long day', as the Christians call Yom Kippur, the Jewish day of atonement, the town council orders the Rabbis to 'make a gift of their long day to the good city of Amsterdam', and when they refuse the town council calls on the citizens of Amsterdam to 'take away their long day by force'. Thus the Jews are allowed to live together with the Christians, albeit in a ghetto, within the same city. If, however, the Christians are short of anything, it is taken for granted that the Jews will have to bear the costs.

The tailors get 'onto their mounts', gallop off and brandish 'their scissors to chop off the beards of the Jews'. The Jews entrench themselves in the synagogue in order to pray and resist the tailors with their 'large, old scapegoat'. 'Scapegoat' is the term used for the goat which the Jews offer as a sacrifice to Jehovah on the day of atonement. Brentano thus links both tailors and Jews to the goat, which is considered in mythology and in Grimms' fairy tales to be the 'creature of the devil'. Neither the external appearance of the orthodox Jews nor their sacred customs escape his derision.

In a study of Judaism in Germany the Christian German Dining Society is mentioned, which was founded in Berlin in 1811 at the instigation of Achim von Arnim. According to its constitution no 'Philistines, French people, women or Jews' were allowed to become members. It was there that Brentano delivered his speech against the Philistines, which is aimed just as much at the Jews.

The figure of the Jew also appears in Brentano's 'Italian fairy tales'. In 'Gockel und Hinkel' (The Rooster and the Hen), a fairy tale which was written at some point after summer 1815, three old Jews make an appearance, again with a goat, this time in order to spirit away the magic ring which is concealed in the neck of the cockerel. In Brentano's source, Basile's fairy tale 'Der Hahnenstein' (The Rooster's Gem) there are not three Jews but 'two ugly sorcerers'. Brentano stopped writing after his religious conversion in the year 1817 and left his fairy tales unpublished. In 1836, some twenty years later, he took up the cockerel fairy tale again and completely reworked it. One might think that in the meantime he might have become better informed, or moderated his position as far as his anti-Jewish disposition was concerned. Quite the opposite. He extended the anti-Jewish passages of this fairy tale quite considerably and made them even more intense.

In the later *Kunstmärchen* Jews are not mentioned as such, which does not however mean that they are not present. Thus the principal figure in Theodor Storm's fairy tale 'Bulemanns Haus' (Bulemann's House) appears to be a caricature of a Jew. Bulemann has the Jewish first name Daniel, whilst his half-sister and her son are called Christine and Christian. He is a pawn-broker by trade, and stingy to boot, and wears a dressing-gown, sleeping-cap and slippers, all attributes which can be found in contemporary caricatures of Jews. Other examples of indirect representation of this type can also be found elsewhere, such as, for example, in Charles Dickens' fairy tales.

The Image of the 'Gypsy' in Fairy Tales

Kunstmärchen

The fact that Gypsies were not allowed admission to the Christian German Dining Society either is not mentioned specifically in the constitution because it went without saying. The longest tale from the manuscript collection of fairy tales of the Brothers Grimm

'Murmelthier' (Marmot)[10] was not included in the *Kinder- und Hausmärchen* but was expanded by Brentano into the 'Märchen vom Murmelthier' (Tale of the Marmot), the third of the Rhine fairy tales.

Towards the end of the tale when everything is 'resolved', the girl marmot finds out that she is the daughter of the King of Burgundy and that her step-mother is a 'Gypsy' and stole her from the King's garden when she was a baby. 'So did the wicked Gypsy wild / steal the tender little child'. In his use of poetic licence Brentano shows no inhibitions about making a rhyme about the most scurrilous prejudice about the Gypsies. In the annotated edition published by Hanser in 1965 and in the historical critical edition of 1983 there is not a single word of comment on this grave alteration of the source.

In his *Novelle* 'Isabella von Ägypten' (Isabella of Egypt), which also shows the influence of the *Volksmärchen* and which was also written in spring 1812 in Berlin, Achim von Arnim, unlike Brentano, does not criminalise the image of the Gypsy, but idealises it. In so doing he distorts it just as much.

Arnim not only uses a fairy tale-like tone and many motifs from fairy tales, but also keeps to the typical pattern of events of the fairy tale. He begins with the expulsion of the Gypsies from Egypt (here he uses the legend of the denying of a bed for the night) and then tells of the romantic relationship between the Gypsy princess Isabella and Charles V and concludes with a fairy tale happy ending: the return of the Gypsy people to their original homeland.

In her excellent dissertation on 'The Image of the Gypsy in German Literature' Heidi Berger evaluates this *Novelle* as a 'valuable contribution to the image of the Gypsy', because Arnim is the only person to see the fate of the Gypsies from the viewpoint of the Gypsies.[11] The happy ending does, however, bear more resemblance to a romantic utopia than to the interpretation Berger puts on it. Is it not also a model for 'the Final Solution to the Gypsy question'?

Gypsies also feature in Ludwig Tieck's fairy tale 'Die Elfen' (The Elves), even if they only 'look like' Gypsies. In answer to his wife's question as to 'who on earth the people could in fact be who live there and why they had in fact kept so far away from everyone in the community, as if they had a bad conscience', the tenant replies: 'Poor riff-raff. They look like Gypsy folk who go around robbing and cheating people in faraway places and perhaps have their hideout here. The only thing that surprises me is that my gracious lady tolerates them'.

At any rate the woman is puzzled as to why the people keep their distance from the community and the church, but does not hit upon the idea that the reason behind this might lie with the community. As far as her husband is concerned, he is clear in his own mind, right from the start, that they are robbers and cheats who really ought not to be tolerated at all.

Tieck developed his fairy tale (which is in fact, to be more precise, a legend, as the rest of the story shows) out of the juxtaposition of 'desolate place' and 'flower garden' and the juxtaposition of 'Gypsies' and 'elves' or 'rogues' and 'benefactors'. It is probable that he did not intend to draw the Gypsies in a negative way, but wanted to merely use the Gypsy children, who are depicted as 'ugly' and 'dirty', as a dark background against which the shining children of the elves stand out. He does, however, allow the tenant's view that real Gypsies are 'rogues who rob and cheat' to stand uncontradicted. And by transforming the Gypsies into elves, he awakens or reinforces in us the notion that Gypsies are creatures from another world. If the Gypsies need to be got rid of, as the tenant demands, where would there be a place for them in the world? Nowhere. (The comparison of Gypsies with elves has incidentally already been made in Arnim's postscript to 'Des Knaben Wunderhorn' of 1806.)

In the fairy tale of the *Biedermeier* and Realism period, Gypsies are sometimes depicted without actually being referred to as 'Gypsies', and sometimes mentioned without themselves appearing in the story. In Wilhelm Hauff's cycle of fairy tales of 1828, *Das Wirtshaus im Spessart* (The Tavern in the Spessart), the robber chief takes the travellers whom he has taken prisoner in the tavern to the place where the gang of robbers have camped in a small, narrow, wooded valley. This site, on which 'dirty women' look out of their wooden shelters and large dogs jump around barking, is apparently supposed to represent a Gypsy camp.

In Theodor Storm's fairy tale 'Der Spiegel des Cyprianus' (Cyprianus' Mirror), published in 1865, a Countess asks Cyprianus for advice because she is childless, and he replies: 'it's possible that I have better advice for you than those travelling folk who may understand how to swindle the gullible but do not understand the future at all!' He promises to send her a magic mirror. This 'should soon bring you better tidings than the misleading people on the heathland'. Why should the mirror of the 'mighty magician' Cyprianus – or why should the horoscope of a present-day astrologer – tell the truth, whereas on the other hand the fortune-telling of a Gypsy woman is 'deception'? As the fortune-telling in both cases could equally well be true or untrue, the difference can only lie in the nature of the people who are telling the fortunes. The Gypsy woman is fraudulent because she is not a fellow-citizen, but camps out on the 'heath', in other words, because she is a Gypsy.

Literary critics are divided about the images of Gypsies in the *Kunstmärchen*. Some believe that the Romantic movement shows a positive image, whereas the Realist movement shows a negative image, and others feel that the Romantic movement shows an unreal image whereas the Realist movement show a realistic image of the Gypsy. Both views are flawed. In the post-Romantic *Kunstmärchen* there are exclusively negative clichés such as theft, lies and deception, but it is also the case in the Romantic movement that 'Gypsies', and especially 'Gypsy women', are not only changed into elves and angels but also, as in Brentano's tale, 'Die mehreren Wehmüllers' (The Various Wehmüllers) are transformed into witches and in both cases are changed into extraterrestrial creatures or demonised.

Zigeunermärchen

As far as *Volksmärchen* are concerned, 'Gypsies' are not encountered at all in the *Kinder- und Hausmärchen*, and only on rare occasions in German or French collections of fairy tales, but are to be found relatively often in the fairy tales of Hungary, Romania or Serbia, that is, those nations where many Roma live. The fact that the 'Gypsy' is mostly depicted here in negative terms does not come as a surprise after what has been revealed about the *Kunstmärchen*. It is, however, surprising and initially incomprehensible that even Gypsy fairy tales contribute to the demonising of the Gypsy.

Demonic Figures and Demonic Powers

In the *Zigeunermärchen* we naturally find the same extraterrestrial figures who are familiar to us from the magic fairy tales of other nations. The hero or heroine, not infrequently the youngest of the numerous children of a poor Gypsy, has to fight against very powerful opponents such as witches, magicians, cannibals, giants, dragons or devils, and furthermore the giant is perhaps even taller and the dragon has more heads than normal. The hero does not act here as a demonic creature, but rather as the person who liberates the world from demons. As a rule he triumphs over them through tricks, boasting or simply by good fortune, (and that is where the particular charm of these fairy tales lies), unlike the hero of the magic fairy tale who triumphs thanks to miraculous assistants or magic potions which he gets from these assistants. It is striking how many Gypsy fairy tales fall into the category of farcical fairy tale, which seems to be a typical and genuine narrative genre of the Sinti and Roma. When the latter read about the heroes of these farcical fairy tales who have to prove themselves by showing courage and common sense against superior opponents, they can recognise themselves not only as isolated individuals, but also as members of an ethnic group.

There are a particularly large number of extremely humorous examples of farcical fairy tales to be found in Gypsy fairy tales, such as the tales about the outwitting of the devil or the fight with the dragon. Super-human strength, sorcery, lying, stealing and cheating, in other words, all the qualities which are frowned upon and despised in everyday life, are rated positively if the hero grows up with a giant or is suckled by a witch and gains strength from this, if he enters an apprenticeship with his god-father, the devil, learns the craft of magic from the devil's daughter or conquers the devil after an exciting battle to transform him into something else, or if he strikes fear into his opponent merely by bragging, or if he steals a magic item from him. This is because these qualities are legitimised by the plot of the fairy tale.

Fairy Tales about Lying and Stealing

Fairy tales about lying and the fairy tale about the master-thief belong to the sub-genre of the farcical fairy tale. Here it is announced that the hero or his task-master will lie and steal. We are therefore not surprised or shocked that they do this, but are waiting to see how they do it. Here lying and stealing are an art admired by the narrator and listener, although this admiration has its limits if the hero of these fairy tales is a Gypsy. It is to be feared that listeners or readers who approach the fairy tales with the 'expectation' or previously held view that a Gypsy would lie and steal will feel that their prejudices are well founded. The collectors of fairy tales should have watched out for this when they were working on the texts.

In the volume entitled 'Romanian German fairy tales' there is one version of the 'Der Teufel und der Zigeuner' (The Devil and the Gypsy), a farcical fairy tale which has been handed down in many forms, which initially impresses the reader because of its apposite final twist. The devil goes stealing pigs with the Gypsy. When he is cheated out of his share of the booty he says: 'Right then. I am no longer going to go stealing pigs with a Gypsy. He even cheats the devil!' The devil naturally means that as a compliment, but a listener or reader could hear or read into it: 'A Gypsy steals and cheats and is even worse than the devil!'

The Gypsy Woman as Witch

In many fairy tales 'Gypsies' appear who not only acquire demonic powers, but turn out to be demons themselves. This stereotyping almost always refers to women. Some 'Gypsy women' are in reality witches, and furthermore not only ugly old women like those in Grimms' fairy tales, but preferably pretty young women who are not instantly recognisable as witches.

In a fairy tale related by Wlislocki, 'Die Hexe und die Eierschalen' (The Witch and the Eggshells), a beautiful young Gypsy woman once came to a southern Hungarian Gypsy tribe: 'No-one knew who she was, nor what tribe she belonged to. If she was asked about this, she always replied: "My tribe lived far away from here in the Empire of the Turks, and there came a time when the Turkish Emperor there had all Gypsies killed! I alone was able to escape".'

When the listener later finds out that she is a witch, he may well think that the story of the destruction of her tribe was a fabrication. Indeed many people even think that reports by reliable witnesses about the annihilation of the Sinti and Roma in this century are lies.

There are, however, also positive counter-images of witches, such as those in a fairy tale of the Slovakian Roma 'Die schöne Zauberin' (The Beautiful Sorceress).[12] Here the narrator makes it clear right from the start: 'An old Gypsy woman had a beautiful young daughter and the daughter was a sorceress'. He adds the explanation: 'Witchcraft is not a trade that can be learnt, like for example making kettles; you have to be born to be a sorcerer or sorceress'. He says you can recognise this immediately by certain innate physical characteristics, thus ruling out the possibility that the reader will see every Gypsy woman as a sorceress.

How does the girl's witchcraft or magic-making manifest itself? It is seen firstly when she 'enchants' a blacksmith with whom she has fallen in love, secondly when she grows 'younger and more beautiful' after each of her five children and thirdly when she changes herself into a red rose, when her husband, at his mother's bidding, tries to burn her. Thus she never does anything evil. When she finally loses her magic power, and thus also her beauty, and becomes a middle-aged 'normal woman', the blacksmith is not disappointed but loves her all the more. A convincing ending, even if it is not a conventional fairy tale happy ending.

The Gypsy who Looks like the Devil

Men in the fairy tales are not directly demonised, but are 'only' compared to the devil in terms of their external appearance. A farcical fairy tale related by Friedrich Krauss entitled 'Warum die Zigeuner teufelsfürchtig sind' (Why the Gypsies Fear the Devil) is about how the Gypsies caught the son of the Emperor of the devils and 'although they were already black by nature, they rubbed soot on their skins to make themselves look even blacker, so that they looked like devils incarnate'. The rubbing-in of soot is a trick they use to deceive the young inexperienced devil, and is thus a key part of the plot of this fairy tale. The son of the king of devils also falls for it immediately. He believes that they are 'devils who were having fun' and joins in the group of dancers despite having been banned from so doing by his father, whereupon a Gypsy pulls his cap off his head and thus catches him. Whereas the soot is part of the story, the statement that they are 'already black by nature' is superfluous to the plot of the fairy tale, and is thus clearly an addition of the narrator and evidence of his prejudice.

In the farcical fairy tales published by Krauss, the tale 'Wie der Zigeuner den Teufel überlistete' (How the Gypsy Outwitted the Devil) is a further example of how the narrator embellishes the tale. The Gypsy catches the devil out with two tricks, which have nothing to do with skin-colour, be it that of the devil or the Gypsy. Nevertheless, their appearance and, on top of that, their smell, are compared here too, 'The devil is in any case by nature black as an Arab, is dirty, and stinks like a badger. Likewise the Gypsy is by nature dark-skinned, and in addition sooty and evil-smelling from working as a blacksmith and not washing, and that is why the devil considers him to be one of his own kind'.

This comparison is superfluous to the plot and thus again probably an added flourish of the narrator. Certainly it is the devil and not the narrator who considers the Gypsy to be 'one of his own kind'. Nevertheless the dirtiness and evil smell of the Gypsy are not just put down to the fact that he works as a blacksmith (a plausible reason), but are furthermore gratuitously attributed to his 'not washing'. That is, however, not part of being a smith and can thus only represent what the narrator sees as the nature of the Gypsy. A clear-cut case of racism.

In a farce published by Krauss it is explicitly stressed that the Gypsy is honest and therefore resists the devil longer than other people. Yet the narrator cannot refrain from describing the Gypsy as having a close affinity with the devil. He begins with the words: 'The devil seduced his chosen brother, the Gypsy'.

In view of these examples, the question is raised as to the identity of this narrator. Would the Roma who told the story orally speak in this way about himself and his kind, and furthermore do so in front of a non-Roma? Or was the person who wrote down, edited and translated the fairy tales, in this case Friedrich Krauss?

The racist prejudice of the narrator is shown quite explicitly in a Russian Gypsy fairy tale entitled 'Wie der Teufel den Zigeuner auf seinen Platz stellen wollte' (How the Devil Wanted to Put the Gypsy in his Place). He introduces the hero, a really strong Gypsy, as follows: 'The Gypsy looked black and awe-inspiring like a devil. Except that he didn't have any horns. The peasants were afraid of him'. When the devil seeks him out, the narrator comments: 'His face looked like the spitting image of a Gypsy'. When the devil comes back the narrator puts the suggestive question: "Were they perhaps really *Doppelgänger*?" Finally he puts the following words in the devil's mouth: 'he looks so like me about the face that no- one can tell us apart'. But the Gypsy does not fall for his attempt to make him into his surrogate and finally puts an end to the devil look-alike.

This would be an original, funny, farcical fairy tale in terms of plot, if the narrator did not suggest to us four times in a row how much the two resemble each other. In so doing he reveals to us how important it is to him to demonise the Gypsy in the truest sense of the word.

In a Hungarian Gypsy fairy tale the narrator does not bother to demonstrate to the reader at length how similar the Gypsy is to the devil. He simply acts as if he himself mistakes one for the other. After the devil has sent the Gypsy to a fountain the story goes as follows: 'The devil ... , thingummy ... , the Gypsy grabbed a pickaxe'. And when the devil wants to go chopping wood with the

Gypsy, we then read: 'the Gypsy had second thoughts, took a roll of string and the devil ... no, the Gypsy took the string with him'. Both cases of mistaken identity go against the flow of the plot, because it is only the Gypsy who is planning to do something with the pickaxe and the string. Thus the malicious intent of the narrator becomes apparent despite the supposed mistaken identity.

In a fairy tale from 'Janitschek im Räuberschloß' (Janitschek in the Robbers' Castle) a story is told which goes against the prejudice of the similarity of the Gypsy to the devil. Robbers have captured Janitschek and want to burn him, but he escapes in the smoke. The youngest robber says: "'Was this prince supposed to have been a devil?" "Yes, Yes, Yes," cried the others, "What does it matter if he was a devil? Then we have helped him to get to hell." "Rubbish", said the oldest, "there aren't any devils. He has disappeared and that's all there is to it! Come on, let's look for him".'

It is true that in reality there are no devils, but they were invented and live on in fairy tales to the present day, in order to demonise people who think or live differently or look different to the majority of the population.

Aetiological Tales about Jews and 'Gypsies'

At the beginning I referred to the Christian, or rather racist, legends from the Middle Ages, the legend about the descent of the Gypsies from Cain, about the bed for the night being refused and about the forging of the nails for the Cross. Among the *Zigeunermärchen* there is a variation of this last legend, which was possibly invented and narrated by the Romanies as a positive counter-story. The Gypsy who forged the nails does not forge one nail too many for the cross, but one too few, in order to spare Christ additional pain. This does of course not counteract the lie that a Gypsy was also involved in the crucifixion.

Another tale which also dates back to medieval sources, that of the journey of the Jews across the Red Sea, is related in a *Zigeunermärchen* from Hungary. Gypsies were also supposed to have belonged to King Pharaoh's army, for they were 'Pharaoh's own people, his relatives'. They stayed back on the shore of the Red Sea, waiting to see 'how things would turn out', and therefore remained alive. But God created a 'second further miracle' and set a storm loose on them which dispersed them to the four winds. 'In the end God also dispersed the Jews throughout the whole world'. Despite this mental leap from the fall of Pharaoh to the crucifixion of Christ there is an unambiguous lesson to be learnt from this story. Anyone who drives away Jews or Gypsies is carrying out God's work.

Both the Christian legends and the aetiological stories supposedly narrated by Roma are deliberate falsifications of history, because they smuggle in Sinti and Roma to the history of the Jewish people. And both serve a dual purpose: they serve to allocate blame to the Jews and to transfer this blame to the Sinti and Roma. At the same time they thus serve as a justification for their expulsion, which is where their joint history of suffering then begins.

Outlook

The examples presented here, which are only the tip of the iceberg, show that even fairy tales which seem extremely harmless have contributed to demonising Gypsies and Jews. Images of Jews and Gypsies which were created by the Christian churches of both confessions towards the end of the Middle Ages were passed down through the centuries through the oral and written traditions of *Volksmärchen* and *Kunstmärchen*.

The logical consequence of this demonising was the increasingly striking marginalisation of Jews and Sinti and Roma. It gave new impetus to their persecution and annihilation in Germany, and in the areas of Europe conquered by German troops. Contrary to what many people still think, the 'Gypsy question' not only affected isolated individuals who were without work and a permanent place of residence and were therefore labelled as 'antisocial', but all 'Gypsies', as well as the so-called 'half-Gypsies'. The legal basis for this categorisation was created as early as 1935 with the Nuremberg Race Laws, which also affected Sinti and Roma. From 1937 to 1944 Sinti and Roma were locked up in labour camps and concentration camps, and were investigated by the Racial Hygiene and Demographic Biology Research Unit with the support of the German Research Foundation. On 31 July 1941, shortly after the invasion of the Soviet Union, Heydrich brought out the directive to include the 'Gypsies' in the 'Final Solution to the Jewish question' as well.

After the war the extent of the genocide of the Jews and the Sinti and Roma was not spoken about in Germany for a long time. The Federal Republic claimed to be the sole legal successor to the German Reich, and took the resulting responsibilities on itself. Since the 1950s the state has thus paid 'compensation' (as if it were ever possible to compensate) to the Jews who survived, and has helped with the rebuilding of the state of Israel. Since the beginning of the 1980s, literary historians have begun to investigate the image of Jews in German literature, again funded by the state via the German Research Foundation.

In contrast, many Sinti both in the Federal Republic and in the German Democratic Republic tried in vain to seek recognition as persecuted and maltreated people. Hardly any academic research has been conducted into the image of the 'Gypsy' in German and European cultural history. The dissertation I quoted earlier was written in Ontario. The so-called 'Gypsy fairy tales', which not only reflect the narrative art of the Sinti and Roma, but at the same time also reflect the prejudices of the majority population, are still in circulation today. What is the explanation for the fact that we, the researchers into and connoisseurs of fairy tales, have not queried this, indeed have not even noticed it? Perhaps the demonic image of the Gypsy which is to be found in the fairy tales also corresponds to our own prejudiced view?

Notes

1. Genesis 4:14.
2. H. Mode, ed. *Zigeunermärchen aus aller Welt : Vier Sammlungen*, No. 78, Leipzig, Insel, 1984.
3. Ibid., No. 118.
4. Ibid., No. 221.
5. Ibid., No. 230.
6. Brüder Grimm, *Kinder- und Hausmärchen*, Ausgabe letzter Hand, ed. H. Rölleke, Stuttgart, Reclam, 1980, No. 7.
7. Ibid., Anhang 17c.
8. Ibid., No. 115
9. Ibid., No. 110
10. In the manuscript collection of the Brothers Grimm it was No. 37.
11. See H. Berger, 'Das Zigeunerbild in der deutschen Literatur des 19. Jahrhunderts', Diss., Waterloo, Ontario, 1972, p.86f.
12. M. Voriskova, ed., *Singende Geigen: Slovakische Zigeunermärchen*, Hanau, Dausien Verlag, 1973, p.187.

CHAPTER 8

Images of Sinti and Roma in German Children's and Teenage Literature*

Michail Krausnick

Vested Interests

I would like first to declare my own vested interests: as a literary critic I consider myself committed to objectivity, as a supporter of the civil rights movement I stand up for people who are made into the objects of literature, and as an author I myself am in the glass house. Given these vested interests, I have three questions to ask with reference to the texts: what are the author's intentions? What effect does this have on the reader? What consequences does this type of representation have for the Sinti and Roma? The interrelationship between intention, effect and consequences forms the basis of my analysis.

The Outsider Perspective: Observations on a Widely Held Prejudice

For centuries lack of knowledge, misinformation and prejudice have made Sinti and Roma, and thus 'the Gypsy', ideal figures for

* Translated by Susan Tebbutt

writers to project. A closer inspection is not welcome. Otherness and sinisterness are desired, in order to allow exotic fantasies to proliferate. Even authors claiming to be critical tend more towards tracking down and underlining supposedly exotic peculiarities. It is not in normal everyday life that they seek to appreciate the Sinti, but in the deviant, the 'other', the exotic, the sinister and the marginal.

Notions of the wandering 'Gypsy' who is blindly driven by a mythical urge to travel are still extremely prevalent. As was the case in the literature of the nineteenth century, Sinti and Roma are still described as creatures outside time and history, and Roma from western, central, eastern and south eastern Europe are still all simplistically lumped together, which adds fuel to the fire in terms of the fateful process of presenting them as an enigma, shrouded in mystery and strangeness.

On the other hand, short shrift is given in almost all the media to the Sinti as our (the Germans) fellow citizens and contemporaries who have lived in German-speaking territory for six hundred years. There is no ethnological interest in registering their current concerns, problems and demands. It is therefore no wonder that Sinti civil rights activists are wary of all experts and people who 'register' them, and object in particular to being sorted and pinned down like dead butterflies.

The 'outsider perspective' – as it were looking through the wrong end of the binoculars – makes it possible for the experts (mostly self-appointed) to pass on ostensibly unusual information and make fake claims to their audience about the uniqueness of research findings. We are dealing here with jargon used by journalists or ethnologists, which often serves to legitimise their own research premise or to ensure their professional survival. Even well-meaning so-called 'saviours' and helpers, be they in Christian or multi-cultural guise, cannot abstain from looking through the wrong end of the binoculars. It is necessary to protect nations which are under threat by loving them, and in order to make them lovable it would seem that they must be made 'interesting and exotic', but such glossy magazine revelations are nothing more than the dogged perpetuation of nineteenth-century colonialist ethnology.

It is in the nineteenth century that the roots of modern racism can be located. In the wake of imperial power interests and colonial expansionist efforts, ethnologists rediscovered the Sinti and Roma, the most popular images being of them as 'nomads', an 'enigmatic primitive people', 'Europe's Red Indians', 'heathens' to be converted, or 'strangers in our midst'. In the children's and teenage literature of the Wilhelminian era this new, racially determined way of seeing the world came increasingly to the fore. The 'Gypsy' was made not only into an 'exotic' person, but into the 'negro' or the 'primitive' on their own doorstep, in analogy with the native 'Hottentots' or 'Hereros' of the German African colonies. It was against this distorted image of the Sinti as an enemy that our white conquering, exploiting and genocidal culture tried to legitimise itself as a superior form of culture.

Yet even if today people no longer go on sabre-rattling safaris kitted out with tropical helmet and binoculars, the arrogance of the outsider perspective has remained, and continues to be far from harmless. In the search for a particular culture, people generalise from unusual events of peripheral importance, chance perceptions, one-off observations and the glaringly obvious. They transfer these generalisations lock, stock and barrel to the whole ethnic group, ignoring the fact that such impressions are mostly deceptive and superficial.

With reference to our own culture, we could in fact recognise very quickly that perceiving what is perceptible would not permit any adequate conclusions to be drawn about the culture and character of, for example, all 'Germans'. Since normality and individuality generally remain inconspicuous or private, the 'outsider perspective' would mainly reveal the so-called 'German' in terms of his public image, probably drinking beer and listening to folk music, or even in negative terms as a wearer of a martial uniform invading the world with war and genocide, or as an arms-dealer, arrogant wheeler-dealer, march-music-loving sauerkraut-eater or right-wing xenophobe.

Such superficial perceptions are thus closer to illusion than reality. When the outsider looks through binoculars, both the long-distance and the close-up view can be deceptive. The milkman is familiar with milk drinkers, the social worker knows underdogs, the special-school teacher knows those with learning difficulties, the police reporter knows criminals and the dentist knows people with dental problems, whether they be residents of a particular town, Turks, Jews, Catholics or 'Gypsies'. And the campsite warden would in fact see *the* 'Germans' — if they really did exist at all — as a restless, non-sedentary, caravanning people driven by a mythical *Wanderlust*.

When we look at children's and teenage literature about Sinti and Roma we have to deal particularly with these two general types of prejudiced perception, the all-too-myopic close-up view and the all-too-long-sighted perspective. The following features are clear:

a) No ethnic group in Germany is more mercilessly and indiscriminately slandered than the Sinti and Roma. Prejudices, once acquired, are defended with particular obstinacy (especially by those who do not possess any other information about the group).

b) People show a great deal less restraint and critical distance with respect to clichés and prejudices about the Sinti and Roma than to those about other ethnic groups. According to opinion polls, anti-Gypsyism in Germany is at the moment growing continuously and is roughly ten times higher than anti-Semitism (68 percent as opposed to 7 percent according to EMNID,[1] March 1994). It should be noted at this point that only 2 percent of those questioned had ever had any personal contact with Sinti or Roma. First-hand knowledge is thus hardly a factor.

c) Prejudices about the Sinti and Roma are not of the sort which might be excused, but virulent, life-threatening prejudices in the racist tradition of the Nazi period.

d) There is no other ethnic group for whom prejudice is more threatening and disastrous. The relatives of the victims of the Nazi genocide are again being collectively insulted, physically attacked, threatened with death (whether it be in Rostock or Hemsbach) and even murdered (in February 1995 in a bomb attack in Burgenland in Austria) by the successors of the perpetrators. In autumn 1992 others, like the Gypsy refugees from Romania, were collectively excluded from the Basic Right to Asylum by Seiters (the Minister of the Interior at the time), and deported *en masse*.

e) Furthermore, in recent times we have seen the circulation of liberal, multi-cultural, romanticising concepts of the Roma as a European nomadic people, as the 'true' Europeans. That sounds enticing, but tends rather to weaken the struggle of the Sinti and Roma for civil rights in the countries in which they have been resident for centuries.

Even among otherwise enlightened people a type of 'philo-Gypsyism' may be observed, a stifling love of the 'other', which stipulates that the objects of this love must lead a different type of life, and does not allow the Sinti and Roma any scope for self-realisation and development, or for normality and proximity to the majority population. People like to feel they are tolerant, but are inflexible in the way that they expect the 'other' to lead a different way of life and expect them to have a different attitude to work, love, money, blocks of flats and to the bureaucracy of building societies. In short, the Gypsy is too good to be true.

Children's and teenage literature dealing with Sinti and Roma thus has consequences for the minority and does not exist in a poetic vacuum, but continues to have a social responsibility and has to come up to high moral expectations.

The Image of Sinti and Roma in Schoolbooks

Right into the 1970s, schoolbook publishers had a predilection for myths and fairy tales featuring the Gypsies' carefree, romantic, nomadic life close to nature, but also featured 'monster-Gypsies' who stole washing and children, tortured animals, told fortunes and were even cannibalistic. Even famous writers such as Werner Bergengruen (*Der Zigeuner und das Wiesel*, 1967), (The Gypsy and the Weasel) were responsible for such images, but after the protests of the Sinti organisations, such tales seem hardly to feature any longer in school books. The 'Gypsy' as bogey man seems to have had his day.

It is nevertheless irritating that a writer of the calibre of Wolfdietrich Schnurre is condemned to do more harm than good to his friends, thanks to the inclusion of his short story 'Jenö war mein Freund' (Jenö was my friend) in countless German school readers. This is yet another example of how the *intentions* of the author, the *effect* on the reader and the *consequences* for the minority are worlds apart. Time and time again these three criteria will be our yardstick.

It is obvious that Schnurre was Jenö's friend, and that he was not prejudiced against catching and eating hedgehogs, and even shows an understanding of a particular relationship to property, when the barometer on the wall suddenly goes missing after Jenö's visit. There is no doubt that this story is set unambiguously in an anti-fascist context, when there are references at the end of the story to a real crime, the deportation and genocide of the Sinti and Roma. Nevertheless it is annoying that it is precisely this story which is reproduced in school readers for the fifth and sixth grades and that it is this image of young Sinti and Roma which leaves its mark on millions of children. In most cases what sticks in the mind is the image of a petty thieving, animal-torturing, strange 'Gypsy boy' who might even, given the chance, have eaten Schnurre's own guinea-pig. Given that the children are at an age at which they are particularly fond of animals, who can blame them if they do not find the Sinti very endearing after this. It is, however, very hard to deconstruct these prejudices once they are fixed emotionally in children's hearts.[2]

Incidentally, Schnurre's story is based on a grave error, a case of mistaken identity. Jenö was in fact not a Rom or Sinto at all. The language which he tries to teach his friend is without a shadow of a doubt *Rotwelsch*, the language of the German vagabonds dating back to the Middle Ages, and not Romani, the language of the Sinti and Roma. Thus Jenö is anything but the 'Gypsy' who apparently still haunts the classrooms. He is a so-called *Jenischer* or 'white Gypsy', a traveller and a descendant of the German 'vagabonds'.

Do more recent, more realistic documentary texts paint a picture which shows less prejudice and is less damaging? I would like now to examine the volume *Ich bin ein Zigeuner* (I am a Gypsy), first published in 1991 by Klett. It is hard to understand why this prestigious publisher of schoolbooks still employs editors who do not have the courtesy to address the Sinti and Roma by their correct name. It is, however, even more disturbing that the focal figure in this first source of information for children, a book which is sent into schools as part of the imposing-sounding series 'Knowledge and Education', is a Sinto with a criminal record.

The thin volume contains two short texts, the short story 'Die Truhe' (The Chest) by Marie-Therese Schins and 'Ich bin ein Zigeuner' (I am a Gypsy), a brief autobiographical account by Stefan W., a young Sinto.[3] In the former the author tells an unlikely but apparently true autobiographical story about an old chest which she gives to a seventeen-year-old Sinto to restore. According to the foreword the despised 'Gypsy' who has been chased away is supposed to have been turned into the 'saviour' of an 'oppressed woman'. The chest is restored and takes pride of place in the brother's living room and now suddenly reminds the writer of her grandmother, who had hidden a young 'Gypsy' girl and her small child from the Nazis. All three were betrayed and sent to a concentration camp, where the grandmother was killed.

Immediately after this somewhat flat tale we find a short, trite, true-life story, *Ich bin ein Zigeuner* by Stefan W., who has been persuaded to write it by the author. What Stefan W. writes has at best the quality of a barely adequate school essay. He draws a veil over the reason why he ended up in jail, and is merely said to have gone 'off the rails'. At the same time the young Sinto complains about prejudice against his ethnic group, and declares that he wants to write a book about it.

It is obviously very positive if a young man turns out to be rehabilitated into society, and one may smile at the naivety with which the well-meaning author implies that the transgressor has a talent for writing, but what is more than offensive is how complacently and irresponsibly this thoughtless *kitsch* is passed off as 'Education and Knowledge' by a prestigious publisher of schoolbooks. How can it be justified that young readers' first introduction to the topic of Sinti and Roma is the case of a person who has committed a criminal offence? How can it be overlooked that this is effectively establishing an ethnic base for criminality and thus defaming and stigmatising a whole ethnic group? With what other ethnic group, with what other minority, would such an insensitive step be taken?

Even Stiftung Lesen[4] does not seem to be aware of the particular responsibility they have in view of the Nazi genocide of the Sinti and Roma. How can people forget that prior to the deportation and later annihilation of the Jewish minority and the Sinti and Roma minority in Nazi Germany, these ethnic groups were systematically represented as criminals and condemned? In 1935, for example, the then Minister for the Interior, Frick, had given orders that 'racial affiliation' was to be highlighted in the report when so-called 'non-Aryans' were sentenced.

Children's and Teenage Literature

There are two pieces of research which have focused particularly on the mythical figure of the 'Gypsy'. In her study entitled 'Children's Literature and the Role of the Gypsy' (1984), Denise Binns, an English teacher-trainer, concludes that the use of negative clichés (outsider, child-stealer, thief) has decreased considerably from 1814 to 1983 and that romantic stereotypes are also disappearing. With the progressive thrust of the world-wide student and civil rights movements at the end of the 1960s, the real world is becoming more important in both fiction and non-fiction. Furthermore, more and more Romanies are appearing as autonomous narrators of fairy tales and stories.

These observations, which are based on English literature about 'Gypsies', also apply to German-language children's and teenage literature. In 1989 Petra-Gabriele Briel published a study entitled *Lumpenkind und Traumprinzessin* (Ragged Child and Dream Princess), subtitled 'Zur Sozialgestalt der Zigeuner in der Kinder- und Jugendliteratur seit dem 19. Jahrhundert' (On the Representation of the Gypsy in Society in Children's and Teenage Literature Since the Nineteenth Century), which concentrates primarily on analysing the intentions of the authors. She compares the well meant with the malicious, but does not, however, go into further detail about the effects and the consequences of the resulting image of the 'Gypsy'. Briel also makes a selection from the wide range of material available and identifies three stereotypes:

a) The converted Gypsy child — the Gypsy child is seen as an ideal object to be educated, being wild, heathen and dirty, and is supposed to be integrated into bourgeois society via school and religion. Examples are Ottilie Wildermuth's *Braunes Lenchen* (Little Brown Lena), probably published in the 1860s, and Tony Schumacher's *Komteßchen und Zigeunerkind* (Little Countess and Gypsy Child), published in 1914,

b) the dancing Gypsy child – seen as fantastic foil, romantic ideal or as an erotic figure. Examples are Josef C. Grund's *Rosita, das Zigeunermädchen* (Rosita, the Gypsy Girl), published in 1957, and Dagmar Galin's *Ich heiße Paprika* (I'm called Paprika), published in 1975, and

c) the respected Gypsy child (examples being Zitelmann and Wölfel), although Briel does not go into great detail here.

In the following analysis I would now like to develop a more differentiated theoretical model of my own, which is not limited merely to the *intentions* of the author but includes our criteria, namely the *effect* (on the reader) and the *consequences* (for the minority group).

Theoretical Model

There are fundamentally two types of children's and teenage literature in which Sinti and Roma appear as protagonists, those where they are seen as mythical and those where they are seen as real characters. In the first type, the 'Gypsy' is presented in a stylised and standardised form, as an exotic 'stranger'. I differentiate between three types of representation, firstly the positive romanticising cliché, showing a romantic, alternative, close-to-nature, musical, anti-bourgeois people leading a nomadic caravanning life, secondly the negative cliché of sinister 'Gypsy life' in which members of the ethnic group are demonised, criminalised or condemned, and thirdly the preaching, paternalistic cliché, which stipulates with missionary zeal that the Sinto should either be integrated into bourgeois society or lead the life of an artist. In all three instances, however, the 'Gypsy' has no opportunity to develop independently. He is cast immutably as a mythical figure.

In more recent children's and teenage literature, on the other hand, we meet Sinti and Roma as real people in a specific historical and social context. It is precisely in this category that it is important to differentiate as far as the actual authenticity and credibility of the characters are concerned. Here I distinguish between three forms of representation, firstly the fictional or poetic (Zitelmann, Wölfel), secondly the documentary or narrative (Wedding, Petersen, Schenk, Püschel, Hackl and Tuckermann), and finally the biographical or autobiographical (Krausnick).

The Mythical Figure

For centuries Sinti and Roma have mainly been represented as mythical figures, as 'Gypsies', both in great literature and popular literature (e.g., in detective stories or comics) and also in children's and teenage literature. It is only in more recent literature, particularly since the 1970s, that attempts have been made to allow them to appear as Sinti and Roma and thus as real characters.

The 'Gypsy' as a mythical figure, as an exotic guest, is seen as an essential part of increasing the tension and heightening the emotional appeal of texts. As a protagonist he is sometimes criminal, sometimes romantic, sometimes dreamy, in works such as Karl May's series of novels *Mit Zepter und Hammer* (With Sceptre and Hammer) and *Juweleninsel* (Island of Jewels) and Martin

Walser's *Nanosch*, whose eponymous hero also became famous in a German television detective programme.

As in trivial literature, exotic, adventurous, unusual, strange, frightening, fascinating and exciting elements also play an important role in children's and teenage literature. People who drive large luxury limousines and caravans and deal in antiques and carpets, who may perhaps steal children, who appear sinister, who can tell fortunes and perform magic, and work in a circus or show business, who are fiendish musicians, wear thick gold earrings and have a mysterious urge to be on the move, who beg and read people's hands, peddle goods and steal the washing from the line, who are hot-blooded and erotically attractive, camp bare-foot at the edge of the forest or by the campfire, despise the bourgeois and tread a fine line between deprivation and criminality, such characters are of course more interesting than the German equivalent of Joe Bloggs or the man on the Clapham omnibus. Above all they are more interesting because they contribute to the commercial success of films, television plays and books.

Since time immemorial the 'Gypsy', just like the knight, the robber, the Red Indian or the ghost, has been part of the repertoire of adventure stories, mysteries, sagas and fairy tales in popular culture and children's and teenage literature. Mostly he remains limited to his function of moving on the plot. The advantage of this is that he can suddenly pop up and disappear again unnoticed, or 'move on'. As a totally freely invented product of the author's imagination he has little or nothing to do with reality. For centuries Sinti and Roma were simply not taken seriously as real people.

In the literature of the eighteenth and nineteenth centuries there was a certain romantic *laissez-faire* in the dissemination of ethnic falsehoods and racist (albeit well-intended) clichés. Today, in view of the imperialist, colonialist abuse and in view of the genocide of the Native American Indians, Africans, Vietnamese and Kurds and the death in the Holocaust of Jews, Sinti and Roma, it is no longer an excuse to plead ignorance or naivety. Freedom of expression in art and entertainment is important, but should not be at the expense of humanity. We should not allow our view of real people to be distorted. Even good old favourites from literature such as Carmen, Uncle Tom and Huckleberry Finn should be re-assessed as to their side-effects. Clichéd images of ethnic groups and minorities who are still threatened today should be banished for ever to being a thing of the past.

Sinti and Roma as Real People

The image of the Sinti as 'real people' is of more importance than the Gypsy myth, which is relatively easy to understand and criticise. Furthermore it is important to sort out to what extent the Sinto or Sintezza is seen as an individual personality or whether the individual is supposed to stand for a whole ethnic group.

In the texts where Sinti and Roma appear as real figures there is a far greater danger, namely the danger of the formation of new clichés and myths, and I therefore wish to examine them particularly thoroughly, from the point of view of safeguarding the rights of the minority group rather than the artistic freedom of the writer. It is of course possible that I myself may make mistakes. I too have gone through a learning process and react more sensitively today than thirteen years ago when my first book *Die Zigeuner sind da* (The Gypsies are Here) came out. Today I would express many things differently, but there are some things I would still underline and repeat, such as the introduction:

> A book about Sinti and Roma is thus about us, holds a mirror up to ourselves. The guilt which non-Gypsies have taken on themselves should not be kept silent. The stupidities and prejudices which still clog up German minds must be revealed. But romantic clichés ought to be eliminated, if the Sinti and Roma are to be taken seriously ... *The* Gypsies do not exist any more than do *the* 'Red Indians', *the* Jews, or *the* East Frisians. Such generalisations are at best a joke and at worst a death sentence ... This collection of texts shows the variety, the richness and the liveliness, the suffering and the worries of Gypsy life, but these images, which are pieced together in a mosaic-like fashion, should remain open to change and correction, precisely because we are dealing with a living nation, with human beings.

Today I would not use the outsider term 'Gypsy', which was used at the time, even among civil rights activists, to facilitate communication. The feeling that it could be impolite and uncultivated not to address peoples or nations with their correct name is however not too well developed in Germany.

In my second book, *Da wollten wir frei sein: Eine Sinti-Familie erzählt* (Then We Wanted to be Free: A Sinti Family Tells its Story), published in 1983, the publisher and I deliberately did not use the term 'Gypsy', which might have helped the book sell better. This brought down the initial print-run of the first edition by a third. Relinquishing the exotic is really damaging to business.

In the following section I will discuss some books which fall into the category of fictional narrative, but predominantly depict the Sinti as real people rather than as mythical characters.

Example 1

The short story *Mond, Mond, Mond* (Moon, Moon, Moon) by Ursula Wölfel, published in 1962, is a type of poetic approximation to reality. It has sold very well, is recommended as part of the school curriculum, and was also filmed as a television series. It has formed the image of the Sinti in a very special way. The author tells the story of two Sinti girls. The beautiful fifteen-year-old Nauka and her little sister Pimmi have been selling lace in the village and cannot find their way back to the quarry where the family have camped with their caravan. During the search for their relatives they meet their uncle, old Panelon, who is travelling round with horse and cart, and keeps talking about red rocks, which he absolutely has to find. Both girls sense that Panelon will not rest until he has found the red rocks. Thanks to Pimmi's help they succeed in going together to the place where Panelon's wife and children were taken prisoner by the SS and were taken to a concentration camp. Panelon feels guilty because he had sat too long in a pub and thus had not been taken prisoner, and had survived the genocide. The uncle is helped out of his despair by returning to the dreadful place and by talking to the two kind girls. He gets over his nightmares and is reconciled with those who are dead.

The fate of Panelon is embedded in a plot which features a fairy tale type of close-to-nature, nomadic, caravanning life-style and uses the positive, romantic clichés of bygone times. A family is presented as a 'clan' which gets through life in a timeless way by begging, fortune-telling, stealing the odd bit of food, peddling, dancing, puppet plays and fire-eating. Poverty becomes an idyll. In the first fifty pages a car is the only indication of the century in which the story is set. It is like a child's dream, which arouses a type of understanding for the Sinti which is of little use, because it has next to nothing to do with real people and today's real world.

Mond, Mond, Mond is a book of literary merit, even if the narrative style seems a little antiquated today. Its didactic and progressive qualities are, however, overrated. Wölfel is generally credited with having been the first to introduce the theme of the genocide of Sinti and Roma into the world of children's and teenage literature in the Adenauer era. The humanitarian concern of the author is beyond question, yet when used in schools her story needs to be treated with great caution, especially as a starting point for a more intensive study of the Nazi period. It is precisely because of its non-committal humanity that this story can make it all too easy for teachers to simply tick off the Nazi period and genocide and say they have 'covered' it.

Genocide 'on racial grounds' is seen primarily from the point of view of the victims, as fate. Those responsible remain in the background, but on the other hand the psychological suffering of the survivors is portrayed very sensitively, and even the question of whether Panelon is partly to blame for the death of his family is raised.

In the Adenauer period the mention of historical events in a children's book was certainly an important, courageous achievement. Yet today it looks bad if the Nazis only appear in the shadows as 'wicked bogeymen'. Such a moderate approach would certainly be more digestible for a fairly young readership (the book is recommended for primary school and the first years of secondary school), but it is to be hoped that students ask more concrete questions. Despite being recommended as a source of information about the ethnic group of the Sinti and Roma, *Mond, Mond, Mond* is absolutely unsuitable in this respect. The romantic clichés totally obscure the real world. Sinti and Roma may indeed be seen as 'appealing', in the same way that talking bears, rabbits or tigers in other children's books are 'appealing'. They are 'fixed' in people's minds as fairy tale fantasy figures. Although the image presented to young readers may be positive, it is totally inaccurate.

Example 2

Arnulf Zitelmann's *Unter Gauklern* (Among the Travelling Artistes), published in 1980, is aimed at young people. Linori, a Romani girl, appears both as a mythical and a real character, and is respected as a person. The historical adventure novel gives a colourful picture of the Middle Ages and tells the exciting story, full of atmosphere, of the love of Martis, a fifteen-year-old hunchback shepherd living in a monastery, for Linori. He rescues Linori, who has been dragged away and raped by soldiers, and finds her a hiding place in the house of a woman who is reputedly a witch. Martis gets into danger, flees from the monks and begins to lead a nomadic life. He comes upon Linori (who has also escaped and is looking for her family) among a group of artistes. He falls in love and leads an adventurous life with her 'among the travelling artistes'. In Regensburg they finally meet up with Linori's family again. The Romanies are supposed to be hanged because of their nomadic way of life, but Martis manages to prevent that and lives with them for a while, but when Linori marries a young Romani Martis goes back to the artistes.

Zitelmann seems to have his own special sources of information about the Sinti and Roma. He is certainly the first and indeed the only person who was able to find out about their activities in the thirteenth century, two hundred years before they are first mentioned in documents in the year 1407 in Central Europe. Yet we do not want to take things too seriously. Zitelmann's novel is a historicising product of his imagination, without any direct claim to represent reality, and is full of exotic events and characters. Thus most of what he narrates about the Romanies and their way of life, like their premature appearance, is not verifiable. Zitelmann's information comes from historical speculations about the Roma and from fairy tales and sagas.

On the other hand the social mechanisms which are shown within the historical framework are based on reality and are still relevant today, namely the scapegoat function of the Sinti and Roma in crisis times, hostility to and hatred of foreigners, and the interplay of discrimination, oppression and persecution.

Example 3

Another historical novel with a Sinto as the central protagonist is Wolf Klaußner's *Jüppa und der Zigeuner* (Jüppa and the Gypsy), published in 1979. Told from the perspective of a young boy, the novel depicts life in a Franconian village in the last months of the war and in the immediate postwar period. Wilhelm (known as Jüppa), the son of a landlord, is a quarter Jewish and thus a much bullied outsider at school. In a quarry he comes upon Psomi, a Greek who has escaped from the concentration camp in Esterwege, where he was imprisoned as a Gypsy. Expecting that the war would soon be over, Jüppa decides to rescue Psomi and looks after him, hiding him first in a cave and finally in his own home. A friendship develops between the two, and after the end of the war Jüppa and Psomi attend grammar school together. For some months there is a flickering hope of a better, more humane society in Germany, but soon the old Nazis are back at the helm again in new circumstances. The school system is once more as stultifying and authoritarian as ever. One day Psomi, the Greek Sinto, disappears again.

The exciting adventure story does not portray a closed world, but the chaos of a collapsing world, full of hypocrisy, brutality, falsehoods, hopes, dreams and humiliations. It shows the meaninglessness and idiocies of the time, and the empty heroism in which children are still expected to believe, while the Nazis are already on the run.

In contrast, Jüppa, who has been humiliated and raped, and his almost idolised friend Psomi, are always on the run. Psomi is seen not as a Greek, not as a Sinto, but as a person whose humanity is intact. The most important thing about the book is that what counts is not whether someone is a Sinto, a Greek, German, Jew or American, but what they do, and whether they rescue themselves and others from this chaos. As far as otherness is concerned, the central theme is the extent of the differences between Germans and Germans, Christians and hypocritical Christians, between Nazis, fellow-travellers, onlookers and persecuted people, between teachers, soldiers and farmers, and between the merciful and the merciless.

The second group of books in which the Sinti appear as real individuals are those which I call documentary narratives, as opposed to the earlier fictional poetic works. Most of the authors refer to direct experiences and meetings with Sinti, and the characters are based on real people.

In meiner Sprache gibt's kein Wort für morgen (In My Language There is No Word for Tomorrow), is the extremely dubious claim which teacher and journalist Elisabeth Petersen chooses as the title for her story (aimed at children aged twelve and above), which was published in 1990. She explains what she is hoping to convey: 'The otherness of the *Gypsy world* intrigued me and I felt that an insight into this world would be equally gripping for young people'. Petersen tells the story of the fight of Galo Schawo, a school-weary fifteen-year-old Sinto, against a rival, and tells of the discrimination which he faces every day. We see him peddling goods, with his extended family at the death-bed of his aunt, in the caravan on his travels, at a festival in Arolsen, at the camp-fire, dancing and making music. Finally we learn of his love for Franca, whom he marries on his last day at school without worrying too much (see title) about what the future may hold.

Many young readers will enjoy identifying with Galo Schawo, but at the same time will see his life as a different world, which despite all the discrimination seems freer and more exciting than their own. The author, however, concentrates too hard on elements which appear exotic to us. The distance and the otherness is built up too much, which almost leads to the formation of a new myth, of a slightly marginal 'Gypsy life' which has apparently retained its customs and its code of honour unscathed, yet very few Sinti and Roma today earn a living travelling around in caravans. Anyone who sets out to look for the 'other' will not find the familiar. No cliché is as persistent as that of the nomadic caravanning life. Instead of explaining in socio-historical terms how centuries of persecution forced the Romanies, like the Jews, into certain professions and life-styles, Petersen erroneously represents the travelling around of the craftsmen, artists and trading families as a culturally or even ethnically determined *Wanderlust*.

It would definitely be easier to brush aside the author's highly specific images if they could just be taken as one particular case. Unfortunately she, like many of her colleagues, has a tendency to treat her individual observations about one family as if they were universally applicable to the whole ethnic group. What is even more intolerable is when she presumes in an epilogue (which is superfluous) to attribute to the Sinti an 'unquestionable otherness'. Here an arsenal of defamatory prejudices is heaped upon the whole ethnic group:

A Sinto or Roma child never learns for the distant future.
They do not understand that they are subordinate to the teacher.
Any attempt to limit their urge to move about is total anathema to them.
The term *punctuality* does not exist for them.
You eat when you are hungry.
They are different in temperament to us Central Europeans.
The *prejudice* that Gypsies steal often proves to be true.

Petersen, the 'Gypsy specialist', finally would have us believe: 'that these people can be accepted in their otherness, that they can possibly be loved, but that they can never be registered in rational terms'. The choice of words ('never', 'register', 'rational') is, I feel, significant.

To return to the title, *In meiner Sprache gibt's kein Wort für morgen.* This prejudice goes through the book like a *leitmotiv*, for of course there is a word in Romani for tomorrow, namely 'daissa'. Yet Petersen does not allow this, since it also means 'another day'. She prefers to abide by her prejudice-laden assertion, which culminates in the statement that 'care and planning for the future are concepts unknown to the Sinti', although in fact she ought to know that German Sinti and Roma do indeed have a very keen, existential interest in both the past and the future. They have in no way forgotten the Nazi past and have to worry about the future of their children and grandchildren more than many others in this country (Germany), which is also their country.

We find similar generalisations and supposed expertise in Dieter Schenk's teenage novel *Der Wind ist des Teufels Niesen: Die Geschichte eines jungen Zigeuners* (The Wind is the Sneeze of the Devil: The Story of a Young Gypsy), published in 1988 and recommended for children above the age of fourteen.

Schoolgirl Astrid watches in horror as a young Sinti girl and her brothers are evicted first from a store and then from a toy shop. Shortly afterwards Merzeli is accused by the police of having stolen a valuable toy train. Astrid wants to get him off the hook by speaking up for him, but Merzeli refuses her help, arguing that the police do not believe the word of anyone who stands up for Gypsies anyway. Astrid then does some detective-work and finds out by chance that one of her class-mates had stolen the train. She takes it off him secretly and goes with it to the Romanies, with whom, in the meantime, she has struck up a friendship, and shows it to Merzeli. Astrid finally decides to take the train back to the toyshop and put it back in its place secretly. The ill-considered act makes Merzeli seem even more suspicious, because by now his fingerprints are on the train. At the hearing at the Juvenile Court, the judge reluctantly lets Merzeli off, on the grounds that 'in cases of uncertainty' the accused is given the benefit of the doubt.

Astrid has thus achieved little by trying to help the Sinto. The pardon does not remove the prejudices but perpetuates them. The same must also unfortunately be said of the author and his book. Schenk's story is based on his direct contacts with a Sinti family living on the edge of Bad Hersfeld. Overall a fairly favourable picture is painted of the life of this family, but their world is seen in slightly romantic terms compared to the life of the Gadzos. This romanticising is illuminating. The questioning of the non-Sinti life-style, the whims of bureaucracy and political opposition to Nazis and neo-Nazis gives grounds for thought, yet I have three strong objections, which also apply to many similar 'problem-based' books.

Firstly, the author, the self-designated 'expert on the Gypsies', takes on too much. His ethnological and historical digressions are unconvincing. The presentation of traditional customs does not help people to get to know the Sinti, any more than consulting a handbook of etiquette would enable one to talk about West German culture. Furthermore, there is no need for every author of a story in which a Sinti is featured to prove him/herself to be a Gypsy expert.

Secondly, the author blends his particular knowledge of one particular family with his general observations on the fringes of society and complacently transfers this mixed bag of knowledge to the whole ethnic group along the lines of 'If you know one, you know them all'. The Sinto who lives on the Haune estate is no more representative of the whole ethnic group than the Sinto who lives in a caravan, in a high-rise block or in his own house. Social deprivation and the resulting behaviour patterns must however be seen in a *social* and *political* context and not be interpreted in ethnic and cultural terms.

Thirdly, my final most serious reservation relates to criminal-isation. The novel revolves round the most stupid and dreadful cliché, and the author even says in the epilogue that he must talk 'honestly' about the 'Gypsies' petty thieving'. In doing so he slanders and marginalises the whole ethnic group and thought-lessly replicates the calumny of the Nazi period.

Schenk certainly does not intend to harm the Sinti and Roma. I do not belittle the fact that he writes about their persecution and genocide in the Nazi period, and that he is very committed in his stance against the neo-Nazis and their meetings in Bad Hersfeld, yet 'good intentions' are not enough. We must persist in inves-tigating both the side-effects of children's books on readers, and the consequences for the minority group. And therefore I believe that Robert Meinhardt, the Sinto quoted by Schenk, was not so far off the mark:

> He [the Sinto] had to endure Sachsenhausen concentration camp. When I went to see him some time ago, he welcomed me with the following words. 'They came from the Racial Hygiene and Demographic Biology Research Unit like you are coming now and they interrogated us, apparently in a good cause. In reality this paved the way for our being sent to the concentration camp. The door is over there!'

Finally I would like to present an early successful example of a realistic picture of Sinti in children's and teenage literature, Alex Wedding's novel *Ede and Unku* (Ede and Unku), published in 1931, which is based on a true story.[5] The novel is set in a working-class district of Berlin before the Nazis came to power, and depicts the friendship between Ede, the son of a working-class family and Unku, a Sinti girl. Together they hide a striking worker, who is hunted by the police, in Uku's grandmother's caravan. The children help the adults, and Unku's family helps the threatened workers. Most of the characters are based on real people. (No less a person than John Heartfield, the Communist artist who invented photo-collage, took photos of Unku and her family.)

The socially committed novel was surprisingly successful, and although put on the index of forbidden books when Hitler came to power, was also quickly translated into Czech, English and Danish. After 1945 there were over twenty editions published in the GDR, where it was part of the school curriculum, and it was filmed in 1982.

For the first time Sinti appear in a children's book as real people, as fellow citizens, without being defamed or romanticised. It is taken for granted that people help their fellow men in need, and that the oppressed and striking workers show solidarity. Ede and Unku themselves are depicted as individuals with the same rights, each in their specific milieu. The world of tenement blocks of Ede the working-class boy is, one suspects, probably just as exotic to the reader as Unku's caravan site. Unku is portrayed as a very pleasant, self-confident, independent, helpful, modern girl. She stands as an individual and does not to have represent all 'Sinti girls'. The supportiveness of Unku's family towards the others is also portrayed as very natural, and no attempt is made to present this willingness to help as an ethnic or cultural trait. This is simply how things are.

Valuable background information about the novel is contained in two essays by the Berlin writer Reimar Gilsenbach, namely 'Unkus letzter Tanz' (Unku's Last Dance), and 'Das Sinti-Mädchen Unku' (The Sinti Girl Unku).[6] Gilsenbach has researched the fate of the title figure (Erna Lauenburger) and her family in the Nazi period, has looked into the files of her persecutors and has questioned surviving relatives.

> Unku's family had moved to Magdeburg, where she and many other Sinti were forced to go to a 'Gypsy site', as the Nazis mockingly called it. The Sinti could not leave this site without a police permit, even for a day, and had to do unpaid forced labour and received just enough food to survive. At the start of March 1943 the police surrounded the 'site' at first dawn, heavily armed, accompanied by police dogs. The Sinti were taken off to the railway station,

locked into freight wagons, and finally arrived at the concentration camp Auschwitz-Birkenau. Former stables served as accommodation, and soon some twenty thousand Roma and Sinti men, women and children were herded together, facing dreadful suffering.

And what about Unku? She was the mother of a small child, whom she had named Mariechen. Thousands of Sinti died of hunger and illness. Mariechen died too. Unku was beside herself with pain, and it is said she rushed screaming out of the barracks and started to dance outside, one of the old Sinti dances, where the dancer hardly stirs from the spot and yet is full of wild passion. As she danced, Unku laughed, such a shrill laugh that the hearts of all who were watching her dance turned cold. Then every prisoner sensed that her dance was induced by madness. Brave men grabbed hold of her and took her into the sick bay. Instead of help and a cure she found her murderers there. An SS doctor gave her a fatal injection. This was how Unku, the young, beautiful Unku died. Unku's mother died, her grandmother Nutza died, Heinrich and Feini died. *Mulo, mulo, mulo.* Dead people, dead people, dead people.

Conclusion

In this analysis of the image of the Sinti and Roma in contemporary children's and teenage literature and in schoolbooks, what is most evident is the lack of sensitivity, the tendency towards the exotic and the unthinking readiness of these authors to display prejudice. The 'Sinto' is not perceived as a fellow human being, a fellow citizen, or a fellow contemporary, but is used as a stock figure, and is seen to a greater or lesser degree as a romantic character, in other words, as a 'Gypsy'. In more recent literature there is a trend towards depicting him as a criminal or member of a shadowy group on the fringes of society. This overemphasis is another form of stigmatisation, especially when the causes of deprivation and criminal behaviour are not seen to be of a political or social nature, but are depicted vaguely, in a racist way, as having ethnic and cultural origins, with blame put completely on 'Gypsies' themselves. It is alarming that even people who are otherwise enlightened (both authors and editors) still take the liberty to make such sweeping generalisations, although, mind you, this only happens in the case of the 'Gypsies'.

Neither the fairy tale romantic images of Gypsies, 'philo-Gypsyism', operetta-like idealisation, nor the well meaning clichés of Schnurre and Wölfel have helped in the past to undo the damage done by the negative distorting images, prejudices and slanderous allegations. There is no mention in literature of the real life of all those of the ethnic minority group who are integrated into society. That would seem not to make interesting literature, or relate to readers' needs or market forces. What is wanted is the strange and the exotic, not the proximity and normality of the Sinti, who are after all fellow citizens. This approach has had fatal consequences once already.

In view of the devastating consequences of prejudice, ranging from genocide to the pogroms and arson attacks today and the murders in Burgenland in 1995, the time has finally come to demand a responsible and sensitive representation of the Sinti and Roma in literature and the media. This representation must do justice to our particular responsibility to this threatened minority group, with its particular need for protection.

Therefore the three questions about the texts dealing with Sinti and Roma which were posed at the start can help to evaluate their moral quality and humane understanding. What are the author's intentions? What effect does this have on the reader and what consequences does the representation have for the Sinti and Roma?

Finally, I would like to recommend Anja Tuckermann's story *Muscha* (1994), set in the Nazi period, which is educational, exciting and extremely topical, and shows via an authentic case the fatal threat to all humanity, civilisation and culture posed by the Nazis and racists. When little Josef starts school, he becomes increasingly aware that he is supposed to be different, because he looks different. Although he wants to be one of the gang he is pushed to one side, ostracised and beaten up. Nobody can tell him why. Not even his parents. He is an adopted child. Muscha does not know why the other children call 'Gypsy pig' as he goes past. His foster parents cannot save him from persecution by the Nazis. Tracked down by racial researchers from the Racial Hygiene and Demographic Biology Research Unit, he is supposed to be sterilised and has to hide in a garden shed.

Tuckermann writes from Muscha's perspective, through the eyes of the child, and describes the closeness and human warmth and the bonds that link people. Muscha cannot understand why he is considered different and marginalised. He asks why all this is happening to him. It is only after the war that he puts the pieces of the jigsaw together, and learns that he is a Sinto, and that the total annihilation of his ethnic group had been decided upon. The question of why it happened is not distorted or restricted by Gypsy myths or exotic clichés. Despite concrete references to the Nazi genocide, the person who is subject to racial hatred could come from Ghana, Vietnam or Turkey, and this is what makes the novel so topical.

The historical background is seen chronologically as part of a dynamic process. The growing threat to the victim is easy to comprehend, but so too is the increasing dehumanisation of society, and the danger of become embroiled as spectator, participant or perpetrator. Readers are called upon to re-examine their own moral and ethical positions.

Notes

1. EMNID is the German institute for demographic research.
2. In 1994 I was invited to a reading to fifth-grade children in a school in Mannheim. Yet again the teacher had read the story of Jenö to give the class a lead-in to the 'Gypsy' theme. In the course of the conversation it emerged that some of the children had gained the impression that being deported to the concentration camp was perhaps a punishment (admittedly too severe a one) for catching the hedgehog and stealing the barometer. But one of the children was a ten-year old Sinto boy who told me in a depressed tone that most of his school-mates would now think that he was also given to petty theft and eating hedgehogs. The teacher asked me to sort it out quickly, as I was, he said, the expert. I tried to do so, but I fear that most of the children were more inclined to believe Wolfdietrich Schnurre than me, and would carry this with them for the rest of their lives. Prejudices are hard to dislodge.
3. There is also a foreword by Professor P. Budweg from Hamburg Technical University as well as information under the rubric 'Key word: Gypsy' by the editor J. Genuneit. In addition there is the commentary by Professor Dr E. Ockel from the University of Osnabrück/Vechta.
4. Stiftung Lesen is a German organisation whose aim is to encourage young people to read.
5. Alex Wedding is the pseudonym for the Jewish author Grete Weiskopf.
6. R. Gilsenbach, 'Unkus letzter Tanz', in *Kaleidoskop*, Berlin, Der Kinderbuchverlag, 1976, pp.166–176 and 'Das Sinti-Mädchen Unku', in *pogrom* 130/1987, pp.52–54.

CHAPTER 9

Challenging New Literary Images of Sinti and Roma

Susan Tebbutt

Creating Alternatives

There are many parallels between the treatment of black people by white people and the treatment of Gypsies by non-Gypsies. In the introduction to her study of race and representation, bell hooks, a leading American black feminist critic, argues:

> For some time now the critical challenge for black folks has been to expand the discussion of race and representation beyond debates about good and bad imagery. [...] The issue is really one of standpoint. [...] It is also about transforming the image, creating alternatives, asking ourselves questions about what types of images subvert, pose critical alternatives, and transform our worldviews and move us away from dualistic thinking about good and bad.[1]

For the Sinti and Roma, often singled out because of the different colour of their skin and because of what is perceived as their 'otherness', the challenge is similar, since it is rare to find images which subvert or which actually portray the persecution of Sinti and Roma on grounds of ethnic affiliation. There is thus a need to challenge existing images of Sinti and Roma in German-language literature and to highlight challenging images, images which do in fact move readers away from dualistic thinking about good and bad, and increase awareness of the diversity within the ethnic group. bell hooks argues that the exploration of racial difference can represent a breakthrough, a challenge to various systems of domination, but that the 'over-riding fear is that cultural, ethnic and racial differences will be continually commodified and offered up as new dishes to enhance the white palate — that the Other will be eaten, consumed, and forgotten'.[2]

In the post-1980 period in German-language literature there is strong evidence that issues relating to racial difference are actually being explored with reference to the Sinti and Roma, but it is important that the commercial publishing boom is not based solely on the desire to commodify the group. It is particularly difficult to find an appropriate name for this writing, since the Sinti and Roma community includes both members of the majority (German or Austrian) population and foreign Romanies living in Germany or Austria. There is no term equivalent to *Gastarbeiterliteratur* which would include both writing about and writing by the Sinti/Roma, and since most Sinti/Roma writing in German have German or Austrian nationality their work cannot all be subsumed under the heading of *MigrantInnenliteratur* (loosely translated as 'literature written by immigrants').[3] In today's multi-cultural society there is an awareness of the need to acknowledge and accredit the contribution of people from minority cultures to the culture of the majority population, and the contribution of the Sinti and Roma should be no exception.[4]

The principal studies of the representation of Sinti and Roma in German-language literature were published in the late 1980s and 1990s. They do not, however, devote much space to contemporary images. Briel looks in *Lumpenkind und Traumprinzessin*[5] at the modern period, but only deals with children's and teenage literature. Strauß in *Die Sinti/Roma-Erzählkunst*[6] highlights the importance of the oral tradition, but concentrates on older literature and fairy tales in particular, and raises the question of whether and how there can be a different type of literature which breaks down the myth of the 'Gypsy' as a type of 'noble savage', living a 'natural' life free from the cares of the industrial world. In *Roma und Sinti im Spiegel der deutschen Literatur* Djuric[7] takes in such a broad sweep of literature from the seventeenth century to the present day that only some eight out of the 273 pages are devoted to discussing post-war literature. Eder is one of the very first critics to devote an entire book, *Geboren bin ich vor Jahrtausenden*, published in 1993,[8] to writing *by* rather than writing *about* Roma, but although her excellent comparative study of seven Roma writers of different nationalities (including one German and one Austrian writer) includes a section on autobiographical writing and the representation of the Holocaust, she does not look at any other genre. Thus none of the existing works acknowledge the diversity to be found among post-1980 images and self-images of the Sinti and Roma in German-language literature.

Images of an Innocent Victim of the Holocaust

Erich Hackl's much-acclaimed *Abschied von Sidonie* (Farewell Sidonia), published in 1989,[9] is based on the true story of an abandoned Austrian Gypsy girl who is adopted by a non-Gypsy Austrian family, the Breirathers, but eventually deported to Auschwitz. Hackl goes beyond merely reflecting negative emotions and responses towards the minority group, and constructs a more complex web of images.

Born in Austria, Hackl studied German and Romance languages, and it was during a spell in Madrid as an assistant lecturer that his interest in the Gypsies first developed. *Abschied von Sidonie* is a milestone in the history of German-language literature. Here for the first time the persecution of the Romani ethnic group occupies a central position. The narrative begins with the abandoning of Sidonie Adlersburg, an infant, a bundle of rags, on the threshold of the hospital in Steyr. There is no doubt from the start that she is of Gypsy descent. The narrative has a certain symmetry, in that it closes with the narrator taking leave of Sidonie in the widest sense.

Hackl does not portray the world in an idealised, romanticised way, but shows the prejudices harboured by the majority of the population, who hold Gypsies in low regard, and have inaccurate images of them. Skin colour is an important factor here. Hackl quotes references to Sidonie as 'a friendly Moorish child', 'the black object' and 'negro child'.[10] The apparent confounding of two very different ethnic minority groups, the Gypsies and the Moors, is a very common phenomenon, and underlines the fact that the majority population do not take the time to appreciate the differences between minority groups. The narrator later refers to people who rejoice that their town is free of Jews and make references to 'Negroes and Gypsies, these alien pests'.[11] The otherwise seemingly liberal doctor says to the Breirather parents: 'Why on earth are you bringing the black girl to see me? She doesn't belong here at all'.[12] Although Sidonie, 'even if she stood out because of her dark skin colour and her blue-black shimmering hair',[13] is accepted by her playmates, the latter are quick to use the word 'Gypsy' as a term of abuse, and call after her: 'Gypsy lass. Gypsy child. You're only a Gypsy after all',[14] but on the other hand they are quick to look after her if they hear other Gypsies are in the area, taking her by the hand and running into the house. Although this is presented as helpfulness towards Sidonie, at the same time it indicates the depth of the misconceptions about the group, despite fondness for a particular person.

Hackl fictionalises the fate of one individual, but in so doing gives insights into the fate of countless others, in much the same way that the *Diary of Anne Frank* touches a nerve because it represents the horror of the atrocities committed against an innocent victim. The socio-political setting is conveyed through the descriptions of conditions in and around Steyr. The poverty of the Gypsies is seen within a community in which hardship, poor health and low life expectancy is rife. Within the narrative the authenticity of the account is backed up by mention of the setting up of a centre in Vienna to combat the 'Gypsy Nuisance'. The objective is to register and fingerprint all Austrian and foreign Gypsies in the area. It is when the regulations are tightened up that Sidonie herself is rounded up and taken to Linz and deported from there. Hackl points out the fragility and vulnerability of an ethnic group, symbolised in the character of Sidonie, last seen by her parents clutching her doll as she departs on the transport to the concentration camp. It is the incorporation of authentic historical evidence into the narrative, itself based on real events, which makes the message of Hackl's work so convincing.

Persecution on ethnic grounds is highlighted. The narrator reflects that Sidonie is not able to conceal her otherness by, for example, pulling on a white skin or dyeing her hair, because even if she did that she would still be in danger, because even someone who has changed into a lamb is still hunted by the wolves. The narrator concludes: 'It is conceivable that the town is divided in the years of momentous events into those who howl with the wolves and those who keep silent. There are hardly any of the latter; the former are ten a penny'.[15]

The social criticism is not only of the crimes committed under Hitler, but also of the continuity of persecution. Hackl criticises those who howled with the wolves and still fail to acknowledge their complicity in crimes against the Sinti and Roma and contrasts them with the Breirather family, who have a sense of justice and belong to the minority who are not prepared to keep silent. Significantly, Breirather himself was incarcerated for eighteen months because of his left-wing convictions.

Whereas the account of Sidonie's life is told in a seemingly objective manner, in the final section of the work the narrator becomes angry and mocks the supposed justification for deporting Sidonie, quoting opinions voiced that she might not be paying enough attention in school and that she did not show enough respect to teachers. The novel is about coming to terms with the past, with the majority society firmly accused of being responsible for the death of Sidonie, taken to task for not having re-examined the past during the fifty or so years after the war, and reminded of the need to take positive steps to commemorate the dead by erecting monuments.

Differentiated Self-Images of Sinti and Roma

For marginal groups, such as the Romanies, who are traditionally seen from an outsider perspective, as alien, foreign and inferior, writing is seen as an act of empowerment, of laying claim to a place in the cultural heritage. A key development in the last quarter of the twentieth century is the blossoming of a new genre, that of socially critical German-language autobiographical writing by members of the Sinti/Roma community. Given that Romani is largely an oral language and that for many generations the nomadic life-style meant that the level of schooling was low, with a high incidence of illiteracy, it is hardly surprising that there are relatively few written works by Romanies.

Since the identity of each writer is determined by a number of factors such as gender, age, family status, life-style and place of origin, there is great diversity in the writing. Unlike in much contemporary English-language writing by Roma, which focuses on family and personal events, the political element is far more important, and experiences of the 'hidden Holocaust', the genocide of the Sinti and Roma during the Hitler regime, and the continuity of discrimination in the post-war period cast a long shadow.

Four Generations of a German Sinti Family Narrate

There is a long tradition of story-telling among Romani families, and in *"Da wollten wir frei sein!"* (Then We Wanted to be Free!), published in 1983,[16] the age-old tradition takes on a new, more politicised dimension. The oral narratives of four generations of a Sinti family living in Germany were recorded and transcribed. A selection was made together with the family, who amended and approved the various drafts until they were willing to authorise publication. Michail Krausnick, the collector and editor of the tales, prefaces each account with a thumb-nail sketch of the speaker, but keeps his editorial presence to an absolute minimum.

There is no attempt to portray a typical family, but within the four generations we meet men, women, people with different occupations and life-styles, ranging from the eighty-five year old fortune-teller Elisabeth Kreutz (born 1896), whose father was a horse trader, violin-maker and musician, to Anton Franz (born 1941) and Dronja Peter (born 1946) who are both active members of the Sinti and Roma civil rights movement and take part in events such as the rally in Bergen-Belsen and the Dachau hunger strike (described in Chapter 4), and to Jaqueline Lagrenne (born 1964) who was unemployed at the time of the recordings.

The work is on the borderline between documentary literature and autobiographical writing, and although the Sinti are recounting their experiences as Germans living in Germany, the work has a similar function to other German works for teen-agers which introduce readers to the life and culture of foreign minority groups living in Germany. Each person speaks both as an individual and as a member of an ethnic group, and the resulting mosaic gives insights into the world of the Sinti in an extremely accessible form, with a number of photographs and illustrations included which acknowledge the identity of the family members as individuals.

The family are not seen as outsiders, or foreigners, and regard Germany as their home, even though at times they are treated like undesirable aliens. Hildegard Lagrenne (born 1921) relates how they were liberated by the Russians from the concentration camp on 27 January 1945. When asked where they wanted to go, she and her family replied: 'Home. Germany. That is our home when all's said and done. That's where we belong'.[17] This feeling of belonging is, however, tinged with regret that this same homeland has taken their best years from them.

For the Kreutz family the noose begins to tighten with the law passed during the Nazi period forbidding all Romanies from travelling. Friedrich Kreutz recalls being seized in police raids, herded into a compound in Cologne and finally being deported to Auschwitz. After managing to escape he obtains a German identity card and joins the German army, but comments on how ironic it is that he is permitted to fight for Germany, but is not rewarded for his sacrifices. His case typifies the way in which the supposed boundary line between the Gypsy and the non-Gypsy is drawn arbitrarily.

Although the title refers to a 'family' narrative, the content is far from being a cosy family yarn. Explicit mention is made of the suffering of the family. The torture, sterilisation and medical experimentation to which they and other Romanies were subjected during the Nazi period is described in an uncompromising way, and it is important to remember that although *Da wollten wir frei sein!* is written for teenagers, major sections of the history of the Sinti and Roma in the twentieth century are presented with more immediacy and vividness than that normally found in most works for adults about the Holocaust. The continuity of the persecution in the post-war period is also represented, as is the rise of the Romani civil rights movement in Germany, with its campaigns for recognition of the suffering in the Nazi period in the labour and concentration camps ending in laughable sums being paid as compensation.

The aim of the work is to raise awareness of the existence and diversity of the ethnic group and to build bridges between the Sinti and non-Sinti community in Germany. Anton Franz talks about the importance of a cultural centre where Sinti can re-establish the customs and traditions of the group and find a way back to their cultural identity, and he feels that such a cultural centre would give non-Gypsies a place and an opportunity to meet Gypsies in a relaxed atmosphere, and to get to know their customs and traditions, which might help break down some of the prejudices harboured by Gadzos towards Gypsies. It is indicative of the chord which the volume has struck with readers that it has been reprinted with a new introduction after the resurgence of overt racial violence against Romanies in the late 1980s and early 1990s. It continues to serve an extremely useful purpose.

Alfred Lessing: Coming out of Hiding

The title of Alfred Lessing's *Mein Leben im Versteck: Wie ein deutscher Sinti* (sic) *den Holocaust überlebte* (My Life in Hiding: How a German Sinto Survived the Holocaust), published in 1993, is important.[18] He is at once writing about how and why he spent time in hiding, concealing his identity as a Sinto, but at the same time in doing so he is coming out of hiding and talking openly about his ethnic affiliation. The fact that he does this in the 1990s, almost fifty years after the end of the war, is partly because it was difficult for him to bring himself to write down his experiences, and partly because of the need to counter accusations of the myth of the Holocaust and to demonstrate that the German Sinti are 'completely normal people'[19] with feelings, fear and hopes.

Born in 1921, Lessing lived in the family flat in Herford in north Germany from the age of four. Although the family had given up their nomadic life-style and the children attended the local Catholic school, Romani was spoken at home. Intertwined with the picaresque, unusual, exciting, adventurous, even melodramatic account is the serious case study of a Romani who is on the run for no reason other than that he is a Gypsy. From an early age he realises that in order to survive it is necessary for him to pass himself off as someone he is not.

Being a Sinto can have fatal consequences. His first memory of the impact of discrimination against the Romanies is the brutal murder of his father by some forestry workers who suspect the father of poaching. The body is given an unceremonious burial without the family being notified, and it is only through a series of coincidences that his murder is found out at all. Lessing learns his lesson. He has a natural talent for music and when he meets members of an American jazz band (rejected as 'nigger music' by the Nazis) he passes himself off as a South American because of his swarthy skin, but is sent packing by the porter at the door of the concert hall, who says 'What do you want here, Gypsy, get the hell out of here, or I'll kick you out'.[20]

Lessing is a German Sinto, and at times he is accepted as a German, but when it is found out that he is a Gypsy the authorities cannot conceive that he can be both a German and a member of the Romani community. He writes about his life and his adventures as a musician with a travelling circus, his time in the German army and later in Russia during the Second World War, and how he finally escapes from his persecutors one last time during the air attacks on Dresden.

One of Lessing's survival strategies is to pass as someone else, such as when he passes himself off as an Italian musician playing for the Nazis as part of the *Kraft durch Freude* (strength through joy) programme, although he finds it extremely hard when he has to entertain the Nazi 'torture-mongers'[21] in Buchenwald, but cannot afford to refuse to play in case the authorities then suspect that he is a Sinto. It is interesting that when he returns to Germany he records that he feels, like members of the Kreutz family, that it is his home. 'So I now went back to my native country. Germany was always my home, but there again it meant fear. Time and time again fear of persecution and terror, fear of being discovered and locked up as a Romani, fear of becoming a victim of the Nazi racial policy'.[22]

Later after the war he moved to Bavaria and got a job playing for the Americans, then acted in films and eventually acquired a fairground stall in a show, but the legacy of his ethnic affiliation lingers on. Despite repeated requests he only received a miserly compensation. His is a story of excitement, colour and the exotic, but he is deliberately coming out of 'hiding' to make his case public.

The Memories of Ceija Stojka, an Austrian Roma

Like members of the Kreutz family and Alfred Lessing, it was almost fifty years after the end of the war that Ceija Stojka felt moved to write about her experiences. She too wanted to share her memories with a wider audience, and to make more people aware of the suffering of the Roma during the Holocaust. She too has a strong sense of belonging to her home country, and *Wir leben im Verborgenen: Erinnerungen einer Rom-Zigeunerin* (We Live Concealed Lives: Memories of a Rom-Gypsy), published in 1988,[23] opens up new dimensions in that it presents an Austrian Romani woman's memories of her life from the 1930s to the 1980s, of prewar Vienna, concentration camps and post-war discrimination in Austria. Ceija Stojka is writing from what in many ways is a marginal position. Women writers have always been in a minority, she belongs to an ethnic minority group, she is Austrian but is not writing in her mother-tongue, Romani, and she is one of the few Austrian Roma survivors of the Holocaust.

The account was written with the help of editor Karin Berger and extracts from interviews with Berger are included at the end of the volume. The language is spontaneous and lively, coloured with numerous Austrian dialect words and expressions. Her happy memories of her early childhood in the east of Austria, near the Hungarian border, with her descriptions of playing with other children in the back-streets of Vienna and going to the local swimming pool give no indication of how the story is going to continue. It is hard for a non-Roma to imagine how hard it must have been to suddenly become the recipient of discrimination and persecution, as the Nazi policies become enforced and she and other Roma are harassed at school and made to feel inferior.

How is this persecution represented? It begins in earnest with the murder of her father, who was deported to Dachau and then transferred to the brutal concentration camp at Mauthausen. The father's remains are returned in an urn. Ceija reports how her mother screams 'Wackar, ande san du katte?'(Wackar, are you in there?),[24] and puts the bones in a handkerchief and carries them round her neck as a memento, only to have them confiscated later by the Nazis. It is particularly remarkable that Ceija actually quotes the Romani words uttered by her mother at this moment of extreme stress, and at a number of other points in her account she quotes in Romani, giving the German/Austrian equivalent in each case. The mother is portrayed as a loving, caring, deeply religious woman, who is extremely protective towards her children, but she is powerless against the immense Nazi German bureaucracy.

The woman's perspective is very much in evidence. Ceija, together with her mother, brother and sisters, is transported to Auschwitz in a freight wagon and is later sent to the women's camp at Ravensbrück. There are no taboo zones in her writing, and Ceija records her experiences of tattooing, disinfection, delousing, sterilisation, insanitary conditions and the omnipresence of death in a chilling, but self-effacing way, praising the way her mother struggled to keep the spirits of the family up in the face of adversity. She talks with Karin Berger about how the act of writing down her experiences was painful, but how she chose to record her experiences of the Holocaust lest the events pass into oblivion or are denied. She explains how she still has nightmares about Auschwitz:

> Sometimes when I open my eyes in the morning, my God, I have the smell in my nose again, the smell of the cremations. Yes, the dreams, they come quite

of their own accord, without you doing anything, and you can't just sweep them aside and say 'I was only dreaming'. I really did go through it all, and experienced tremendous fear, every day. Every day in there was a year, every hour was an eternity.[25]

In the final part of her interview with Karin Berger she cites instances of post-war harassment and her fear of attacks, and explains how she sees instances of discrimination against Roma in everyday life, and that the situation has not altered much: 'All of us, whether we were Roma or Sinti, kept ourselves to ourselves, and only waited for what was coming to us. Unfortunately only misfortune befell us, both before the concentration camp and afterwards'.[26]

In her later autobiographical work, *Reisende auf dieser Welt* (Traveller in this World), published in 1992,[27] Ceija Stojka writes more about her life in the post-war period, and of the problems she has faced as a mother of a son who became addicted to drugs. Rather than writing primarily as a member of the Roma community, she is first and foremost writing of her intense maternal feelings of frustration at not being able to help her son and of sadness at his death. In the second half of the work she writes of her love of music and her mission to convey her love of the Roma musical tradition to others, and through the music to increase understanding of the minority group.

The two works are very different in content and mood, but they complement each other, and emphasise the fact that each person's identity is constructed from a number of elements, of which ethnicity is one. Stojka is writing in *Wir leben im Verborgenen* as a daughter, woman, Austrian, survivor, Romani and educator, whereas in *Reisende auf dieser Welt* she is writing as a mother, mourner, Romani, Austrian, music-lover and cultural ambassador. The many different facets of her identity help to illustrate that each member of the Gypsy population is as complex a person as the Gadzo, rather than a one-dimensional cardboard figure.

Karl Stojka's Travels at Home and Abroad

Karl Stojka, now a much acclaimed artist, has travelled a great deal, not only out of choice, but because he was forced to travel and was persecuted. He, like the other Sinti and Roma who have written about their lives, underlines the fact that he has his worries like all other people. In his autobiography *Auf der ganzen Welt zu Hause* (At Home in the Whole World), published in 1994,[28] he writes both of his suffering during the Holocaust and of the post-war period. He describes in detail his recollections of suffering, including the brutal carving of the tattoo on his arm, Z5742, which is still there as a reminder, and of his travels and work selling carpets in the United States, where he stayed until 1973. In all the other accounts by Sinti and Roma discussed above, the conflict between being a member of both the Roma community and the German or Austrian community is described, but Karl Stojka also talks about how he is perceived in relation to black Americans. He says: ' As Gypsies we hardly had any problems with the coloured people in our neighbourhood. They always in fact made a distinction between us and white people, just as the latter counted us among their number. So we always stood between the two worlds and did not really quite belong to either'.[29] Like the other Sinti and Roma, he too stresses that the Roma are first and foremost human beings with emotions like all other people. Despite the permanent scars he has from his treatment by the Nazis he shows remarkable reluctance to fall into the trap of stereotyping a national group:

> I am not angry with the Germans, because it was not one particular nation or another which robbed me of my childhood and my health, it was human beings who did that to me, and if there is something I can't understand, then it is how human beings can inflict something like that on other people. If I hear on the radio today that there are more outbreaks of violence against Gypsies in countries like Romania, Poland and Slovakia, it makes me very sad, because I can see that it is starting all over again.[30]

The fact that he and the other Sinti and Roma have chosen to write down their memories at the end of the twentieth century is a sign that they wish the majority population to take note of the reality of their lives rather than continue to live in a cloud of half-truths, misconceptions and lies. Each person locates himself or herself firmly within the culture of the country in which they live, but the dichotomy between the bitterness and resentment at how they are treated by their homeland and their wish to create more positive, optimistic images of the future for Sinti and Roma in Germany and Austria is a constantly recurring motif.

German-Language Texts by Eastern European Roma

The anthology of some twenty short accounts by Eastern European Roma, *Die Roma: Hoffen auf ein Leben ohne Angst* (The Roma: Hoping for a Life Without Fear 1992), was published shortly after the series of right-wing extremist attacks on foreigners and on Sinti and Roma, and was designed to give the majority population insights into the concerns and hopes of the ethnic group, and diffuse some of the ill-feeling aroused by sensationalist journalism which depicts all 'Gypsies' as a threatening mass (see Introduction). Three Roma, two from Slovakia and one from Serbia, write about their experiences of arriving in Germany. Both Slovakians stress that they had left their country because of the political persecution in Slovakia, and that they would like to stay in Germany. Ivanka Jovanovic, a Serbian woman who had spent some time in Austria many years previously, had fled with her husband to Berlin in the 1980s. He was later deported as an illegal immigrant, and when his wife tried to appeal for political asylum for him, she and the children were also threatened with deportation. Ivanka writes about how she does not look like a 'typical' Roma: 'Really we ought to be ashamed, that we are happy not to look like Roma. If I am a Romani woman then I ought to be proud of my people. There were, however, some moments in our lives when we simply had to hide this fact. That is very sad. But our very existence was at stake'.[31]

In these brief personal cameos the dilemma of the ethnic group becomes evident. The solution of returning to their country of origin is unacceptable, because they would face even greater persecution. Individuals tell their story and the reader is given a chance to form personal opinions based on eyewitness narrative, rather than hearsay or prejudice. It is important that more such accounts are published, both to increase awareness of the diversity of the Roma population in Europe, and to present the Roma as individuals rather than media scapegoats.

Before concluding this study of images and self-images of Sinti and Roma in German-language literature, it is important to note the publication in 1989 of Rajko Djuric's *Zigeunerische Elegien* (Gypsy Elegies),[32] a dual-language edition in Romani and German. The poems draw their inspiration from the world of nature, with death, fire, wind and water being common motifs.

'Ohne Haus (Heim) ohne Grab' (Without House [Home] Without Grave), 'Der Mond' (The Moon) with its images of Gypsies sitting round a fire by moonlight, and 'Obdachlos' (Homeless), are typical of the collection, in that they convey images of a group of people living a nomadic life close to nature. The poems may be seen either as romantic and nostalgic, or as anachronistic. Djuric, Yugoslavian by birth, is eager to promote a standard written form of Romani, but does not presume to offer readers a blueprint, since his variant of Romani has a predominantly Serbian influence, and is not identical with forms found in Germany and Austria. Since Romani is primarily a spoken language, there is only a very small corpus of work written by members of the ethnic group in this language, and Djuric's work takes its place alongside writing by other ethnic minority writers such as the Italians, Japanese or Turks, and helps to give the Romani community a sense of owning a written, cultural heritage as well as being famous for their oral tradition.

Conclusions

Contemporary writing in the German language by Sinti and Roma challenges traditional stereotypical images of the demonised or romanticised Gypsy and presents instead images of an ethnic group with its own traditions and its own very specific history of discrimination and persecution.

Hackl's *Erzählung* marks a watershed in that it introduces a wide audience to the crimes perpetrated against the Roma and also focuses on the need to acknowledge the omissions of the post-war period and the importance of marking respect for those who perished in the Holocaust, particularly since smaller groups can easily become submerged and suppressed, if they do not have a strong influential lobby to campaign on their behalf.

The diversity of the experiences of the Sinti and Roma is reflected in the autobiographical works. Rather than being treated as objects, passive sufferers at the hands of the majority, people who are registered, photographed, archived, and documented in the interests of science, the Sinti and Roma in Germany and Austria are now feeling the necessity to tell their own story and reflect on their lives, and in particular their suffering in the Holocaust. The autobiographies cease to resemble those of members of the majority society at the point at which the personal becomes political, the membership of the ethnic minority group becomes a liability and human rights begin to be infringed.

Fear is a central emotion in the lives of all those Sinti and Roma who have recorded their experiences, and it is the wish of the authors that this fear be eliminated, by making the majority of society more aware of the rights of the Romani ethnic minority group, in order that further attacks on the minority group may be averted.

Writing is only one expression of culture, and through their writing many of the Sinti and Roma themselves underline the importance of their own Romani culture and tradition, in narration as much as in music and art. They are not exotic, colourful 'Gypsies' pulled out of context, pinned to the board like butterflies assembled by a collector, commodities, but human beings with human rights. Each person living in Germany and Austria has the right to contribute to the cultural heritage, and it is to be hoped that the contribution of Roma and Sinti to the German-speaking community will continue to gather strength and inspiration from the pioneering work already done. The challenge is to move beyond the polarity of good and bad images towards a challenging new reflection of the diversity of the culture and traditions of the Sinti and Roma today.

Notes

1. b. hooks, *Black Looks: Race and Representation*, London, Turnaround, 1992, p.4.

2. Ibid., p.39.

3. See D. Horrocks and E. Kolinsky, eds, *Turkish Culture in German Society Today*, Providence, Oxford, Berghahn, 1996, which includes a chapter by Sabine Fischer and Moray McGowan, 'From "Pappkoffer" to Pluralism', pp.1-22, which provides an overview of migrant writing in the Federal Republic of Germany.

4. See the collection of essays edited by R. King, J. Connell and P. White, *Writing across Worlds: Literature and Migration*, London, New York, Routledge, 1995, which includes articles on images of the Irish and Jews in Britain, and analyses of the work of Algerian writers in France and migrant writing in Germany.

5. P-G. Briel, *'Lumpenkind und Traumprinzessin': Zur Sozialgestalt der Zigeuner in der Kinder- und Jugendliteratur seit dem 19. Jahrhundert*, Giessen, Focus, 1989.

6. D. Strauß, ed., *Die Sinti/Roma-Erzählkunst*, Heidelberg, Dokumentations- und Kulturzentrum Deutscher Sinti und Roma, 1992.

7. R. Djuric, *Roma und Sinti im Spiegel der deutschen Literatur*, Frankfurt am Main, Peter Lang, 1995.

8. B. Eder, *Geboren bin ich vor Jahrtausenden ...: Bilderwelten in der Literatur der Roma und Sinti*, Klagenfurt, Drava, 1993.

9. E. Hackl, *Abschied von Sidonie*, Zurich, Diogenes, 1989.

10. Ibid., Sidonie is referred to as 'ein freundliches Mohrenkind' (p.31), 'das schwarze Ding' (p.59) and 'Negerkind' (p.79).

11. Ibid., p.75. 'Neger und Zigeuner, diese artfremden Schädlinge'.

12. Ibid., pp.29–30.

13. Ibid., p.50.

14. Ibid., p.50.

15. Ibid., p.125.

16. M. Krausnick, *'Da wollten wir frei sein!': Eine Sinti-Familie erzählt*, Weinheim, Basel, Beltz, 1983.

17. Krausnick, *'Da wollten wir frei sein!'*, 2nd edn, 1986, p.39.

18. A. Lessing, *Mein Leben im Versteck: Wie ein deutscher Sinti den Holocaust überlebte*, Düsseldorf, Zebulon Verlag, 1993.

19. Ibid., p.14.

20. Ibid., p.35.

21. Ibid., p.122. 'Ich konnte doch nicht in einem Konzentrationslager Musik machen. Ich konnte doch nicht die Folterknechte unterhalten, während im gleichen Lager Sinti, Juden, Roma und andere gequält und mißhandelt wurden'.

22. Ibid., p.106.

23. C. Stojka, *Wir leben im Verborgenen*, ed. by K. Berger, Vienna, Picus, 1988.

24. Ibid., p.19.

25. Ibid., p.105.

26. Ibid., p.150.

27. C. Stojka, *Reisende auf dieser Welt: Aus dem Leben einer Rom-Zigeunerin*, ed. K. Berger, Vienna, Picus, 1992.

28. K. Stojka and R. Pohanka. *Auf der ganzen Welt zu Hause: Das Leben und Wandern des Zigeuners Karl Stojka*, Vienna, Picus, 1994.

29. Ibid., p.107.

30. Ibid., p.9.

31. G. Fienbork et al., eds, *Die Roma — Hoffen auf ein Leben ohne Angst*, Reinbek bei Hamburg, Rowohlt, 1992, p.187.

32. R. Djuric, *Zigeunerische Elegeien: Gedichte in Romani und Deutsch*, Hamburg, Buske, 1989.

Conclusion

Susan Tebbutt

In this volume issues relating to society, language and literature have been examined in turn. By way of conclusion, the three strands are pulled together with reference to the Gypsy/Gadzo relationship, centuries of marginalisation and persecution, and postwar developments.

The Gypsy/Gadzo Relationship

More than fifty years have passed since the 'hidden Holocaust', the genocide of half a million European Romanies, the culmination of over five centuries of persecution of the ethnic group, but the Gypsy/Gadzo relationship still remains far from harmonious. In common with Gypsies in other countries in Europe, Gypsies in German-speaking countries face many problems with respect to their identity and image. Unlike members of other minority groups in Europe, such as the Catalans or Basques in Spain, the Bretons, Alsatians or Corsicans in France or Frisians in Germany, the Sinti and Roma in Germany and Austria are not associated with one particular geographical region. Some, such as those living in Baden-Württemberg near the border with France, or in Burgenland in Austria, near the Hungarian border, live near borders with other countries (a phenomenon explained in part by the fact that during the centuries of persecution, groups often found that moving across a border could mean temporary freedom from harassment, or escape from a potential death penalty), but many others live in cities which are nowhere near a border. While most Sinti and Roma in Germany/Austria have German or Austrian nationality, some of the most recent Romani immigrants, such as those from Romania or Yugoslavia, are foreign. Thus whereas members of, say, the Catalan minority are both Catalan and Spanish, not all Roma in Germany and Austria are both members of the Roma ethnic group and German or Austrian.

It has been pointed out that the majority population has viewed the Sinti and Roma with caution, suspicion and disapproval over the centuries. Traces of the hierarchical relationship can be seen in the disparaging use of the word *Zigeuner* in the German language. Public signs relating to the 'Gypsies', whether they be in the form of the posts with pictures of Gypsies hanging from the gallows which were intended to deter other Gypsies from entering towns in bygone times, or modern signs at the entrance to campsites banning Gypsies, are tangible signs of the way the majority population considered the Gypsy minority to be undesirable elements. It is paradoxical that given how 'other' these 'swarthy-skinned' people were considered to be, and how frequently they feature (erroneously) in lists of foreigners in Germany and Austria, the Germans were still prepared to enlist them in the army during both the First and the Second World War. On 9 December 1944 the Party Chancellery issued a decree that both Gypsy and Jewish *Mischlinge* of the Second Degree (with one alien grandparent) could serve in the *Volkssturm*, but that Jewish and Gypsy people of the First Degree (with two alien grandparents) were prohibited from serving.[1] Military service was compulsory for German Sinti, which explains why Sinti deportees sometimes arrived at Auschwitz-Birkenau and other camps in their uniforms, since they were deported from the front when the decision for mass killing was made.

Attempts to stigmatise, hound, assimilate and contain the Sinti and Roma have been based on spurious logic and pseudo-scientific methods. The very act of defining who exactly is part of the Sinti and Roma community is fraught with difficulty. For most Germans and Austrians the 'Gypsies' form part of a homogeneous mass, a nomadic people with a different, by implication inferior, culture and life-style, who have a lower status in society. In cases where members of the Romani community may appear to conform to the stereotype, such as the Roma who came to Germany and Austria after the fall of Communism, closer examination reveals that they were forced to flee pogroms in their own country of origin, bringing with them almost nothing but the clothes they were wearing. The act of migrating is thus not automatically part of an intrinsic wish to lead a nomadic life. These very 'visible' Roma may beg or offer to tell fortunes, and thus reinforce the clichéd image, but for each of these Roma there will be hundreds of members of the Roma community going about their everyday business, working in banks, shops, hospitals or firms, outwardly indistinguishable from the rest of the population, not least because it is rare for Roma to speak their own language, Romani, in the presence of non-Roma.

Romani is not one language used throughout the world, but has over sixty different dialects. Far from being a homogeneous group linguistically, the Sinti and Roma community in Germany and Austria consists of many groups which have been in these countries for periods of time ranging from a few months to many centuries, speaking different dialects, and coming from different countries. As Anthony Grant points out, there are almost as many speakers of non-German Romani as there are speakers of German Romani in the German-speaking world. Although Sinti is one of the more distinctive dialects and has been influenced by different varieties of German, it contains borrowings from other languages, just as the dialects which evolved in other countries were influenced by the language of the majority population there too. It is thus not surprising that Roma living in Germany and Austria are not all able to communicate freely with one another in 'the Romani language'.

The wariness of the majority population towards the Roma is replicated in the wariness the Roma community feels towards the Gadzos. Given the history of persecution, assimilation and annihilation, it is hardly surprising that the Roma are happy to organise events to promote the image of their own culture in Germany and Austria, but do not wish to hand over aspects of that culture to outsiders as a type of researchable or quantifiable commodity.

Centuries of Marginalisation and Persecution

From their very first arrival in Europe from India, the Gypsies have been treated with great suspicion and frequently outlawed. Countries such as Germany, Austria, Hungary, France, Spain,

Portugal and Britain implemented a range of discriminatory laws ranging from the death penalty to deportation to colonies as far afield as South America. Within individual countries the authorities took pains to keep moving the Gypsies on from one village to another, from one town to another, and even from one country to another. From the first official records of their presence in Germany in the fifteenth century, the authorities in Germany and Austria have viewed Gypsies as a threat and as a nuisance and have taken steps to move them on. Measures taken in the eighteenth century under Empress Maria Theresa further restricted the freedom of the Gypsies, and even lead to the setting up of special colonies or villages to which the Gypsies were assigned.

In the nineteenth century the growing urbanisation and industrialisation led to a backlash of Gadzo interest in rural life and a hankering after greater communion with nature, but the sympathy with the Gypsies was accompanied by increased motivation to assimilate them to the way of life of the majority of the population, and even involved taking steps to prevent the Romanies from using their own language.

The relationship between the Gadzo and the Gypsy was one of researcher and research object, reflected in the first wave of works in the eighteenth and nineteenth century which attempt to trace the roots of the Romani language and classify and describe the life and language of the Gypsies. Many of these works include what is now acknowledged to be suspect material, as it has been shown that some of the evidence given to the collectors of Romani words and compilers of anthropological accounts did not always correspond with reality, since members of the Romani community did not always give accurate information to the researchers, fearing that they were handing over their heritage to the researchers in much the same way that archaeologists in the past frequently assumed ownership of foreign artefacts and remains which they found and illegitimately claimed for their own country.

The interest in the language is paralleled in the interest of the Romantic literary movement in the Gypsies, who tends to be idealised, romanticised and exoticised. Whereas the image of the Jew has been the subject of many studies, images of Gypsies have been largely ignored, although there is at least as much material to appraise.

Some of the earliest images are to be found in the nineteenth-century collections of fairy tales made by the Brothers Grimm, where Gypsies are seen as wicked, criminal or frightening, or in the *Kunstmärchen*, the fairy tales composed by writers such as Brentano and Arnim. Although writers might argue that they felt sympathetic towards the Gypsies, the figure of the Gypsy is often demonised and reduced to stereotypical dimensions, in the same way that the Jew is seen as a negative or demonic figure. Wilhelm Solms points out how ironic it is that even the so-called *Zigeunermärchen*, the tales supposedly related by Gypsies, also reveal a prejudiced way of looking at the world, with negative images of the Gypsies in the tales, and there is thus some doubt as to whether the works were in fact simply the tales recorded from Romanies' oral accounts, or whether the person who wrote down the tale embellished it and altered it so that it fitted into the world view of the Gypsies which was prevalent.

Despite the upsurge of interest in Gypsies in the nineteenth century, there was a growing feeling in Germany that the 'Gypsy nuisance' was a problem which had to be tackled. More and more states introduced laws controlling the movements of the group, and the setting up by the Bavarian Police under Alfred Dillmann of a central office in Munich in 1899 to control Gypsy affairs, was an important date in the history of the persecution of the Gypsies. The laws regulating the movements of the Gypsies were tightened up, and the registering and recording of the activities of the group, both normal and criminal, became more systematic. The passing of the Nuremberg Race Laws in 1935 meant severe restrictions not only for the Jewish community but also for Sinti and Roma. Hitler considered both groups to be unfit to mix with or marry Germans, and he later even included the Gypsies in the Final Solution to the Jewish question. The 1936 cleansing of Berlin of Gypsies in preparation for the Olympic Games (echoes of which were seen in the clearing of Gypsies from the centre of Barcelona for the Olympic Games in 1992) was yet another step down the road towards the planned annihilation of the ethnic minority. The supposedly academic basis of the Berlin Racial Hygiene and Demographic Biology Research Unit, under the directorship of Robert Ritter, included lengthy interviews conducted by Eva Justin and other colleagues, and the listing, registering, photographing, fingerprinting, taking of anthropometric measurements and constructing of family trees. Academic scientific research was coopted into the process of bureaucratic planning and state planning. Genealogy was required to prove Aryan ancestry and thus political loyalty. The family trees and the attendant bureaucratic registration provided for social control and intimidation, determining whom one could marry and if one could be employed, and also segregated some minorities, such as Jews, Gypsies and disabled people, as alien and undesirable, excluding them from the 'national community'. The programme of action of the Research Unit was a crucial part of Hitler's plan to rid the country of people who were perceived as alien, although the Roma are in fact of Indo-Aryan descent. The deportation of the Gypsies to the concentration camps was facilitated by the existence of the lengthy lists of family members and family trees.

The *Festsetzung* legislation of 1938/1939 used traditional propaganda stereotypes about Gypsy 'nomadism and vagrancy' to achieve comprehensive registration of the Sinti and Roma as well as of the entire population of Germany. This enabled the state to mobilise its citizens for labour and military service, and made it simpler for the police to round up and deport Gypsies, who could be found at registered addresses. The process of identification, registration, concentration and deportation could not be implemented without police legislation on 'fixed compulsory domiciles', which is really closer to a form of house arrest and the creation of assembly centres.

In the past decade the literature on municipal internment camps for Gypsies after 1933 has improved dramatically, with good analytical essays and monographs on Cologne, Düsseldorf, Frankfurt, Essen and Hamburg,[2] and there are now many essays and monographs on the concentration camps and labour camps, where conditions were bleak and freedom severely limited. Similarly, the full extent of the exploitation of Sinti and Roma workers in munitions factories, quarries and industrial firms has only recently been revealed. Ludwig Eiber's case-studies of Munich Sinti families from 1933 until 1945 give an indication of the horrific range of ways in which suffering was inflicted on innocent people whose only crime was to be part of the Sinti community. Accounts of the degrading treatment in the concentration camps are similar to those provided by members of other ethnic groups, such as the Jews, but it is only recently that accounts by Sinti and Roma, including reports, for example, of medical experiments and compulsory sterilisation, have become more widely accessible and acknowledged. Even the fact that many Sinti and Roma were forced to wear a cloth triangle with the letter Z, in the same way that the Jews had to wear a yellow cloth Star of David, is rarely mentioned in accounts of the Holocaust.

Sometimes Sinti and Roma were assigned a black triangle, when they were subsumed in the 'asocial' prisoner category. At two concentration camps, Auschwitz and Majdanek, the letter Z, together with a number, was tattooed on each Sinti or Roma's arm on arrival, but this is omitted from almost all historical accounts of the Holocaust. It is thus important that individuals counteract this final degradation and reduction to an anonymous number or invisibility by reclaiming their experiences of the past for posterity.

It is in a work of teenage literature, the account of the experiences of a Sinti family in the course of the twentieth century, recorded by Michail Krausnick, that the historical events outlined above come to life as each member of the family recalls how the major political decisions of the day affected their everyday lives. Since very few members of the majority population have personal acquaintances who belong to the Romani community, these eyewitness autobiographical accounts form a particularly important source of knowledge in an extremely accessible form. It is significant that none of the autobiographical works dealing with the Holocaust was written immediately after the end of the war, because the suffering of the group at the hands of the Nazis was so deeply disturbing that it was only after a period of time that some of the survivors felt able to record their feelings about and impressions of this traumatic time. The time gap also required the ability to publish and distribute this literature. Even today, most of the Roma/Sinti history is distributed by small publishing houses, although this is gradually changing. There is, moreover, a time gap on all Holocaust memoirs and histories, including Jewish ones. The first books on the Sinti and Roma appeared in the early 1970s, and growing interest in the Holocaust has changed and expanded available publications for all victim groups.

Postwar Developments

Difficulties in gaining access to the relevant documents and archives containing information about the Nazi crimes against Sinti and Roma meant that many decades elapsed before the continuity of the persecution of the Sinti and Roma in the postwar period was acknowledged. Officials in the police service, housing, health and welfare departments were often the same people who had previously discriminated against the minority group during the Third Reich, and they harassed and humiliated survivors. The extent of the failure of the German government and academia to assume collective responsibility for the crimes committed during the Nazi period is astounding, and the failure to de-Nazify the postwar German civil service and academia is very widespread.[3] People with a background of involvement in inhuman, racial discrimination, such as Robert Ritter, Eva Justin and Sophie Ehrhardt, were allowed to continue unhindered in positions of academic responsibility and abuse the research data collected under Hitler. There is a need to re-examine history from the point of view of the Sinti and Roma minority, a minority without a strong official lobby, and to refocus historical interest on all victims of the Holocaust, and not just the Jews, and in particular to reconsider the case of the persecution of groups such as the Sinti and Roma.

It is against this background of continued discrimination and persecution that the Romani civil rights movement has evolved in the postwar period. Initially based on individual and family initiatives designed to provide solutions to problems concerning housing and jobs, the formation of local associations in the 1950s and 1960s led to the strengthening of the regional groups into umbrella organisations. The 1980s were marked by a number of campaigns to draw attention to the position both of indigenous Sinti and Roma who had suffered in the Holocaust, as well as to the position of those more recent Roma immigrants who were again being hounded by the government of the day. As Yaron Matras points out, in the 1990s there is greater cooperation between the organisations based in Germany and international Romani groups, and this international dimension offers new scope to influence the course of politics. Involvement of Sinti and Roma organisations in the work of bodies such as the United Nations and the Council of Europe is helping to put pressure on German and Austrian authorities to afford all members of the ethnic minority group equal treatment to that given to the majority population.

Alongside efforts to improve the lot of the Romanies, and to build up regional, national and international support mechanisms, there is a move to promote the Romani language. At the end of the twentieth century it is now possible to study the Romani language at universities as far apart as Austin/Texas, London, Prague and Paris. It is possible to hear speakers of most Romani dialects somewhere in Germany today, but this is one of the problems which has made it harder to work towards standardising the language or settling on common forms. The setting up of an International Congress to discuss issues such as this standard-isation should help to heighten the sense of pride in their linguistic and cultural roots on the part of members of the ethnic group. There is optimism about the setting up of a World Romani Congress and about the growing academic interest in the Roma minority, with new Europe-wide initiatives being undertaken in the fields of human rights, language, education and culture.

Has there been a marked change in the image of the Gypsy in post-1945 German language literature? Anti-Gypsy stereotypes have abounded in literature and must be seen as similar to anti-Semitic images. As Daniel Strauß explains, historically there is a difference between traditional anti-Gypsy images and the racially motivated anti-Gypsyism, although both are closely associated with the treating of Gypsies as scapegoats. Even at the end of the twentieth century people should remain vigilant in rejecting images of prejudice against Gypsies.

For many people, their first encounter with the Gypsies will be through literature, and the schoolbook thus has a crucial role to play. Even prestigious German publishers of schoolbooks do not automatically treat the ethnic group with respect, and works which appear in a series called 'Education and Knowledge', but which spread misinformation, may help to perpetuate stereotypes and give the wrong impression to young people who have no other way of judging an ethnic group of whom they have no first-hand knowledge.

Writers who claim to be familiar with the Gypsies are not necessarily bound to present an accurate or prejudice-free picture, and the mere presence of a Gypsy in a story is no guarantee that the writer is sensitive in portraying customs. It is easy to distort reality and give the impression that the Gypsies are prone to thieving and criminal behaviour. What tends to be missing, even in the twentieth century, is the literary image of the Gypsy as a real person, notable exceptions being Alex Wedding's *Ede und Unku* and Erich Hackl's *Abschied von Sidonie*.

There is not a long history of writing by Roma, because the Romani language is an oral language which has traditionally been held to be a secret language (Ceija Stojka is one of the few Romani writers to intersperse her work with snippets of the Romani language), but from the 1980s onwards a number of Romanies have begun to attempt their own form of *Vergangenheitsbewältigung* (coming to terms with the past). All the writers find it extremely painful and difficult to write about their own extremes of suffering and about the tribulations of close members of their family, but the works are written in the hope that they will enable non-Gypsies to understand the experiences of the Sinti and Roma in the Holocaust.

Accounts of the Holocaust are by definition survivors' accounts, and the writings about the various methods employed by different people to survive the persecution have to be read bearing in mind that the great majority of the Roma community did not survive. The role of the literature is to introduce the wider public to the diversity of the experiences of the ethnic group, and to present the writers as individuals as well as members of a group, and the most recent publications of the writing of eastern European Roma living in Germany add a further dimension to this body of work.

Outlook

Despite the increase in right-wing attacks on Romanies in the late 1980s and 1990s throughout Europe, the development of civil rights groups on a local, regional, national, European and international level gives some grounds for optimism, but should not give rise to complacency. It is to be hoped that the German-speaking countries will enter the twenty-first century with a determination to allow members of the Sinti and Roma community to contribute fully to the political, social and cultural life of each country. It is important to learn from the past, and not treat the Gypsies as yet another exotic group, or as foreigners, or as a commodity to research.

Not all Gypsies wish to be called Sinti or Roma, not all object to being called Gypsy, and most but not all speak the Romani language, but this does not automatically mean that they will understand each other. There is a certain amount of overlap between the dialects and customs, but it is important to remember that the members of the Sinti and Roma community should not all be lumped together and classified in an Orientalist fashion as different. It remains to be hoped that the new millennium will see the rights of the group strengthened and the attitudes of the majority population become more tolerant and understanding. In multi-cultural Germany and Austria it is all too easy to ignore a group without a homeland and without a strong presence in the media world. It may be that the Internet with its websites, communication networks and new technology may assist the Sinti and Roma to gain a higher profile and to be treated as equals rather than as inferiors. The setting up of the Dokumentations- und Kulturzentrum Deutscher Sinti und Roma in Heidelberg gives a national focus to both political and cultural initiatives and activities.

Whereas before there was little literature about the group and its culture and traditions, a number of works were published in the 1980s and 1990s which help the majority population to gain a more balanced picture. New publishing initiatives in Germany in the Romani language help to give the language greater status and promote the idea that the Romani language is on a par with other minority languages in the German-speaking world. The fact that writers from the Roma community are beginning to make their voices heard is an important step in German-language literature.

This volume on Sinti and Roma in German-speaking society and in German-language literature aims to present some of the many pieces of the jigsaw and show how they fit together into a complex and fascinating picture. Much work remains to be done on charting the comparisons between the experiences of Roma in different European countries and how the language, culture and literature have developed in each country against varying socio-political backgrounds.

There has been little space to mention images of the Gypsy in art by non-Gypsies and works of art created by members of the Sinti and Roma community. Such a study would help the majority population to understand the factors underlying the way in which visual images of the group are projected, and at the same time would give greater prominence to the role of the minority group as contributors to the culture of the German-speaking countries.

Unlike the generally romanticised images in nineteenth-century art, when Gypsies were often depicted on the move, and the caravan and horses tended to be represented with more care and in greater detail than the people, twentieth-century artists such as Otto Pankok and Otto Müller depict members of the Sinti and Roma community as individuals. In the last quarter of the twentieth century the striking colours of Karl Stojka's art reflect the violence of his experiences of the Nazi period, and the inclusion of individuals wearing the Z cloth badge gives a rare opportunity to see the persecution of the Sinti and Roma depicted in art. His painting of the murder of almost three thousand Gypsies in one night at Auschwitz-Birkenau is a horrific and gruelling reminder of the atrocities of the regime, and should serve as a reminder of the barbaric inhumanity of humans towards their fellow humans, and of the dangers of anti-Gypsyism.

Notes

1. Bundesarchiv Koblenz, NS6/98, p.95ff.
2. See S. Milton, 'Vorstufe zur Vernichtung: Die Zigeunerlager nach 1933', *Vierteljahrshefte für Zeitgeschichte 43*, 1/1995, pp.115-130, K. Fings and F. Sparing, *'Zur Zeit Zigeunerlager': Die Verfolgung der Düsseldorfer Sinti und Roma im Nationalsozialismus*, Cologne, Volksblatt, 1992, and M. Zimmermann, *Rassenutopie und Genozid: Die nationalsozialistische 'Lösung der Zigeunerfrage'*, Hamburg, Christians, 1996, pp.93-100.
3. See N. Frei, *Vergangenheitspolitik*, Munich, Beck, 1996, where it is demonstrated how pervasive was the rehabilitation of compromised individuals.

NOTES ON CONTRIBUTORS

LUDWIG EIBER is a historian working at the Bayerische Staatskanzlei, Haus der Bayerischen Geschichte in Augsburg. Publications include his volume on the persecution of the Sinti and Roma in Munich from 1933 to 1945, *Ich wußte, es wird schlimm* (1993), and many periodical articles on the Sinti and Roma and on aspects of the Nazi period and its aftermath, including the role of the police and the judiciary in Munich and the activities of the Hamburg State Police.

ANTHONY P. GRANT lectures in Linguistics in the Department of Social Anthropology at the University of St Andrews. A historical and comparative linguist, he has published many articles on Romani linguistics in Britain and abroad and has presented papers on the study of Romani lexicon, the Greek linguistic influence on Romani, and the history of Shelta, the language of Irish Travellers.

MICHAIL KRAUSNICK's numerous award-winning books for children and teenagers range from biography, satire and cabaret to science-fiction, poems and radio plays. His publications include *'Da wollten wir frei sein!'* (1983), the theatre play *Die Sinti-Revue* (1985), *Abfahrt Karlsruhe* (1990) and *Wo sind sie hingekommen?* (1995). He was awarded the Civis' 95 prize for his film about the deportation of Roma children to Auschwitz, *Auf Wiedersehen im Himmel!* (SWF 1994).

YARON MATRAS is Researcher at the Department of Linguistics, University of Manchester. He has published on Romani Linguistics, including the volumes *Untersuchungen zu Grammatik und Diskurs des Romanes* (1994) and *Romani in Contact* (1995), and was editor of Romnews Information Service, and worked with Romani civil rights organisations in Germany from 1989 to 1995. He has also published a number of articles on the civil rights situation of the Roma in Europe, and Germany in particular.

SYBIL MILTON was Senior Historian at the United States Holocaust Museum in Washington D.C. from 1986 to 1997 and is now an independent historian, serving as Vice-President of the Independent Experts Commission on Switzerland – World War II. An official member of the US delegation to the CSCE Seminar on 'Roma in the CSCE Region' in Warsaw (1994), she has lectured widely in Germany and the United States on the Roma and Sinti and is on the executive board of the Gypsy Lore Society and President of the Conference Group for Central European History of the American Historical Association. She is co-author of *Art of the Holocaust* (1981), co-editor and contributor to *The Holocaust: Ideology, Bureaucracy and Genocide* (1980), co-author of *In Fitting Memory* (1991), series co-editor of the 26-volume *Archives of the Holocaust* (1990–1995), and has published a number of articles about Roma and Sinti in both German and English.

WILHELM SOLMS has been Professor for German Literature at the Philipps University of Marburg since 1977. He is Chairman of the *Arbeitsgemeinschaft Literarischer Gesellschaften* and was Vice-President of the European Fairy Tale Association from 1989 to 1993. He has written numerous publications on Goethe, contemporary German literature and research into fairy tales, and is author of *Tiere und Tiergestaltige im Märchen* (1991) and editor of *Das selbstverständliche Wunder: Beiträge germanistischer Märchenforschung* (1986) and *Phantastische Welten: Mythen, Märchen, Fantasy* (1994).

DANIEL STRAUSS is Chairman of the Landesverband Deutscher Sinti und Roma in Heidelberg, and was Public Relations Director of the Dokumentations- und Kulturzentrum Deutscher Sinti und Roma from 1987-1996. Since 1996 he has been Project Director at the Fritz Bauer Institute in Frankfurt, preparing teaching material about the genocide of the Sinti and Roma and about anti-Gypsyism. He is active in opening up dialogues between the Sinti and Roma and the majority society on a basis of equality, and has organised a number of conferences and events in Germany on anti-Gypsyism. He is the editor of *Die Sinti/Roma Erzählkunst* (1992), co-editor with Professor Wilhelm Solms of *Zigeunerbilder in der deutschsprachigen Literatur* (1996), and has forthcoming publications on Christian Resistance in the National Socialist state and on anti-Gypsyism in Germany.

SUSAN TEBBUTT is a lecturer in German at the University of Bradford, researching into contemporary German society, culture and literature. Her publications include *Gudrun Pausewang in Context* (1994), an edition of Gudrun Pausewang's *Die Wolke* for Manchester University Press (1992), and a number of articles in German and English on German socially critical teenage literature, on young people, foreigners and violence in Germany, and on minority groups and their representation in German society and literature, and on the work of Ceija Stojka.

SELECT BIBLIOGRAPHY

Acton, T. *Gypsy Politics and Traveller Identity*, Hatfield, University of Hertfordshire Press, 1997

Acton, T. and Mundy, G. eds *Romani Culture and Gypsy Identity*, Hatfield, University of Hertfordshire Press, 1997

Antoni, E. 'Die Roma und die Würde der Gedenkstätte', *Geschichte quer* 3/1994, p.32

Arnim, A. von. *Werke*, 2 vols, Munich, Hanser, 1962

Bakker, P. and Cortiade, M., eds *On the Margin of Romani: Gypsy Languages as Contact Languages*, Studies in Language Contact 1. Amsterdam: Publikaties van het Instituut voor Algemene Taalwetenschap 58, 1991

Bamberger, E. and Ehmann, A., eds *Kinder und Jugendliche als Opfer des Holocaust*, Heidelberg, Dokumentationszentrum Deutscher Sinti und Roma, 1995

Bartos, T. *Zigeunermärchen aus Ungarn*, Frankfurt am Main, Fischer, 1976

Basile, G. *Das Märchen aller Märchen, Der Pentamerone: Dritter Tag*, transl. by F. Liebrecht, Frankfurt am Main, Insel, 1982

Bauer, R. et al., eds *Sinti in der Bundesrepublik: Beiträge zur sozialen Lage einer verfolgten Minderheit*, Bremen, Universität Bremen, 1984

Bayerisches Hauptstaatsarchiv (Bavarian State Archives). Ministry of the Interior 72576–72579 (General files on the Fight against the Gypsy Menace)

Benz, W. *Der Holocaust*, Munich, Beck, 1995

Benz, W. *Feindbild und Vorurteil: Beiträge über Ausgrenzung und Verfolgung*, Munich, dtv, 1996

Bergengruen, W. 'Der Zigeuner und das Wiesel', in *Schwarz auf weiß, ein neues Lesebuch*, 7. Schuljahr, Hannover, Schroedel-Verlag, 1967

Berger, H. 'Das Zigeunerbild in der deutschen Literatur des 19. Jahrhunderts', Diss., Waterloo, Ontario, 1972

Bhabha, H. K. *Nation and Narration*, London, Routledge, 1990

Biester, J. E. 'Über die Zigeuner, besonders im Königreich Preussen, II. Von ihrer Sprache', *Berlinische Monatsschrift* 21/1793, pp.108–168 and pp.360–393

Binns, D. *Children's Literature and the Role of the Gypsy*, Manchester Travellers' School, 1984

Bischoff, F. *Deutsch-Zigeunerisches Wörterbuch*, Ilmenau, 1827

Björgo, T. and Witte, R. *Racist Violence in Europe*, New York, St. Martin's Press, 1993

Boretzky, N. and Igla, B. 'Zum Erbwortschatz des Romani', *Zeitschrift für Phonetik, Sprachwissenschaft und Kommunikationsforschung* 45/1992, pp.227–251

Boretzky, N. and Igla, B. *Wörterbuch Romani-Deutsch-Englisch für den südosteuropäischen Raum*, Wiesbaden, Harrassowitz, 1994

Brand, M. ' ... nach Auschwitz überführt ...': Verfolgung und Vernichtung von Sinti-Familien aus Hamm (Westfalen) während des Dritten Reiches, *Der 50. Jahrestag der Vernichtung der Roma im KL Auschwitz -Birkenau. '3. August 1944–3. August 1994' Einführung in die Ausstellung*, ed. W. Dlugoborski, Auschwitz, Vereinigung der Rom in Polen, 1994, pp.49–57

Brand, M. 'Die vergessene Verfolgung: Der Zigeunerbeauftragte aus Soest und seine Opfer', *Soester Zeitschrift* 107/1995, pp.103–120

Brentano, C. *Italienische Märchen*, in Clemens Brentano, *Märchen*, ed. by W. Frühwald and F. Kemp, Munich, Hanser, 1978

Brentano, C. *Sämtliche Werke und Briefe*, Historisch-kritische Ausgabe, vol. 17, 'Die Märchen vom Rhein', ed. B. Schillbach, Stuttgart, Kohlhammer, 1983

Briel, P-G. *'Lumpenkind und Traumprinzessin': Zur Sozialgestalt der Zigeuner in der Kinder- und Jugendliteratur seit dem 19. Jahrhundert*, Giessen, Focus, 1989

Bundesarchiv Koblenz. Bestand R 165, Sammlung Schumacher 399

Burleigh, M. and Wippermann. W. *The Racial State: Germany 1933–1945*, Cambridge, New York, Port Chester, Melbourne, Sydney, CUP, 1991

Calvet, G. and Formoso, B. *Lexique tsigane II: dialecte sinto piémontais*, Paris, Publications Orientalistes de France, 1987

Cammann, A. and Karasek, A. *Donauschwaben erzählen*, 4 vols, Marburg, Elwert, 1976

Cech, P. and Heinschink, M.F. 'Sepecides-Romani', *LINCOM-EUROPA Languages of the World: Materials 106*, Munich, LINCOM-EUROPA, 1996

Crowe, D. and Kolsti, J., eds *The Gypsies of Eastern Europe*, New York, London, M.E. Sharpe, 1991

Djuric, R. *Zigeunerische Elegien: Gedichte in Romani und Deutsch*, Hamburg, Buske, 1989

Djuric, R. *Roma und Sinti im Spiegel der deutschen Literatur*, Frankfurt am Main, Peter Lang, 1995

Ebert, C., ed. *Der Nachtvogel: Zigeunermärchen aus Rußland*, transl. by R. Landa, Berlin (East), Verlag Volk und Welt, 1986

Eder, B. *Geboren bin ich vor Jahrtausenden ...: Bilderwelten in der Literatur der Roma und Sinti*, Klagenfurt, Drava, 1993

Eiber, L., ed. *'Ich wußte, es wird schlimm': Die Verfolgung der Sinti und Roma in München 1933–1945*, Munich, Buchendorfer, 1993

Eiber, L. 'KZ-Gedenkstätte Dachau', *Geschichte quer* 3/1994, p.32

Fienbork, G. et al., eds *Die Roma – Hoffen auf ein Leben ohne Angst*, Reinbek bei Hamburg, Rowohlt, 1992

Finck, F. N. *Lehrbuch des Dialekts der deutschen Zigeuner*, Marburg, Elwert, 1903

Fings, K. and Sparing, F. *Nur wenige kamen zurück: Sinti und Roma im Nationalsozialismus (Katalog zur Ausstellung)*, Cologne, Selbstverlag, 1990

Fings, K. and Sparing, F. *'z. Zt. Zigeunerlager': Die Verfolgung der Düsseldorfer Sinti und Roma im Nationalsozialismus*, Cologne, Volksblatt, 1992

Fings, K. and Sparing, F. *'Ach Freunde, wohin seid ihr verweht ...?': Otto Pankok und die Düsseldorfer Sinti*, Düsseldorf, Der Oberstadtdirektor — Mahn- und Gedenkstätte Düsseldorf, 1993

Fings, K. and Sparing, F. '"tunlichst als erziehungsunfähig" hinzustellen: Zigeunerkinder und -jugendliche: Aus der Fürsorge in die Vernichtung', *Dachauer Hefte* 9/1993, pp.159–180

Fonseca, I. *Bury Me Standing*, London, Chatto & Windus, 1995

Franz, P. *Zwischen Liebe und Haß: Ein Zigeunerleben*, Freiburg, Herder, 1985

Fraser, A. *The Gypsies*, 2nd edn, Oxford, Cambridge (Mass.), Blackwell, 1995

Friedlander, H. *The Origins of Nazi Genocide: From Euthanasia to the Final Solution*, Chapel Hill, London, University of North Carolina Press, 1995

Galin, D. *Ich heiße Paprika*, Stuttgart, Boje, 1975

Geigges, A. and Wette, B. W. *Zigeuner heute: Verfolgung und Diskriminierung in der BRD*, Bornheim-Merten, Lamuv, 1979

Gesellschaft für bedrohte Völker, ed. *pogrom*, 130/1987, Göttingen

Giere, J., ed. *Die gesellschaftliche Konstruktion des Zigeuners: Zur Genese eines Vorurteils*, Frankfurt, New York, Campus, 1996

Gilliat-Smith, B. 'Lalere Sinte', *Journal of the Gypsy Lore Society*, new series, 2/1908–1909, pp.2–14

Gilsenbach, E. and R., eds *Janitschek im Räuberschloß: Märchen der slowakischen Rom*, collected by M. Hübschmannová, Berlin, Der Kinderbuchverlag, 1983

Gilsenbach, R. 'Unkus letzter Tanz', in *Kaleidoskop*, Berlin, Der Kinderbuchverlag, 1976, pp.166–176

Gilsenbach, R. 'Das Sinti-Mädchen Unku', in *pogrom* 130/1987, pp.52–54

Gilsenbach, R. *Oh Django, sing deinen Zorn!: Sinti und Roma unter den Deutschen*, Berlin, BasisDruck, 1993

Grellmann, H. M. G. *Die Zigeuner: Ein historischer Versuch über die Lebensart und Verfassung, Sitten und Schicksahle dieses Volkes in Europa, nebst ihrem Ursprünge*, Dessau, Leipzig, 1783

Grimm, Brüder. *Kinder- und Hausmärchen*, Ausgabe letzter Hand, ed. H. Rölleke, Stuttgart, Reclam, 1980

Gronemeyer, R. *Zigeuner im Spiegel früher Chroniken und Abhandlungen*, Gießen, 1987

Grund, J. C. *Rosita, das Zigeunermädchen*, Reutlingen, 1957

Haaken, F. *Django: Eine Geschichte in Bildern*, Ravensburg, O. Maier Verlag, 1979

Hackl, E. *Abschied von Sidonie*, Zürich, Diogenes, 1989

Halwachs, D. W. et al., 'Romani', *LINCOM-EUROPA Languages of the World: Materials 107*, Munich, LINCOM-EUROPA, forthcoming

Hancock, I. 'Introduction', and 'Gypsy History in Germany and Neighboring Lands: A Chronology Leading to the Holocaust and Beyond', in *The Gypsies of Eastern Europe*, ed. D. Crowe and J. Kolsti, New York, London, M.E. Sharpe, 1991, pp.3–9 and pp.11–30

Hancock, I. 'The Roots of Inequity: Romani Cultural Rights in their Historical and Social Context', *Immigrants and Minorities*, 11/1992, pp.3–20

Hancock, I. F. 'On the Migration and Affiliation of the Domba: Iranian words in Rom, Lom and Dom Gypsy', in *Romani in Contact: the History, Structure and Sociology of a Language*, ed. Y. Matras, Amsterdam, John Benjamins (Current Issues in Linguistic Theory 126), 1995, pp.25–51

Hancock, I. 'Responses to the Porrajmos (The Romani Holocaust)', in *Is the Holocaust Unique?*, ed. A. S. Rosenbaum, Colorado, Westview Press, 1996

Hase-Mihalik, E. von and Kreuzkamp, D. *'Du kriegst auch einen schönen Wohnwagen': Zwangslager für Sinti und Roma während des Nationalsozialismus in Frankfurt am Main*, Frankfurt am Main, Brandes & Apsel, 1990

Hauff, W. *Sämtliche Werke*, 2 vols, Stuttgart, Cotta, 1962

Heinschink, M. and Hemetek, U., eds *Roma: das unbekannte Volk*, Vienna, Cologne, Weimar, Böhlau, 1994

Hohmann, J. S. *Geschichte der Zigeunerverfolgung in Deutschland*, rev. edn, Frankfurt am Main, Campus, 1988

Hohmann, J.S. *Robert Ritter und die Erben der Kriminalbiologie: 'Zigeunerforschung' im Nationalsozialismus und in Westdeutschland im Zeichen des Rassismus*, Frankfurt, Bern, New York, Paris, Peter Lang, 1991

Hohmann, J., ed. *Sinti und Roma in Deutschland: Versuch einer Bilanz*, Frankfurt, Peter Lang, 1995

Hohmann, J. and Schopf, R., eds *Zigeunerleben*, Darmstadt: ms-edition, 2nd edn, 1980

Holzinger, D. *Das Rómanes: Grammatik und Diskursanalyse der Sprache der Sinte*, Innsbrucker Beiträge zur Kulturwissenschaft, Sonderheft 85, Innsbruck: Institut für Sprachwissenschaft der Universität Innsbruck, 1993

Holzinger, D. *O Latscho Lab o Jesus Christsester* (Gospel according to St Mark), 2nd edn, Florshain, 1994 (transl. D. Holzinger, though this is not mentioned in the title)

Holzinger, D. 'Romanes (Sinte)', *LINCOM-EUROPA Languages of the World: Materials, 105*, Munich, LINCOM-EUROPA, 1995

hooks, b. *Black Looks: Race and Representation*, London, Turnaround, 1992

Horrocks, D. and Kolinsky, E., eds *Turkish Culture in German Society Today*, Providence, Oxford, Berghahn, 1996

Igla, B. 'Entlehnung und Lehnübersetzung deutscher Präfixverben im Sinti', *Prinzipien des Sprachwandels*, ed. J. Erfurt, B. Jessing and M. Perl, Bochum, Brockmeyer, 1992, pp.38–55

Jean, D. 'Glossaire de gadškeno manuš', *Etudes tsiganes*, 1/1970, pp.2–69

Jühling, J. 'I. Kriminalisches. II. Alphabetisches Wörterverzeichnis der Zigeunersprache', *Archiv für Kriminal-Anthropologie und Kriminalistik*, 1908–1909, vols 31 and 32

Kenrick, D. and Puxon, G. *Sinti und Roma: Die Vernichtung eines Volkes im NS-Staat*, transl. by A. Stegelmann, Göttingen, Gesellschaft für bedrohte Völker, 1981

Kenrick, D. and Puxon, G. *Gypsies under the Swastika*, Hatfield, University of Hertfordshire Press, 1995

King, R., Connell, J. and White, P., eds *Writing across Worlds: Literature and Migration*, London, New York, Routledge, 1995

Klaußner, W. *Jüppa und der Zigeuner*, Frankfurt, Sauerländer, 1979

Klüger, R. 'Jüdische Gestalten aus der deutschen Literatur des 19. Jahrhunderts', in *Katastrophen: Über deutsche Literatur*, Göttingen, Wallstein Verlag, 1994

Kluyver, A. 'Un glossaire tsigane du seizième siècle', *Journal of the Gypsy Lore Society*, new series, 4/1910–1911, pp.131–142

Knobloch, J. 'Volkskundliche Sinti-Texte', *Anthropos* 45/1950, pp.223–250

Köpf, P. *Stichwort: Sinti und Roma*, Munich, Heyne, 1994

Kovács, A., ed. *Ungarische Volksmärchen*, Düsseldorf, Cologne, Diederichs, 1965

Krausnick, M. *'Da wollten wir frei sein!': Eine Sinti-Familie erzählt*, Weinheim, Basel, Beltz, 1st publ. 1983, 2nd edn 1986

Krausnick, M. *Abfahrt Karlsruhe: Die Deportation in den Völkermord*, Neckargemünd, Verband der Sinti und Roma Karlsruhe e.V., 1990

Krausnick, M. *Wo sind sie hingekommen?: Der unterschlagene Völkermord an den Sinti und Roma*, Gerlingen, Bleicher, 1995

Krauss, F. S. *Zigeunerhumor*, Leipzig, 1907

Landeshauptstadt Düsseldorf, ed. *Verfolgung und Widerstand in Düsseldorf 1933–1945*, Düsseldorf, Landeshauptstadt Düsseldorf, 1990

Leidgeb, E. and Horn, N. *Opre Roma! Erhebt Euch!*, Munich, AG Spak Bücher, 1994

Lessing, A. *Mein Leben im Versteck: Wie ein deutscher Sinti den Holocaust überlebte*, Düsseldorf, Zebulon Verlag, 1993

Liebich, R. *Die Zigeuner in ihrem Wesen und in ihrer Sprache*, Leipzig, Brockhaus, 1863

Liégeois, J-P., transl. from French by S. ní Shuíneár. *School Provision for Gypsy and Traveller Children*, Brussels, Commission of the European Communities, 1987

Liégeois, J-P. and Gheorghe, N., transl. from French by S. ní Shuíneár. *Roma/Gypsies: A European Minority*, London, Minority Rights Group, 1995

Lindemann, F. *Die Sinti aus dem Ummenwinkel*, Weinheim, Basel, Beltz, 1991

Ludolf, J. H. *Ludolfi ad suam Historiam Aethiopicam antehac editam Commentarius*, Frankfurt a.M., 1691

Maciejewski, F. 'Elemente des Antiziganismus', in *Die gesellschaftliche Konstruktion des Zigeuners: Zur Genese eines Vorurteils*, ed. J. Giere, Frankfurt, New York, 1996

Markefka, M. *Vorurteile – Minderheiten – Diskriminierung*, 7th rev. edn, Neuwied, Kriftel, Berlin, Luchterhand, 1995

Martins-Heuß, K. *Zur mythischen Figur des Zigeuners*, Frankfurt am Main, 1983

May, K. *Die Juweleninsel*, Nördlingen, 1987

May, K. *Mit Zepter und Hammer*, Nördlingen, 1987

Meister, J. 'Die "Zigeunerkinder" von der St. Josefspflege in Mulfingen', Sonderdruck aus *1999: Zeitschrift für Sozialgeschichte des 20. und 21. Jahrhunderts*, 2/1987

Mihaly, J. *Michael Arpad und sein Kind*, Berlin, Litpol Verlagsgesellschaft, 1981 (1st publ 1930)

Miklosich, F. X. R. von. 'Über die Mundarten und die Wanderungen der Zigeuner Europas', *Denkschriften der kaiserlichen Akademie der Wissenschaften, philosophich-historische Klasse*, vols 21–31, Vienna, Karl Gerolds Sohn, 1872–1881

Miklosich, F. X. R. von. 'Beiträge zur Kenntnis der Zigeunermundarten', *Sitzungsberichte der kaiserlichen Akademie der Wissenschaften, philosophisch-historische Klasse*, vols 77–90, Vienna, Karl Gerolds Sohn, 1874–1878

Milton, S. 'Antechamber to Birkenau: The Zigeunerlager after 1933', in *Die Normalität des Verbrechens: Bilanz und Perspektiven der Forschung zu den nationalsozialistischen Gewaltverbrechen*, ed. H. Grabitz, K. Bästlein, J. Tuchel et al., Berlin, Hentrich, 1994, pp.241–259.

Milton, S. 'Sinti und Roma als "vergessene Opfergruppe" in der Gedenkstättenarbeit', in *Der Völkermord an den Sinti und Roma in der Gedenkstättenarbeit*, ed. E. Bamberger, Heidelberg, Dokumentations- und Kulturzentrum Deutscher Sinti und Roma, 1994, pp.53–60

Milton, S. 'Holocaust: The Gypsies', in *Genocide in the Twentieth Century: Critical Essays and Eyewitness Accounts*, ed. W. S. Parsons, I. W. Charny and S. Totten, New York, London, Garland Publishing, 1995, pp.209–264

Milton, S. ed. and transl. *The Story of Karl Stojka: A Childhood in Birkenau*, Washington, D.C., United States Holocaust Memorial Museum, 1992

Miskow, J. and Brøndal, V. 'Sigøjnersprog I Danmark', *Danske Studier*, 1923, pp.97–145

Mitscherlich, A. and Mielke, F. *Medizin ohne Menschlichkeit: Dokumente des Nürnberger Ärzteprozesses*, Frankfurt am Main, 1960

Mode, H., ed. *Zigeunermärchen aus aller Welt: Vier Sammlungen*, Leipzig, Insel, 1984

Müller-Hill, B. *Tödliche Wissenschaft: Die Aussonderung von Juden, Zigeunern und Geisteskranken 1933–1945*, Reinbek bei Hamburg, Rowohlt, 1984

Okely, J. *The Traveller-Gypsies*, Cambridge, CUP, 1983

Petersen, E. *'In meiner Sprache gibt's kein Wort für morgen'*, Recklinghausen, Georg Bitter, 1990

Petzold, L. 'Der ewige Verlierer: Das Bild des Juden in der deutschen Volksliteratur', in *Das Bild des Juden in der Volks- und Jugendliteratur vom 18. Jahrhundert bis 1945*, ed. H. Pleticha, Würzburg, Königshausen und Neumann, 1985

Pott, A. F. *Die Zigeuner in Europa und Asien*, Halle, Heynemann, 1844–1845

Pross, C. and Aly, G., eds *The Value of the Human Being: Medicine in Nazi Germany 1918–1945*, transl. by M. Iwand, Berlin, Ärztekammer Berlin and Edition Hentrich, 1991

Puchner, G. *Sprechen Sie Rotwelsch: 2446 Wörter und Redewendungen der deutschen Gaunersprache*, Munich, Heimaran, 1975

Püschel, W. *Die zerbrochene Melodie*, Stuttgart, 1992

Reemtsma, K. *Sinti und Roma: Geschichte, Kultur, Gegenwart*, Munich, Beck, 1996

Reinhard, M. A. 'The Formation of Occupational Terms in German Romani (Dialect of the Sinte)', *International Journal of the Sociology of Language* 19/1979, pp.19–32

Riechert, H. *Im Schatten von Auschwitz: Die nationalsozialistische Sterilisationspolitik gegenüber Sinti und Roma*, Münster, New York, Waxmann, 1995

Rinser, L. *Wer wirft den Stein?: Zigeuner sein in Deutschland; Eine Anklage*, Stuttgart, Edition Weitbrecht, 1985

Rose, R. *Wir wollen Bürgerrechte und keinen Rassismus*, Heidelberg, Zentralrat Deutscher Sinti und Roma, 1985

Rose, R. *Bürgerrechte für Sinti und Roma: Das Buch zum Rassismus in Deutschland*, Heidelberg, Zentralrat Deutscher Sinti und Roma, 1987

Rose, R. ed. *Der Nationalsozialistische Völkermord an den Sinti und Roma*, 2nd rev. edn, Heidelberg, Dokumentationszentrum Deutscher Sinti und Roma, 1995

Rose, R. and Weiss, W. *Sinti und Roma im 'Dritten Reich': Das Programm der Vernichtung durch Arbeit*, Göttingen, Lamuv, 1991

Rüdiger, J. C. C. *Von der Sprache und Herkunft der Zigeuner aus Indien*, Leipzig, 1782

Sampson, J. *The Dialect of the Gypsies of Wales*, Oxford, Clarendon Press, 1926

Sattler, J. ed. by Pastor F. Zeller. *O voyako-hiro katar o Jesusesko Christuskero banasgimmo ä Johannestar*, Berlin, British and Foreign Bible Society, 1930

Schenk, D. *Der Wind ist des Teufels Niesen*, Reinbek, Rowohlt, 1988

Schins, M-T. *Die Truhe / Ich bin ein Zigeuner*, Stuttgart, 1991

Schnurre, W. 'Jenö war mein Freund', in *Lesezeichen A / B 7*, Stuttgart, Klett, 1985

Schumacher, T. *Komteßchen und Zigeunerkind*, Stuttgart, Levy & Müller, 1914

Senzera, L. 'Il dialetto dei Sinti Piemontesi', *Lacio Drom* 22 / 1986

Sibley, D. *Geographies of Exclusion*, London, New York, Routledge, 1995

Stadtarchiv München (Munich City Archives). Bestand Polizeidirektion Munich 581

Stadtarchiv München. Bestand Polizeidirektion Munich 7033

Steinmetz, S. *Österreichs Zigeuner im NS-Staat*, Vienna, Frankfurt, Zurich, Europa Verlag, 1966

Stenographischer Bericht des Bayerischen Landtags 1925 / 26, Bd. V., 116. Sitzung 12.5.1926

Stephani, K., ed. *Märchen der Rumäniendeutschen*, Düsseldorf, Diederichs, 1991

Stojka, C. *Wir leben im Verborgenen: Erinnerungen einer Rom-Zigeunerin*, ed. K. Berger, Vienna, Picus, 1988

Stojka, C. *Reisende auf dieser Welt: Aus dem Leben einer Rom-Zigeunerin*, ed. K. Berger, Vienna, Picus, 1992

Stojka, K. *Ein Kind in Birkenau*, Vienna, Karl Stojka (Eigendruck), 1995

Stojka, K. *Gas*, Vienna, Karl Stojka (Eigendruck), 1996

Stojka, K. and Pohanka, R. *Auf der ganzen Welt zu Hause: Das Leben und Wandern des Zigeuners Karl Stojka*, Vienna, Picus, 1994

Storm, T. *Werke*, Vol. 4, Frankfurt am Main, Deutscher Klassiker Verlag, 1988

Strauß, D., ed. *Die Sinti / Roma-Erzählkunst*, Heidelberg, Dokumentations- und Kulturzentrum Deutscher Sinti und Roma, 1992

Strauß, D. and Solms, W., eds *Zigeunerbilder in der deutschsprachigen Literatur*, Heidelberg, 1995

Stuckart, W. and Globke, H. *Kommentar zur deutschen Rassengesetzgebung*, Vol. 1., Munich, Berlin, 1936

Supple, C. *From Prejudice to Genocide: Learning about the Holocaust*, Stoke-on-Trent, Trentham Books, 1993

Thurner, E. *Nationalsozialismus und Zigeuner in Österreich*, Vienna, Salzburg, Geyer Edition, 1983

Tieck, L. *Werke*, Vol. 11, 'Die Märchen aus dem Phantasus', Munich, Winkler, 1963

Tuckermann, A. *Muscha*, Munich, Erika Klopp Verlag, 1994

UnterstützerInnengruppe 'Bleiberecht für alle Roma' Tübingen / Reutlingen. 'Antirassistische Arbeit – Linksradikaler Anspruch und realpolitische Praxis', in *'Ein Herrenvolk von Untertanen': Rassismus – Nationalismus – Sexismus*, ed. A. Foitzik et al., Duisburg, DISS, 1992, pp.185–198

Urban, R. and Wittich, E. *O Evangelio Jezus Kristusesko pala Markus*, Berlin, British and Foreign Bible Society, 1912

Verband der Roma in Polen, ed. *Das Schicksal der Sinti und Roma im KL Auschwitz-Birkenau*, Warsaw, Kanzlei des Sejm, 1994

von Sowa, R. *Wörterbuch des Dialekts der deutschen Zigeuner: Abhandlungen für die Kunde des Morgenlandes*, XI. Band, I. Teil, Leipzig, Deutsche Morgenländische Gesellschaft, 1898

Voriskova, M., ed. *Singende Geigen: Slovakische Zigeunermärchen*, Hanau, Dausien Verlag, 1973

Watson, A. *The Germans: Who are They Now?*, London, Methuen, 1992

Wedding, A. *Ede und Unku*, Berlin, Basis, no date (1st publ. 1932)

Wildermuth, O. *Braunes Lenchen*, Berlin, probably 1860s

Wippermann, W. '*Wie die Zigeuner*': *Antisemitismus und Antiziganismus im Vergleich*, Berlin, Elefanten Press, 1997

Wlislocki, H. von, ed. *Volksdichtungen der siebenbürgischen und südungarischen Zigeuner*, Vienna, 1890

Wölfel, U. *Mond, Mond, Mond*, Düsseldorf, Hoch, 1962

Zentrale Stelle der Landesjustizverwaltungen Ludwigsburg. Az: 410 AR - J 214/76 Bd. 1

Zimmermann, M. *Verfolgt, vertrieben, vernichtet: Die nationalsozialistische Vernichtungspolitik gegen Sinti und Roma*, Essen, 1989, 2nd edn 1993

Zimmermann, M. *Rassenutopie und Genozid: Die nationalsozialistische 'Lösung der Zigeunerfrage'*, Hamburg, Christians, 1996

Zitelmann, A. *Unter Gauklern*, Weinheim, Beltz & Gelberg, 1980

Zülch, T., ed. *In Auschwitz vergast, bis heute verfolgt: Zur Situation der Roma und Sinti in Deutschland und Europa*, Reinbek bei Hamburg, Rowholt, 1979

INDEX